Occupy This Body
A Buddhist Memoir

Sharon A. Suh

D1603542

The Sumeru Press Inc.
2019

OCCUPY THIS BODY
A Buddhist Memoir
Sharon A. Suh

Published by
The Sumeru Press Inc.
301 Bayrose Drive, Suite 402
Nepean, ON
Canada K2J 5W3

Library and Archives Canada Cataloguing in Publication

Title: Occupy this body : a Buddhist memoir / Sharon A. Suh.
Names: Suh, Sharon A., author.
Identifiers: Canadiana 20190144572 | ISBN 9781896559506 (softcover)
Subjects: LCSH: Suh, Sharon A. | LCSH: Buddhists—United States—
Biography. | LCSH: Korean Americans—
    Biography. | LCSH: Eating disorders—Patients—United States—
Biography. | LCSH: Body image.
Classification: LCC BQ988.U34 A3 2019 | DDC 294.3092—dc23

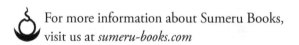 For more information about Sumeru Books,
visit us at *sumeru-books.com*

Contents

Prologue

I HAVE ALREADY STOPPED trying to count my breaths up to ten because I never make it past number four. And I know I should be focusing on the barely perceptible sensations gently tickling my nostrils with each long inhale and exhale of the breath, but I am focusing instead on everyone else. Everyone else looks so calm with their serene Buddha-like faces, but I am fidgety. My foot has fallen asleep and I am still disappointed that I didn't grab one of those crunchy vegan cookies during registration because my stomach is growling. I glance around the meditation hall and start to imagine how I will redecorate my living room in Seattle so that it looks like this retreat center with its warm light, artfully placed Buddha statues, and remarkably polished floors. How do they manage to keep the floors so shiny? I will have to learn their secret. I can hear the college student behind me breathing like a master monk. Bejeweled in layers of wooden mala beads, grandma with the blue mirrored sunglasses props herself up in a stadium seat as she sits in perfect lotus position. Why didn't I get one of those when I first chose my meditation space for the week? Rookie mistake.

I glimpse down at the thin cushions I selected earlier thinking that it would be good thing to be moderate. But my attempts to be a successful Buddhist meditator have been sabotaged by my ankle bones grinding painfully into the wood floor. I peer around at the luxuriously pillowed meditation spaces I could have chosen and begin to plot my next move. Next time, I will select a cushion throne like the seasoned meditators whose serene faces and upright postures are supported by the right props. In the meantime, I stare out the windows of the meditation hall and fixate on the sun slowly descending the parched hills of Marin County.

But I must *sit*. I must *stay*. I am only on the first hour of day one.

As a second-generation Korean American woman, I jumped at the opportunity to attend this silent Buddhist meditation retreat that touted itself as a safe space for people of color. I was so used to being one of the few Asian Americans in the meditation centers I visited in the U.S. that when I saw the advertisement for this opportunity, the 16-hour drive from

Seattle to California seemed worth every minute. And I was right. As soon
as I drove up to the parking lot and saw all the other people of color, I felt
like I had finally found my spiritual center.

"May you take up space and be like the Buddha who touched the
earth to bear witness to his enlightenment," our lead teacher Asha says in
her calm, lilting voice. I ignore the searing pain developing in my back
muscles and round my shoulders a few times to release the accumulating
tension. I feel like I have put my entire body on ice for hours on end. I am
surrounded by meditation cushions with people perfectly propped upon
them. I am sitting amidst a tranquil sea of flawless mountains.

Following Asha's cues to pay close attention to how our bodies feel
on the cushions, I breathe deeply into my belly and imagine filling out
the contours of my body from the inside out. My breath feels jagged and
forced. I try to visualize myself growing bigger and taking up space while
Asha says out loud what we have all felt at one time or another—that as
people of color we are often invisible, people have not always wanted to
see us, and sometimes we are made to feel small.

Then, with a twinkle in her eyes, she smiles widely and says something
that I have never heard in a dharma talk before. "I see you."

There is a palpable shift in the room and I can feel my own body
begin to ease into its cushion while taking in this radical message. Despite
thirty years of visiting meditation centers and temples as a grad student,
professor, and Buddhist, I have never had a dharma teacher, let alone a
female lay Buddhist of color, tell me exactly what I needed to hear. It was
as if she could see straight into my head, my heart, and into my past.

I sit in rapt attention with laser-like focus as the teacher's words reveal
a nuanced insight into the Buddha's teachings that all my years of studying Buddhism never could. And that is that Buddhist practice is an act
of taking up space and generating self-love and self-care. "Buddha's beautiful journey is akin to ours on the mat as we are assailed by doubt and
other hindrances," Asha says. "It takes radical courage to sit, be aware, be
mindful, and investigate our reality and our truth."

Asha encourages us to generate gentle appreciation toward ourselves
as if we are our own beloveds.

What a noble and intriguing concept, I think. Can I even do that? Have
I ever one really done that? Will I learn to generate loving-kindness for myself? After all, this practice of self-love comes neither naturally nor easily.
This challenge is perhaps my life-long *kōan,* or puzzle, to appreciate this
body of mine, that I am to contemplate until I have a mental breakthrough.

Our second guiding teacher, Jaya, brings me immediately back to the present moment. "Letting go of distractions is one of the bravest things we can do for ourselves," she says as she picks up a large straw basket and invites us—once again—to offer up our cell phones into the donation basket. We all smile as a few of the remaining guilty parties pull their phones out of their pockets, power down, and nervously bid them *adieu* for the next four days. I am feeling smug at this point because I had already offered up my cell phone, my laptop, and my books when I first arrived at the registration desk. But now I wonder how I will remember all the profound things that have already been said and anything else that happens on the retreat if I can't write it down. My monkey mind panics because if something isn't put in writing, it will forever be lost. So I hatch a plan—after this session, I will pretend to write a note to the teachers but instead of posting it on the message board, I will stash it in my pockets. By the end of the retreat, I have amassed a thick pile of recycled rectangles full of hastily jotted chicken scratch. The researcher in me prevails.

Over the next few days, the muscles in body loosen up and this room full of strangers starts to feel like a long-lost *sangha* (community of support) even though we haven't spoken a single word to one another. I stop sizing up the other bodies in the room, wondering if they are better meditators than I am or if they look better than I do. Even my body, which has been silenced all the way down to its bowels on this retreat where there is little privacy, begins to relax. This room full of people of color engaged in silent meditation has become the sangha I have always been looking for in the U.S., one where I am not a racial minority and my Asian American body melds into the larger space, a space filled with more diversity than I have ever encountered in a meditation hall. It starts to feel like Dr. King's "beloved community."

The teachers tell us that during the retreat, we should follow the five ennobling precepts: To undertake the commitment to protect life. To undertake the commitment to only take what is offered to me. To undertake the commitment to abstain from sexual activity on this retreat. To undertake the commitment to be in noble silence. And to undertake the commitment to abstain from intoxicants while on this retreat.

These precepts create a "container of safety," as Jaya puts it, where we can create a trusting environment and rest in an "incubator for healing and wellness." When we don't have to worry about harsh speech, hateful looks, drunken behavior, stealing, and sexual violence, we can more easily cultivate trust, care, and intimacy where there are fewer barriers between us. "This stuff is important," Asha tells us with a chuckle, "because we have all had our fair share of retreat crushes when we develop these attractions for people we don't even know. Suddenly, after two days of meditating together and seeing the other person across the dining hall, we're creating stories about these people and projecting our future lives onto them. All of a sudden, we're on our first date, then we're a couple, then we're moving in together." She wisely and gently shows us our human propensity to engage in what the Buddha called *papañca* or "mental proliferation" that distracts us from our practice. Many of us laugh because that is precisely what we have started to do. I laugh because I'd done just that. I recently met a man, we went out on a date, then we were suddenly a couple and now, just two days before he dropped me off at the retreat, I agreed to marry him. But since it is a silent retreat, I can't tell anyone I've just gotten engaged.

Despite considering myself a Buddhist and having a doctorate in Buddhist Studies, I usually avoided regular practice because I felt out of place in predominantly white Buddhist centers. Many of them taught insight meditation and encouraged us to focus on controlling the mind but seemed to ignore significant discussion of the body, which I desperately needed. But here, in what looks like a Buddhist summer camp with dormitories, a kitchen hall, hiking trails, and even a resident peacock, Buddhism has come alive for me precisely because the emphasis is on feeling and embracing the body. It is the first time that meditation has been offered to me as the radical act of taking up space and appreciating myself as a woman with a body and a complex history surrounding it.

"Our heads contain incessantly chattering monkeys that swing from thought to thought and we often judge and cling to those thoughts as if they were real," Asha reminds us during the late afternoon sit. She says softly "But over 2500 years ago the Buddha taught his disciples that all thoughts and feelings about ourselves and others are created by the mind. Our experiences are preceded by mind, led by mind, and produced by mind." She stops speaking and we contemplate her words drawn directly from the Buddha's teachings.

Sitting in silence reminds me that my own mind would benefit from putting a stop to its relentless jumping, judging, clinging, and perpetual creation of stories about myself. I settle into the silence and begin my journey into my body. But then my monkey mind breaks the silence and asks, *Why am I so willing to seek out silence?*

After all, I have made an excellent life-long practice of remaining silent in times of worry or conflict. It was a lesson I learned as a child when I fell silent to the goings on in my family even though it never really did much good. Now here I am volunteering to go radio-silent for five full days with no books, no journals (I cheated here), no texting, no phone, no television, and no social media. I have approached the retreat as an academic—detached, intellectually curious, hoping to draw insightful conclusions. But I am unprepared for how personal these five days of respite from work, family, and friends will become. In the penetrating silence, I have found a mental quiet, a quiet that speaks to me. And it says, *occupy this body*. It has taken retreating into silence in the company of one hundred other people of color and escaping from the din of the media and my own thoughts in order to sit, be with my body, and learn to generate the desire to inhabit it and ultimately accept it.

Decades of trying to escape my body have led me to resist any desire to inhabit it. Growing up in Long Island in the seventies, my Korean American body was out of place at home and outside the house. In my mother's eyes, it was never quite right. It was not pretty enough and too chubby. It was unworthy of love. For decades, the perfectionist in me used to think that I could perfect myself into happiness. But the Buddhist in me now tells me to let go of those inherited mental habits; settle in; *occupy this body*.

Asha takes a seat in front of the altar and shares a message that drowns out the nagging pain in my hamstrings that have been folded in lotus position for too long. "When we withdraw our senses to pay radical attention, we can develop the courage to sit still without buying into mediated images of what we think we should look like or be. This process is the radical act of freedom and self-love."

A smile forms on my face. There it is, the direct connection I have needed to make between the Buddha's noble silence and learning how to appreciate my body—rather than treat it like a "neglected family member" bearing the collected burdens of my broken heart. Unlike so many other silences that used to make me feel constricted and anxious, this silence is inviting and compassionate as it gently prods me again to go ahead and dare to *occupy this body*.

And so I do.

Force Feeding

FROM MY HIGH CHAIR, I try to avert my eyes from the huge mound of steaming white rice flanked by an equally tall heap of *bulgogi*, a sweet and savory Korean grilled beef. A small pile of chopped up *kimchi* rinsed in water to nullify its spiciness rests by its side. Each evening my mother ritually arranges the dinner plate on the high chair's removable table. She reaches for the enormous glass of milk and places it exactly at the top front of the plate and a spoon and fork on each side. A soft plastic bib is secured around my neck and the plastic table of my high chair clicks into place. I am once again locked into the rites of eating.

"Don't even think about trying to get out of your chair until you've finished all of it," my mother quietly warns me. "And finish the milk, too."

I know the drill. Eat until I can't eat anymore. Eat because I have no choice. Eat if I am not hungry and don't even bother telling anyone that I am already full. It won't do any good. I pick up my fork and I begin. I know that it is too much for my toddler body to handle, yet I keep at it. I eat what and how much she tells me to even when my cousins shout, "Wow, you can really eat a lot!" My face reddens in shame and my stomach hurts, but I know the consequences to not clearing my plate. So I keep silent, hoping that I won't be punished. Good Korean daughters do what their mothers tell them, after all.

A few hours have passed, I am sick of sitting still, and I still can't finish the rice. I can hear my brother yelling outside with the neighborhood pack of boys playing kickball and running from backyard to backyard as the sun sets. He always got to serve himself and leave the table when he was finished. My head bobs to the side as I grow tired, but I cannot go to sleep. I must stay awake, fork in hand, and eat until all the food on my plate is gone or at least until my father gets home from work. As soon as I hear the car come up the drive and the car door shut, I feel some relief, for I know I will soon be set free from this chair until it is time to return to it in the morning.

When that front door opens and my dad walks in with his briefcase, my mother doesn't skip a beat and says as if it were just a coincidence,

"Oh, she just finished eating." She throws me that familiar warning look to keep quiet and says in exasperation, "at least finish your milk," as if I am the cause of wasted food. I comply, and she finally unlocks the small table. I squirm uncomfortably out of the chair and greet my father with a meek "hello." I am well trained in keeping secrets. And he never asks.

My inability to feel my body and to discern whether I was hungry or full began quite young. As a child, I could never act on my hunger or satiation because my mother always decided when I ate, how much I ate, and when I could stop. I was under her constant surveillance. She had come of age during the Korean war where starvation loomed large and after the war, she moved to the United States in the sixties where food was abundant. Eating as much as possible was necessary for survival in Korea, but here in her new home, thinness was the way to accumulate social capital. Successful American women prevailed in maintaining the latest in body size fashion. In my mother's eyes, the frighteningly thin model, Twiggy, represented the most American ideal of feminine beauty. My mother left the conditions of wartime starvation only to be met with a new kind of food deprivation, but this time it was chosen and culturally desirable to starve for beauty and acceptance.

So why did she choose to force-feed me? How was it that she became ever thinner, her collarbones and ribs growing more prominent while I grew rounder? It was as if each pound that fell off her body through self-starvation landed on mine. She forced me to eat excessively all the things she refused to ingest as if I were eating for two—and in a way I was. Every meal she skipped or later purged through laxatives seemed to appear on my plate to consume until I became the image of what she was hell-bent on avoiding—heavy. I never grew beyond what we might today consider a mildly chubby girl, but I was big enough to become the proxy for, and embodiment of, her fear of weight gain, and the object of my brother's relentless teasing. My father remained curiously silent about the force-feeding practices of my mother, as well as my own body size— perhaps it was because he was usually out of the house early and home quite late and not able to witness most of what transpired in the kitchen. Perhaps it was because she was a master at hiding her behaviors, or perhaps he knew but didn't want to intervene. It was more likely a combination of all three factors. Most of us tend to look away from the things that we know are happening, but are unwilling and afraid to directly address.

The constant pressure to eat but remain thin has become an increasingly common struggle for Asian American women; I was not alone in being forced to eat. Most Asian American women I know grew up bombarded with the constant refrains, "Why are you so fat? How will you get a husband? Eat! Don't leave food on your plate. It's rude!" The warnings were passed down from grandmothers, aunts, and mothers to daughters who are always critiqued for being too fat, but pressured into eating whatever is given as a form of gratitude for those who feed us. This is the Confucian way. My girlfriend Helen is from Korea and even though she is in her mid-fifties, her older sister still nags her for being too fat and chides her for not eating more.

No one is spared this critical gaze. Even my stepmother's friends felt free to criticize my body after I got married in my mid-twenties. There I was in the Korean spa in Manhattan getting ready for a massage. I tried to undress modestly in front of the spa's owner who offered me a glass of wine. Once I took a sip, she looked my body up and down and bluntly remarked, "Huh, your waist was a lot smaller when you got married. I was at your wedding."

A humiliating heat rose in my face and I wished that I could shrink down as small as possible and run out the door while kicking Korean cultural norms out of the bloody way. My stepmother said nothing. She was likely immune to this sort of cultural practice of body shaming. In fact, most of my Korean friends admit that Koreans are very blunt about how you look, but that they do it out of love. Perhaps they are better at letting those bodily assessments roll off their backs, but not me. I felt an immediate tightening of my chest. I was desperate to flee anything that resembled my mother's debilitating assessment of my looks. I took a few breaths, swallowed my humiliation and instead, I played the role of the dutiful daughter and keep quiet. I had been here many times before and knew the rules of the game.

In Korean households children are under the rule of the parents, which makes it difficult to rebel. By forcing me to eat beyond what my body could contain my mother short-circuited my internal cues for hunger and satiation and I so grew more and more estranged from how my body felt. I grew up relying on her to tell me what to do. The basic rule was, "eat, but don't you dare throw up," so I ate everything on my plate and was scared to death to throw up. But sometimes it happened anyway. There are only so many devil dogs that I could eat before I threw it up all over the kitchen table.

Once she took me to the pediatrician and pretended to be utterly confused by my constant throwing up. "I think she does it to misbehave or to rebel," she told Dr. Preston. "I have no idea what to do about her behavior!"

Dr. Preston gave her a look of compassion, turned to me, and asked gently, "Now why would you do something like that?"

My face went hot with embarrassment and the lump in my throat grew heavier as I swallowed yet another lie.

I wasn't the one intentionally expelling food from my body—she was. By this time, I also gained the reputation of a being prone to car sickness, so much so that my parents drove around with brown paper grocery bags in the back seat of the car in case I got car sick. However, this tendency to throw up in the car seemed to have far more to do with the excess volume of food in my belly that I often had been forced to eat prior to getting into the back seat. The worst part about getting sick in the car was not that I would be throwing up into a grocery bag (which my mother had cut down to a shorter height so I could use it more easily), but that in getting sick, I knew that she would get angry at me for making a mess and requiring my parents to stop the car so they could dispose of the mess. There was no winning here. Eat until you feel sick enough to throw up, but don't throw up or you will get in trouble. The logic was terrifying and I did my very best to comply by eating all that she required and holding it in as best I could; however, there was only so much I could control when in the back seat of the car on a bumpy road.

The teachers on the silent retreat encourage us to sit and eat our food in a focused manner. "Smell your food and make sure to take small bites so you can savor the taste and appreciate the meal" says Jake, the former Thai monk.

"Put your fork down between each bite and don't let yourself get distracted so that you eat just until you are full. Trust your body to cue your brain when you have had enough," says Asha. I am not so confident that I will be able to feel my body's fullness once I have eaten enough. I wonder if I could eat what my body wants, desires, and needs without judgment, but I am willing to give it a try. Can I inhabit my body and feel it from the inside out?

Are there others in this dining hall who share the same problem of not knowing how to read their bodies' cues? How do they know when they are still hungry or eating for emotional reasons? Is there is still a voice inside me that I can trust to say that I have had enough?

"Don't eat yourself into numbness. Allow yourself to cultivate awareness and mindfulness about your mind-body process so that you can see how you feel while you eat," Jake continues. I am not feeling terribly confident in my eating skills. I can sit in meditation and feel the weight of my feelings on my chest like Jaya reminds me and I can imagine the Buddha and the bodhisattva Kuan Yin as supports. But can I sit into the silence during my meal and cultivate awareness so that I can hear what my body has to tell me? Years of forced feeding make it hard to feel comfortable enough to have faith in myself. I relied so much on someone else telling me what to eat and how much to eat that I had to learn to trust my own feelings. And here I am in the dining hall of a silent retreat introducing myself to the feeling of satiety and learning to say yes to putting more food on my plate without feeling anxiety or shame and saying no without feeling like I am disappointing someone else.

As a young girl, silence protected me from my mother's rage, but it was detrimental to my ability to feel and listen to my body's needs. Silence was also the Confucian way where we never talked back to our parents, and we kept quiet about bad things in order to save face. It took heading to a meditation hall to check into my body and begin to ask it what it wanted.

"Are you hungry? Do you have physical hunger or emotional hunger? Do you feel full? Have you had enough?"

The funny thing is that I never grew up being asked those questions. Learning how to eat freely without judging my body for what it craved was a new experience. It was a challenging practice, but one whose merits I could see.

> Chop and prepare vegetables, cook up simple grains, and make them available for lunch and dinner with a few sauces and maybe some cheese for the kids. Make a warm breakfast with eggs and put out some yogurt and fruit. Put some small plants on the table to make the meal enjoyable. Put down your fork before each bite and really taste the food. Appreciate that someone took the time to grow your ingredients and try to remember that people work hard to deliver the food to the store. Try to eat only things that taste good, and eat until you are full.

I reread these notes that I wrote on the retreat. They remind me to recreate the peaceful and fulfilling mealtimes I enjoyed at the meditation center. I remember eating what I wanted, however much I wanted, and letting myself eat slowly and remain focused enough so that I could taste my food and observe when I was full. I needed to become the observer and the driver of my own hunger.

We were encouraged not to make direct eye contact with other practitioners as we ate in silence so that we could focus on our own experiences, but that privacy also made me feel safe from the gaze of others on my plate. Maybe I can remember to eat for pleasure and sustenance and learn to taste each bite of food. I did it during the retreat, so perhaps I can do it at home. I chop and wash lettuce, cook pasta, pour tomato sauce from a jar on my daughter Hannah's plate of noodles. I sprinkle a little salt and cheese on her sister Haley's lightly-buttered portion. I have a quick flashback to watching my own mother secretly over-salting my food and adding in extra butter and oil to all my meals; I feel a momentary rise of adrenaline in my blood, but then I remind myself that I am not like her. Haley really does like her noodles with a little butter, salt, and cheese. She has a healthy portion of food on her plate and I am not trying to force-feed her.

I call down to the basement to get Hannah off the computer and up to the table.

"But I'm not hungry!" she shouts up.

I start to wonder why she is not hungry and worry that she might be denying herself food, but then remember that she ate just an hour or two ago. "Then just come sit with us," I yell down to her. I put the plates on the table, grab my own, and we practice eating how I have always wanted—however much we want; no more, no less. I remind myself not to look at what goes into the compost bin from the kids' plates because I want them to learn to trust when their bodies are full and to eat what they want. I have faint echoes of their father sternly telling them, "You have to finish your vegetables and don't waste any food." I shut down the memories of his accusation that I am spoiling them by letting them eat whatever they want. *No, I am saving them from a lifetime of food anxiety and eating out of duty and obligation,* I remind myself silently.

There is no longer a set time for dinner and no demand that anyone finish anything on their plates. Mothers and food is a tricky terrain to navigate, but the ability to listen to my own daughters' internal cues is crucial to their survival as young women. I am determined not to get in their way by repeating the patterns inherited from my mother.

A Good Daughter is a Quiet Daughter

"WHAT ARE YOU TALKING ABOUT? You don't have any problems. Everything's fine with you." So says my girlfriend as I grip the steering wheel, listening to her dismiss the concerns I've been sharing because she assumes that nothing really ever goes wrong with me. As I make my way onto I-5, Natalie goes right back to her monologue about her most recent dating catastrophe, a guy she is convinced is stalking her. I stop listening and begin the conversation that says essentially, everything is not okay. But as is often the case when it comes to me talking about real problems, I recess into my head instead.

Actually, I say to her in my mind, *I do have lots of problems. I have had a fantasy apartment for me and my two kids for years that we move into every time I want to escape. I don't want to be married anymore to a man who never puts us first. I feel trapped in the marriage because we have children, yet I can't imagine keeping up the charade for much longer.*

The trick to seeming like I can do it all and do it well comes from my ability to keep quiet about the negative stuff and the things that seemed almost too hard to endure. But I am well-versed in presenting myself as calm and in charge. By looking put together on the outside by dressing well, staying fit, and refusing to acknowledge how difficult things are, I seem to have had most people convinced that my life has been a seamless success. I do the same now because to fall apart sometimes feels like admitting defeat.

Being quiet has been a both a personality trait and a cultural expectation that has come of growing up as second-generation immigrant kid in Long Island in the 70s. There was a lot of enforced silence and things we simply did not discuss. To the outside world, we were a model minority family, but inside the home madness prevailed. The pressure to contain our mess as Korean immigrants who finally made it into a home in the suburbs of Long Island with a two-car garage, four bedrooms, and a manicured lawn meant that my parents had tried hard to adhere to the story line of Asian American success, but that myth was betrayed each and every day in the confines of our home. Like many Koreans, my mother smoldered with a bitterness of what Koreans refer to as *han*, or a kind of inherited national regret and remorse over centuries of colonization and occupation by foreign powers. Her anger seemed uncontrollable, but it was selectively meted out when my father was traveling the world for a major international corporation and doing what we believed Korean men do—provide for their families, secure the financial well-being of the family, and raise educated, well-mannered children no matter the cost. From the outside, we were doing fine.

Be disciplined, rule-abiding, successful, hard-working children who make the family look good—this lesson was driven home as a kindergartener when my father would line up me and my brother in a military formation as he commanded, "Stand up! Salute! Tell me what you want to be when you grow up."

Although there were no right answers and my father would smile through his façade of sternness, I was expected to answer. My brother always proudly shouted, "Cheetah!" which confused me because at first, I thought he wanted to be a cheater. But he wanted to be the fastest animal in the kingdom.

I always gave my standard answer—"Monkey!" I imagined monkeys to be clever and always liked the cute chimpanzee on television dressed up in a little boy's outfit and saddle shoes holding hands with some kindly adult. Such activities like these weekly military practices confirm the model minority image of my family where success and determination are the most important things. But there is always an underside and backstory.

I learned to be the good quiet daughter and I forced down fear, anger, and resentment as my body became rounder through the forced-eating my mother inflicted, while she remained miraculously thin. Her thinness was the envy of the country club women in Long Island who were forever ordering chef's salads with a bagel whose soft-dough had been scooped out with a spoon and tossed away. The SOB, as this hollowed-out bagel was called, was ordered by the ladies to reduce its carbohydrates. My mother would order the SOB as well and I would cringe with embarrassment because she looked so thin already and I was always worried that others would know how she kept so thin.

"Oh, my god, you are so lucky! Look how thin you are! I bet you can eat anything you want," the ladies would comment enviously as they walked by our table in the dining room. What they never noticed though was that her food was nearly uneaten. It would be pushed from one corner of the plate to the other, but never ingested. "How do you do it?" they'd ask in wonder. I always answered that question myself, but only in my head as I pictured her sitting in the bathroom for hours after swallowing the cotton candy pink laxatives that she popped like SweeTarts into her mouth.

Those smooth, shiny pink pills were a ubiquitous presence throughout the house; they were strewn about her bathroom counter, lodged in her makeup basket, stored in the kitchen cabinet, and crammed in her purse. Much like smokers light up a post-meal cigarette, my mother would often fumble around in her purse after dinner, fish out a little pink pill, wash it down with water after her barely-eaten meal, and retire to the bathroom to await the drug's dangerous magic. It is hard to know when she began using laxatives for weight loss, but when I piece together the bits of information shared by my father over the years, it seems that her misuse of laxatives as a purging method began once she recovered from tuberculosis in Korea and immigrated to the Midwest to meet up with my father in Missouri State in her early twenties.

Because tuberculosis and kidney dysfunction are commonly linked, the medications my mother had begun taking caused puffiness and swelling. Because, as my father put it, she was extremely self-conscious of the water weight gain and especially was worried about appearing to have a "moon-face," she began an extreme diet where she'd eat a single container of strawberry yogurt and barely anything else during the day. Eventually, she added diuretics to the mix to rid her body of the water retention, and the weight came off. Perhaps because she then birthed my brother and me within two years and faced the inevitable bodily changes that come from motherhood, she ramped up her food restriction and added laxatives to the mix.

Contents Under Pressure

THERE IS A LOT to my parents' history that I don't know, but this lack of information is not so unusual. Immigrant parents often don't want to share the stories of the struggles that lead them to leave their home countries and we, their children, know not to ask. Most of the stories I got from my dad about his youth were usually framed around a Korean Horatio Alger theme of beating the odds. My favorite dad story is when he was ill as a teenager and sought relief in a Buddhist temple. My father's stories of this near-death experience usually started with some mysterious bacterial infection that left his life in the balance. The story usually ended with him heroically climbing a mountain outside of Seoul while on the brink of starvation because his body violently rejected whatever food he put into it.

"I was determined to either survive and heal myself or die trying," he'd say in each retelling of his story of living in a remote Buddhist temple for a month. "Nobody knew what to do with me or how to help me. The doctors couldn't do anything." He always taught this story with a triumphalist tone in his voice as if he wanted me to catch the life lesson right off the bat.

If I told the story myself, I'd probably focus on the healing in a Buddhist temple and the ways the monks might have looked after me, but for my dad the crux of the story hinged on the survivalist instinct.

Like a Confucian life coach, he'd share these heroic examples of his life to narrate a model of sacrifice, hard work, and personal commitment no matter the odds. I am still so proud and amazed that he was the first Asian American hired to work as an accountant in New York in the 1960s. An exemplary Asian American life is usually filled with a series of firsts that form a lineage of model minority success and my dad always made sure to contribute to the lineage with his own stories of his exceptionalism that I would then be expected to perpetuate myself. I just needed to make sure that I never bragged about my own accomplishments, for boastful Korean American women were unacceptable. In Korean American culture, humility still reigned supreme.

My father remained a man of firsts even when he was hospitalized for the last time with liver cancer on the critical intensive care ward. "I have never seen anyone do this before on the floor. Your dad is conducting business and signing papers from his gurney with his work partners surrounding him!" his nurse reported two weeks before he finally succumbed to the disease.

As a first-generation immigrant's daughter, I knew to take these narratives of dedication and survival as a guide for how to get through difficult situations and, most importantly, how to persevere. The lesson served me well over the years, but it also had its limits.

Outside of the exemplary Korean traits that were to help mold my life, here are some of the facts that I do know. My parents were among the first Korean students to enter the United States in the late 50s and early 60s on student visas. Both parents landed scholarships to Missouri State when my father matriculated in 1959 after a brief required stint in the Korean army. He was "fresh off the boat" and looked it with his brand-new haircut, perfectly pressed trousers and shirts buttoned all the way to the top. While he never discussed his own encounters with racism in the U.S. outside of breaking through glass ceilings in the corporate world later in his business career, he was such a novelty in middle America that the local Springfield paper wrote an article about him and his recent move from Korea.

"That's how you ended up with American grandparents," he'd often say. "Your grandma and grandpa read the paper, learned that I was from Korea, and just invited me over because their son was there during the war." They became my father's "adoptive" parents from that day forward.

It had never occurred to me that having white grandparents was unusual; we hopped into the Oldsmobile station wagon every Thanksgiving to spend it with our non-Korean family. For me, they were everything I thought grandparents were supposed to be—old, loving, indulgent, and... well, white.

Every Christmas Grandma would send me a tin of mint meringues in the mail from Delaware loaded with chocolate chips and green food dye with a card expressing their love for my brother and me. Eating those melt-in-your-mouth cookies where the meringue gave way to the chunky chocolate chips and ethereal mint flavor was a lesson in food love. I happily assumed my place in their home with their plaid blankets, kitchen full of pies, and Grandpa chasing us around pushing his coke bottle glasses back up his nose and pretending to run slower than he could.

Grandpa reminded me of the grandfather in Johanna Spyri's book

Heidi, a book I read over and over as my own model of survival and exemplary behavior. It did not matter that she was a young girl living far off in the Swiss Alps. Heidi captured my imagination and my own longing because she was orphaned and sent to live with her grandfather in the Swiss Alps, grilling bread and cheese and drinking fresh goat's milk every day. As a seven-year-old, I usually wished I was an orphan and hoped that someday I'd be taken in by a nice old grandfather like Heidi's or my own white Grandpa Karl.

Heidi was plucky and ever cheerful. Her ability to steal little rolls from the dinner table of the home where she was later hired as a lady's companion to a young invalid fascinated me. Her resourcefulness and the fact that she got away with hiding bread in a cupboard gave me some ideas. It didn't occur to me then that she was stockpiling the bread out of a fear of hunger. I was going to stockpile too, only I was stockpiling food that I couldn't eat. When I couldn't possibly eat another bite on my plate, I'd spit out the food into napkins that I would hide behind my dog's wood-paneled gate. Alas, much like harsh housekeeper, Fräulein Rottenmeier, discovered Heidi's secret cache of dinner rolls, so too did my mother discover my secret stash of chewed-up leftovers on the morning of my birthday party.

The other mothers and their daughters were going to be at my house in a few hours, which thankfully kept most of the peace in the house that day. I didn't usually fare so well, but on that day I managed to escape punishment and enjoy the thrill of blowing out the candles on my favorite chocolate cake baked cleverly in a little aluminum coated pan that came with the boxed mix. There were party games like holding plastic straws in our mouths that we tried to stick through the holes of life savers hanging from strings, and of course birthday presents. But toward the end of the party, I had a familiar sinking feeling in my gut because I knew that my friends would eventually go home and everything would return to normal. My mom would stop being the hostess with the mostest and go back to just being herself. True to form, as soon as the last guest left, my mother closed the door and the smile immediately left her face as she uttered, "How dare you! Don't you ever waste food again!" Although I was afraid of her, I stepped away, relieved that she didn't punish me this time.

Nothing was better than being left at white Grandma and Grandpa's house for a week or two when my parents left town. It was a time for my brother and me to live as ordinary kids and not as the peculiar Asian Americans next door. Even if we were an oddity parading around town with our white grandparents, no one ever hinted at anything unusual about seeing us together. I had a white Grandpa and Grandma who showered me with attention, made me great American food that I wasn't forced to overeat, and teased me and my brother with funny nicknames and stories. We even got to paddle around in the old wooden boat they kept moored on the canal by their house. I wouldn't trade them for my stoic and quiet Korean grandparents who sometimes stayed with us in Long Island. When I saw them, gone was the easy intimacy and laughter that I had with my white grandparents. Everyone knew Korean grandparents were formal and you had to "respect your elders" or your parents would get mad at you.

It never seemed fair though that I'd have to be on my best behavior with my Korean grandparents, but my mother didn't. She got to say all sorts of harsh things about her mother-in-law who had a penchant for huge steamy bowls of white rice that she would melt margarine and spicy hot sauce onto. "I can't believe she can eat all that!" my mother would spit out when Halmoni, as we called my Korean grandmother, would go off to her room for a nap. Halmoni didn't speak English so maybe she didn't know what my mother was saying. Or maybe she went to her room just to get away from my mother. I kept a low profile around them.

It took a good year after my father started his freshman year at Missouri State before my mother was allowed to leave Seoul. She was quarantined for tuberculosis, arrived at the age of 20 and married my father in the basement of a little church a year later. My dad liked to toot his own horn and tell me that that my mom had a big crush on him in high school. "Your mom was supposed to get married to someone else but then she met me through your uncle and that was that. Engagement was off, and she ended up with me." He'd then brag about some of the love letters she sent him and act as though she finally caught him. He was ever the narrator of firsts.

My mother looked so young on her wedding day. Fresh out of quarantine, she looked like a Korean Jackie O. at her wedding. She wore a blue and grey wool plaid skirt with matching three-quarter-sleeved fitted jacket and a little pill box hat and gloves. I took to wearing the jacket for a brief stint after she died, partly because I was so delighted that it fit and because it was considered retro cool in my early twenties. My father cut a dashing figure in his black suit, white shirt, and tie. They both looked confident and carefree.

There were no Koreans at the wedding because it was simply impossible to bring their parents from Korea, so their marriage was sanctified by a white minister and some of the elder church women who helped serve the cake and probably donated the flowers. While my dad usually supplied the stories of triumph over the odds and the immigrant success narratives, my mother remained curiously silent about her past. She didn't share much with my brother and me about her childhood and so what I know of her comes from my own memories and from decades of piecing together the tidbits of information my aunts and uncles would quietly murmur to me.

The information was usually offered with a slight shake of the head, the kind that said that they knew that there was abuse going on in my house and the occasional brief snippet was the best they could offer for answers and support. Many of the stories I know of my parents' lives in Korea and as immigrants in the U.S. were often offered as afterthoughts by my extended family members who'd mention details but always cast a little fuzziness around the edges as if they were protecting themselves from revealing hard cold facts. It seemed that they were afraid of my mother and her unpredictable anger, but as a way of reaching out to me, they offered little revelations to lay bare some of the mystery of her life.

"Well, your mom had… well, she had… a… *difficult* time growing up. Her dad and his new wife really doted on your oldest uncle in the family. She was probably a little jealous of all the attention he was getting," they'd say in secretive terms so that my mother would never hear. My great aunt often cited events in my mother's childhood as a way of showing me that she knew what was going on in my house—the gist was that my mom was jealous of her older brother and all the attention showered on him, so she was reliving it at home with me and my brother. I was the stand-in for the less-adored child in my mother's own past, or so I think my aunt was trying to convey without filling in the details.

My father offered similar explanations for her behavior, even noting that he had once taken her to a psychologist to address her anger and treatment of me, but apparently she refused to say much and later claimed that the therapist came to believe that she had no problems with food or mothering. Instead, it was the people around her that were aggravating her—especially me. She did not go back to the therapist apparently because she was too smart for him. I am not sure why my father did not pursue more counseling for her, but my sense is that she could be a fierce opponent and he likely wanted to keep whatever semblance of peace he could. He also managed to cope by playing tennis every weekend and on weeknights with his Korean friends, as well as working all the time. Burying oneself in work and physical activity is certainly one trait that I inherited from my father in response to stressful situations.

These offerings were accepted by me as gestures of acknowledgement that I received gratefully. I knew at a very young age that family did not rat on family, especially Korean families and especially Korean families living in a new culture. But I also knew that others could see into my family and could tell that something was askew. They just couldn't do anything that would draw my mother's attention because they knew that to provoke her would be to poke a sleeping tiger whose force far outweighed the little body that contained it. Sometimes, they'd say, "Well, you know how in Korea, first sons are really important? Well, your mom grew up like that and so maybe that's why…" and I'd be left to fill in the rest of the sentences. Their admission also invoked Korean Confucian culture where the first son is the highest hope for a mother whose worth was solidified through the birth of a son. It hardly seemed fair.

Having a son brought my mother great excitement and joy, something that was evident by his images that adorned the house in Long Island where I grew up. The pencil drawing that she sketched of Mike's cherubic little face sat proudly framed on her dresser along with the photo of him wearing a little blue knit vest smiling out like the happy baby that he was. There were pictures of him in a little plaid checkered suit and cute little white socks and saddle shoes covering his chubby little feet. Mike's calves were smooth and round, soft enough that she'd pretend to take a bite out of them in order to make him laugh. That's the thing with first-born sons to a Korean mother. Mike was a little prince who completed and fulfilled my mother's ever-evolving but not-quite-complete self. Although I didn't have nearly as many photos of me displayed in the house, I did end up in a pastel portrait of me as a three-year-old that hung side by side next to my brother's portrait in the living room.

My mother remains to this day a mystery to me despite being gone for over 23 years. She sketched, she played the guitar, and acted in local community plays at the high school. She was radiant and beautiful onstage dancing to complicated choreography in shows like *Annie Get Your Gun* and *How to Succeed in Business*. She beamed on stage in her high-heeled shoes tap dancing away in a short black dress and belting out the words to "There's no Business, Like Show Business…" I was always so impressed that she had these gifts and so proud of how beautiful she was on stage—

she was also a first because I didn't see any other Korean moms on stage dancing and singing in high heels.

My parents always kept the less sanguine details of being immigrants in a predominantly white land to themselves. Perhaps my dad was trying to shore us up against what he already knew first hand—being Korean in a mostly white world was a constant reminder of the need to bear the invisibility of being an Asian minority, and the swallowing of humiliation for being hyper-visible because of his race. I understand the desire to gloss over the seedy and rough parts of adjustment to a new landscape because I do this myself; I rarely tell the bad stuff or reveal the underbelly of my own details. Somehow, I manage to find the "single mother triumphing over a bad marriage" narrative far more appetizing to give my daughters than to admit defeat. So, whenever I think about some of the things my ex-husband did during our marriage that hurt me, I somehow find a way to rationalize the pain and ignore the damage. I tell myself that I am protecting my daughters' relationship with their father, but I am also suturing up any hint of a rupture or a stitch to keep from unraveling.

Like my parents, I live the Asian American model minority myth where we triumph over defeat against all odds. We remain honorable with stoic faces; we are dedicated to the family and endure all sorts of hardship for the sake of the kids. But we are also contents under pressure and need a safety valve to release the strain of swallowing the difficult stuff that always leaves a dyspeptic feeling in the craw.

I had one other set of grandparents who made an indelible impression on me, yet I never really knew them. I lived with my maternal grandfather and his wife, my mom's stepmother, while my parents and brother remained in New York. I have no memories of this time of my life when my grandparents took me in and no stories of how I got to Korea. Did I travel alone? Did one of my parents drop me off? Did they miss me at all? And why wasn't my brother there, too? I must have been about two years old when I moved into their home in Seoul, and as far as I can tell from the few times my father spoke of this period, I was there for at least six months.

Although it is not so unusual for children to be left with my grandparents while the child's parents immigrate to a new country and settle in before sending for the kids, there is something askew about why I was in Korea. I was born in Flushing, New York and was already an American citizen so I didn't need to be sent for later once my parents found jobs and a home. More important to my own story as a child growing up and my sense of alienation from my mother was the fact that I was sent there while my older brother stayed in New York with my parents. Growing up, I held onto the fuzzy details I garnered through casual attempts at asking my father and I simply assumed that my mother didn't love me enough to keep me at home—or that somehow my birth and presence was so distressing to her that she had to ship me off to Korea while she supposedly found her bearings.

Of course, to any child growing up, the realization that you were sent away will leave an imprint, although in retrospect, I can see that that time away was probably life-saving for me. Although I am a mother of two and couldn't imagine sending one away while holding on to the other, there must have been far more to the story than I was ever privy to. And given the happy little girl looking back at me from photo albums, I am quite confident that the experience was a positive one for me—I had an attentive step-grandmother who raised me as her own daughter and showered me with the kind of affection that I imagine I had craved.

When I found out about living with my grandparents, when I was about ten years old, all I can remember is my father saying with a long pause, "Your mom was sick, and we were so busy, and she couldn't take care of you." I never pried too much for details because my dad would immediately say, "Well, your step-grandmother couldn't have children of her own and so she was delighted to have you and loved you very much." No more details were ever disclosed.

Growing up, I assumed that I was both a consolation prize and the apple of my step-grandmother's eye. I believe this story of her affection for me, for when I look back at childhood photos, I can see her fawning over me and me looking up to her with a big smile on my face while I waited for her to fish a treat from her purse. There she is in the few photos I have of her—a woman probably around my age now who has taken in her stepdaughter's daughter for several months, with her head wrapped in a fashionable kerchief, her long slim legs peeking out from a knee-length skirt, and her feet tucked into two-inch white square-heeled shoes. She casually searches her purse that hangs from one wrist, maybe looking for a piece of gum, or a small toy or something else that obviously kept me in rapt attention. I must have been very loved by my mother's parents, for the black and white photos I have from that time always have me held gently in my grandfather's arms or carrying my own prized balloon with the most natural giant grin on my face, or just laughing readily. I am dressed to the nines in frilly white tights with ruffles on the bottom meant to peak out of the little knit dress I am wearing with a kitty cat embroidered near the hem. I was indeed, it seems, well cared for and loved by grandparents whom I never really got to know after I returned home to New York perhaps a half a year or so later.

Although my mother did not have a close relationship with her stepmother and never spoke with her on the phone or hosted her much at our Long Island home, my step-grandmother often tried to reach out to me, especially after she moved to San Jose, California, once my grandfather passed away. She would send me birthday cards with short abbreviated sentences that would say, "Happy Birthday, Sharon. Love, Halmoni," as she did her best to stay connected to me.

Once she sent me a green jade, rectangular beaded necklace that I cherished and kept with me for years and would twirl around my fingers in secret imagining that they were magnificent gems. I would sit in my room on the floor forever pulling at the necklace and testing how far I could pull without it breaking as if I was exploring the bonds of her love. I could tell that she loved me even though my mother didn't speak with her and would often say that she was not a good person or that she was uneducated when she married my grandfather. Personally, I always thought my mother should be nicer to her since she took me in when my mother couldn't take care of me. My father's explanation that she was too sick to raise me never made much sense to me since she could still take care of my brother, so to this day I assume that she needed a break from raising a daughter. And as things unfolded in my house, it was quite clear that her love for her son was dramatically different from her feelings for her own daughter.

The last time I saw my grandmother was at a family reunion about twenty years ago and though she didn't speak too many words to me, the love that she felt for me was palpable as she grasped both of my hands in hers and looked me straight in the eyes. She gripped my hands tightly, whispered that it had been too long, and as the tears welled up in her eyes, I knew that the feelings of love that showed through in all the photos we have of our time in Korea were in fact real. She loved me, and I got to be raised as a precious daughter, even if just for a short period of time.

It took me years to begin to unpack the significance of this story and how it was that my parents had decided that I was the one to live without them while they continued to care for my brother. It became a lifelong curiosity that I carried inside me, a gendered reminder that being female was a secondary status not only in society, but in my own home. To be born female, was to be unwanted, the child to be sent away. And if not because I had been born female, then because I had been born at all. And having been sent away, I returned to an agreed-upon silence on the matter that suggested it hadn't ever happened, at all. The Korean American installation artist Yong Soon Min says of one of her works that "Invisible wounds are the hardest to heal. They throb with buried memories, telling me that the past is real and that I've survived. Of the visible scars, some are seductive, as if turning a blind eye to the pain that was the source."

One of the greatest blind spots in the Asian American community has been the blanketing oppressive silence in the face of deep atrocities for the sake of the family. Infused with Confucian values of filial piety and deference, Korean Americans may sympathize with the pain of the other but as is the case with my own family, tacit acknowledgement that something has gone awry did not adequately offer a salve to the invisible wounds inflicted in families. We agreed to live in silence and built water-tight boundaries around our struggles—and we addressed our pain and suffering out loud in terms of our ability to gloriously overcome the hardships we'd endured.

As good Confucian Koreans, we suppressed the needs and desires of the individual for the sake of the family, for the sake of the public, for the sake of saving face. The stakes were even higher for our family because we had moved into a predominantly white neighborhood. It felt like all eyes and noses were on us—visitors would sniff the air when they'd come into the kitchen wondering what that "putrid" smell was. The smell of course was the *kimchi*, the lifeblood of the Korean, stored inside a glass jar covered with plastic wrap with lid atop. We were rumored to bury our kimchi in the backyard like they did back in Korea and occasionally we'd be taunted for supposedly being dog-eaters. Kimchi—that potent, spicy, fervent, boiling over, and nearly combustible cabbage—was the perfect symbol for my own family. We were at the boiling point. Occasionally we sizzled. When overripe, we threatened to erupt or seethe. But somehow, we managed to ferment without expanding beyond the limits of the house despite the fear of exposing our stink. We had to; so we stayed quiet.

Like many Korean American households, mine coveted and hid the kimchi from the prying eyes and noses of strangers and friends with the hopes of avoiding that shameful question, "what is that smell?!" We pretended it did not exist by covering it in many layers of plastic bags, we hid it in separate refrigerators as if to hide our shame and dependence. Usually the kimchi remained in the garage so that its odor could meld with that of the car engine's oils at the end of a long day's drive. But could the oily sooty hot smell of the engine mask the contents that lay buried in the refrigerator? We wished it were so. Every day we would open its contents, quickly pulling out a teeming bushel of napa cabbage that has been left to ferment, its contents basically eating away at its own source. We salivate at the thought and we consume it knowing it to be both life force and a source of great shame for so distinctly marking our difference. We desired it, it made us who we were, it marked us as different. There was always a double-bind in that we'd want the kimchi, but then we'd be embarrassed by our very own need.

As a kid growing up in the suburbs of New York, I would usually be greeted on the school bus with the familiar taunt of "Chinese, Japanese, dirty knees, look at these," as groups of kids would take their fingers and turn their eyes up for Chinese, down for Japanese, and pull at one's t-shirt as a gesture of having breasts. These boys were only in the third grade, but they had already been steeped in a racial and gender discrimination that allowed them to exact daily victory because they knew I wouldn't tell. But I did wonder where Korean eyes fit in if they were neither Chinese nor Japanese. It didn't really matter though because in the 1970s no one cared about what part of Asia we were from. Our food stank, we had strange customs, we were invisible yet model minorities, and because we were constantly in the public's eye, we kept bad news under wraps. But the stress from being different would somehow be released. My dad's escape became tennis with his fellow Koreans, parties with other Korean families on the weekends, and traveling abroad to Asia for work for weeks on end. My brother's approach was to run with the neighborhood boys in a herd; he seemed to blend in easily because when moving at a fast pace he was in-distinguishable. Perhaps because she had the inheritance of Confucianism so heavily stamped on her body, my mom remained a *jip saram*, which in Korean literally meant "house person" and was used by a man to describe his wife. My mom mostly stayed home if she was not working part-time for my father's company and it is within the confines of the home that she dealt with her own differences as a minority woman. She exorcised her demons on the one person who would keep her secrets—me.

Women like my mother struggled in the U.S. because they no longer had the familiarity of other Korean women as their confidantes, having left their families behind at such a young age, and because they had to maintain a positive image, they turned their rage inward. Korean culture did allow women to express their hurt, but usually they took it out on their daughters-in-law. Turn on any Korean soap opera and you will find the millennia-old stereotype of the evil mother-in-law meting out her resentment on the son's wife. In olden-day Confucian households, daughters-in-law were the first to rise and make breakfast for the family and the last to bed because they had to clean house. This unequal treatment seeped into the bones of the daughters-in-law who escaped her subordinate position only when her own sons married and the daughter-in-law moved into her rightful spot as the lauded mother-in-law herself, her first position of power in the domicile for Korean women.

The joke on Korean soap operas is that the mothers usually have so much power over their sons precisely because they hide their torment and only offer it in secret. They protect the son who remains the prized possession; after all, he is the gift that makes a woman confident that she has fulfilled her destiny in the Confucian pecking order. My own mom never really had the chance to become that mother-in-law in Korea where she'd eventually inherit the power to exact her revenge. She left Korea to enroll in an American college, married my dad, had kids, and became contents under pressure threatening to explode in secret. I witnessed her secrets, though, and knew how to be dutiful and keep them tucked away. I heard enough successful immigrant stories from my dad to know that I was supposed to triumph against the odds. In my case that meant staying silent at all costs.

Silence is Survival

WEEEEEEOH! WEEEEEEOH! WEEEEEEHO! WEEEEEEHO! WEEEEEEHO! The siren on my brother's GI Joe fort is just far too tempting to leave alone. I have to touch it myself and hit that alarm switch just for the thrill of its shrill-sounding beacon. My fingers move closer and closer to the switch as I ignore my own internal alarm signal telling me that this is a terrible idea. Intuition and warning are simply overridden because I am fixated on getting this thing to make noise. I flip the switch on and a search light suddenly pulses, shooting a beam of light marking a circle around the grounds of the fortress. GI Joe men dressed in combat gear are ready to take down the escapees who dare to break free.

I can feel my own pulse begin to race and I grow as anxious as one of GI Joe's prisoners because I have knowingly transgressed the taboo—I have played with my brother's favorite toy. Mike's Planet of the Apes jungle set was okay to play with, so my Barbies would sometimes pay a visit, albeit to their own demise since they'd end up hung by the hair or lose a head or limb. The jungle was no place for a Barbie though and the proof lay in the plastic graveyard of arms and legs strewn about. I wanted access to that GI Joe fort with the tall gray security walls because it had far cooler features than my Barbie dream house. GI Joe's fort made noise, a loud noise. Barbie's house was cute, frilly, and pink but frankly I wanted more daring action out of her home. Hers only had a doorbell and a very dainty one at that. And besides, maybe Barbie and GI Joe could hang out and protect the fort from invading apes.

So, against my mother's very strict rules that I not touch my brother's fort or even bring my own dolls to play without permission, I have made a bold and calculated move. I know that sounding that alarm will bring on inevitable punishment, but for some reason I don't care. At that moment, safety and reason are tossed out the window in favor of sheer thrill. I want to hear that siren so that I can pretend that Barbie will save the prisoners. But as soon as that siren screeches through the house, my mom flies out of the kitchen and into the living room at rapid speed—just like a real prison guard—coming to a stop where the now-dreaded toy lay. GI Joe had betrayed me by sounding a warning signal far louder than I could have expected. I jump back from the fortress and am immediately tense with anxiety and remorse because my mother told me not to touch, but I did it anyway.

What transpired next occurred in such a flash of fury that even if I didn't go limp with fear, there'd still be no way to stop my mom's anger which could catapult into such a rage that it would barrel down anyone who got in its way. She had gone from nice mom preparing for my aunt's visit later that afternoon into a runaway train whose brakes had spontaneously failed. The sound of the siren provoked a series of events that to this day is so difficult to recount in detail that I often tell myself maybe I am misremembering. But I know that it did happen, that I am not imagining it. I am remembering what I wish I could forget and what I wish I could rewrite as part of my history.

My mother's stony face appeared in front of me, as if conjured by a very scary magic. Her cold eyes narrowed and without breaking her gaze she bore her anger into me. I immediately felt the tears well in my eyes and my throat constrict. How quickly the thrill of play can transform to terror. Her lips formed into a pinched little circle that seethed, "How many times do I have to tell you not to touch his toys!"

I whispered a tiny, "I'm sorry," but saying that never made a difference because her rage was swift, unstoppable, and impervious to apologies when she was in this kind of a mood. She reached out to unload a swift slap to the side of my head, grabbed my hair, and pulled me by the arm toward the basement steps. My feet clunked along the steps heading down to the basement as she pulled at my arm, yanking me down into the cold, damp darkness. She never said a word; she didn't need to. She let go of my hand and went straight to the cardboard boxes that held all sorts of tools, flashlights, and outdoor gear. Finally, she found what she was looking for—an old gray camping rope, the one we had used to lash our suitcases to the roof of our station wagon when we went camping.

I couldn't see her face; it was cloaked in darkness, but I knew as she came closer what she intended to do with that rope. She was going to wrap that rope around me, and there was nothing I could do to stop her, no words that I could utter, no pleas that she would hear. I had touched my brother's prized toy, and for that I would be punished. Severely.

It was a partially finished basement; not quite a room, not quite a cellar. But it was dank and cold as the underground usually is. As she came closer, I could feel myself shiver at her cold fury as she began to tie the rope around my body and my hands. There was nothing I could do to stop what was happening and I began to sink deep into myself looking for some kind of refuge. When she went white hot with her wrath, I went deeper into retreat. But when I our eyes met, I didn't see much of her in there either. She seemed possessed by some other force that wouldn't relent.

She was going to teach me a lesson. A lesson I wouldn't forget. I was not to seek pleasure in my brother's toys. They belonged to him, and him alone.

When she had finally finished knotting the rope, a hasty gesture as if she was running out of time, she walked away, wordlessly. I listened as she walked up the stairs, each step a step toward freedom—freedom from her torment—and each step a step toward utter isolation. I would be left alone.

The door clicked closed, and with it, the last flicker of light. I was left in total darkness. The rope was not tied so tight as to dig into my skin, but that didn't make much of a difference to me because I was too afraid to try to escape. Escape meant more punishment. Acceptance gave me protection.

By this time, I had recessed into my own familiar silence deep inside myself for safety. Pleading and crying would only bring on more punishment and I knew that I simply had to accept the penalty she'd delivered. Much like the enormous plates of food that I'd been forced to consume lest I be spanked, scolded, or held at the table for hours, I swallowed my own anger. The sense of injustice, terror, and desire to defend myself felt like all the meat, rice, and huge glasses of milk that I'd force down in obedience to my mother. And all of it would sit uncomfortably inside me.

I had learned not to defend myself because I was simply too afraid to let it out, not only from fear of her, but also from fear of becoming like her. Like the warning label on the kimchi jar, I too was contents under pressure.

And so it was that I remained tied to that basement pole, a pillar of shame and rage. I had been imprisoned; just like G.I. Joe, captured, but determined to survive.

I stood in that basement for what seemed like a few hours. I wonder if I noticed then that the gray pillars were painted the same color as the GI Joe fort or if I had imagined that I was a prisoner of GI Joe himself. How long would he keep me in solitary? Would he be nicer than my mom? I began once again to play out the fantasy arguments I would have with my mother if I wasn't so afraid of her—the kinds of arguments my own children have with me today when they think I am being unfair. Sometimes I am taken aback by their fearlessness in expressing what they want or don't like, but then I remember that this is what I have always wanted. Children who could say what they wanted, needed, and didn't like. I was not well versed in such expression myself, but I knew growing up that if and when I became a mother, I'd be the kind of mother I fantasized about. While I never think of myself as a terribly imaginative person, I do know that many of my moments of stress were alleviated in some small part by my ability to engage in ideal conversations with those who were threatening me. The only problem was that these conversations would be happening in silence and the person bothering me would usually be right in front of me. But rather than shouting out loud, I'd swallow those screams and let them loose inside my head. I wonder what it must look like to see me stone-faced and trying to remain calm while I rage and triumph in the argument in my own head. Does anybody even see what's going on inside me?

My legs were tired from standing, my chest hurt from choking down sobs, but my eyes had acclimated to the dark. The cold of the pillar seeped through my lower back and I had no other option but to tolerate it. I didn't scream. There was no one to call for help. I was stuck in the basement while my mother probably went back to cooking and cleaning. I envied that my brother was out playing with his friends and wished that he could somehow hear me in the basement through the walls of the house as if he had telepathy. But he couldn't hear me, and he was never raised to pay too much attention to my cries anyway. My mom usually made sure that he was out of the house for the major retributions. She probably didn't want him to see her when she flew off the handle; she was his mother after all and good mothers don't harm their kids.

After what seemed like an interminable time in the dark, the door at the top of the stair quickly opened and light illuminated the basement. My mother swiftly descended the steps, untied my arms, and informed me that my aunt was coming into the house. She didn't make eye contact with me. She didn't need to warn me not to say anything because by this time I was well versed in the practice of silence that protected her from being caught and protected me from further punishment.

I followed behind her up the stairs as she then greeted my aunt at the door saying, "Oh hi! Sharon was just in the basement playing. Say hi to Auntie, Sharon."

I whispered a shy hello and looked up at my aunt and prayed that somehow she could read what had happened just by looking into my eyes.

But I turned my eyes quickly in fear that my mom might notice and sank into my aunt's hugs and sweet voice greeting me. I was safe when my aunt was here and my mom changed into nice mom again all at the flip of a switch. And so back to the kitchen we went to eat.

It was around second grade that I started getting round or "solid" as my relatives would comment as if to spare me the word "fat." As I got heavier from my mother's force-feeding, she got progressively thinner. It was as if I had become the scapegoat and symbol of what she wanted and would not let herself have—lots of food. She was admired for her thin physique and I slowly became her *foie gras* goose, confined to the house, psychologically chained to the table out of fear as I ate and ate, sometimes to the point of throwing up. Each year that I gained weight could be measured equally by her weight loss. Curiously, my father never noticed that I was gaining weight or that I had an enormous appetite, but then again, he never said much about my looks. My mother never let him say positive things about the way I looked because every compliment to me would detract from her recognized beauty. If he or anyone paid me a compliment, she would quickly correct them by pointing out my flaws.

"She isn't pretty, look at her big belly," she would say in Korean, and the listener would accept her judgment as the truth of who I was. It was also common practice to purposefully find the flaws in one's children just to feign humility and also to ensure that the children would end up extremely successful but still retain their Confucian code of moral values. I have never picked up this cultural parenting practice of finding the flaws in my children and then broadcasting them to my friends. I focus on my love for them despite their successes and inevitable failures.

I bore the burden of her fears of gaining weight, her desire to practically disappear, and somehow maintain that ethereal ghost-like appearance. She could stay thin by making me fat.

Koreans have no problem calling a spade a spade to your face and this means that women are constantly being assessed and my mom was no exception in making her assessments. "Mike is such a good boy! Mike is so athletic! Mike is so smart," or some variation of this mantra would be chattered in the telephone as my mom sat at the kitchen table twirling the phone chord with her finger and gushing on about her son's accomplishments. Most of her phone calls included the usual updates of the family's goings on: "Dad is traveling again in China and Korea for another month. Mike got on the baseball team. He is doing so well in school, but his sister is so difficult! She lies all the time. I don't know what to do with her."

While I wasn't exactly a liar, I was complicit in keeping her rage under the radar through my repressed silence, but that was a lie she demanded of me. So I did lie, but mostly by virtue of being silent and for protection—from my mom.

During the mid 70s and 80s, my dad traveled the world on business—he was one of the first Korean Americans to travel to China in 1979 when full diplomatic relations were established during Jimmy Carter's administration. Off he'd go for sometimes up to six weeks leaving my mom alone with two kids—which meant that he'd leave me behind with my mother, and that was always when her behavior became more erratic and frightening. My brother was having a great time in baseball; most of our Saturdays were devoted to his games where my parents would watch and shout for Mike's team and I would wander around on my own, delighted by a bag of Cheese Doodles and a can of orange Fanta. The games were excruciatingly tedious to me, but I made do by making that bag of orange snack last as long as I could, which was no easy feat since they were basically made out of air. One touch of the tongue and the Styrofoam tidbit would magically disintegrate and leave but a slight residue of orange tint on my fingers.

My dad would eventually return home with suitcases full of gifts for us that would somehow make us forget the fact that he was gone all the time—at least that's what I told myself. I hated that he left, mostly because my mom would have free range over the house and much of her abuse would happen when I was alone with her. The sigh of relief when my dad walked through the door would radiate down into my body as I'd begin to feel safe again. And yet, when doling out the souvenirs from his various trips to China and Korea, my father would often catch my eye and give me a doleful look that suggested he knew the time alone with my mother was rough. Nevertheless, he never directly asked me how things went while he was gone and I was far too afraid to initiate any conversation about her various punishments. Instead, I'd often replay the incidents in my head as if they were a television show and hope that somehow he'd magically be able to read my mind.

It's hard to imagine now what it would be like for my mother to have been left back then with two elementary school children and no job outside the home. Perhaps the isolation and entrapment in the suburbs of Long Island were too much to bear and she simply needed an outlet, which was me. Her anger, frustration, and resentment at her own confinement found a vulnerable recipient in me. I can relate to the devastation of having your own dreams and freedom crushed for the sake of your husband's career goals as you become the primary caregiver for your children. I had done that too, but I found different outlets to handle the stress than she did. Yet now, having had to set my own career goals aside for my husband's, I did feel a twisted sort of empathy for my mother. Had she felt the same devastation as I had when my own dreams and freedoms were set aside for the sake of my husband's career goals? Perhaps. Yet I had found different channels to handle the stress of being subordinated to my husband. I had turned to Buddhism; she had turned to violence. We each, ultimately, had made a choice.

My dad always returned with wonderful gifts. His gifts were exquisite, exotic, and fun. On one of his first trips back from China, I got a bright apple-red puffy down coat, a few t-shirts that said silly things on them in poorly constructed English like "Have Happy Day," and a small glossy brown porcelain deer that was so smooth I'd run my fingers along its back and stroke it like a miniature pet. My red puffy coat in the third grade made me so happy because at the time I rarely got clothes that I thought were cool. Most of my outfits were from Billy the Kid brand which back then was targeted toward boys and they were never in the pretty shades of pink I desired.

I walked around in that puffy coat with pride and delight until one day my brother informed me, "You look fat in that." I probably did look like a big shiny red apple in that coat. My body was never thin like his, a fact that my mother often pointed out.

"Mike is so skinny, he has such a fast metabolism," she'd beam with pride.

In the comparative practice of raising kids where Mike was always better than me, I associated thinness with goodness and being better than others. My brother came by his thinness naturally since he was allowed to eat whatever he wanted. My mother came by hers through refusing to eat so that she could incur the envy of the women around her. My thin body didn't come until I left the house for high school because I was forced to eat beyond my natural appetite and it has taken decades for me to figure out what it means to eat naturally and not out of obligation. "Eat more. Finish all the food on that plate," were my instructions and I always tried to do what she told me to do. At least in that way, I'd earn her approval.

Under My Mother's Gaze

THE TELEVISION IS ON in the living room and I can hear the theme song from *Gilligan's Island* playing while my mom and Mike snuggle up on the couch tucking in for a pre-dinner break. My preschool self stands at the step leading down into the wood-paneled den decked out in all shades of seventies complete with crocheted blankets and a floral couch. I can hear the song wind its way into my favorite part, "The millionaire and his wife. The movie star, the professor and Mary Ann, here on Gilligan's Isle," but I cannot see Ginger descending from the stranded plane looking like Marilyn Monroe in her tight-fitting slinky dress or Mary Ann coming out of the plane wearing her shorts and checkered shirt with a corn-fed girl-next-door kind of beauty.

I am not allowed into the room. I must wait to be invited to join my brother and mom. This is her rule. Usually that invitation doesn't come and if it does, it is proceeded by a litany of criticisms about my face and body called out from my mom. "Your profile is so flat. Look how small your nose is and how your lips stick out. Your lips are too big. And look at your stomach poking out."

My face would grow hot at her cruel words, words I had to endure as the admission to the room where the television shows awaited. She'd say the words like a ritual that reminds me of the Buddhist body scan I have often done where we note the parts of our bodies that touch the floor and how we feel the weight of our bodies pressing down on our cushions. The Buddha's body scan aims to develop awareness in the present moment, however, and not to label and judge various body parts. But my mom was no Buddhist. She was a mother in the 1970s hugging her son close and keeping me in close range—but always apart. Whenever I got the go ahead "*Byungshin-ah!* (stupid in Korean) Come in here now!" I'd immediately jump off the step and join them in front of the television, but I tried to keep a safe distance. I was both elated to enter into this sacred space where mom held sway, but also terrified that I would transgress some invisible boundary only to be cast out again.

The emotional push and pull of the living room remains such a difficult and visceral memory because even though I feared my mother and wanted to escape her presence, I was also desperate to be welcomed into her arms like my brother. Mike never had to struggle for my mother's affections, and when he was young he seemed to absorb my mother's criticisms about my face and body. He teased me relentlessly about being fat, would make up songs about my body, and even took to calling me "Beluga Ton Kid" or would snidely whisper "BTK" out of the side of his mouth in mixed company. This self-devised moniker came from the brand label on the back of the corduroy pants that my mother would dress me in, BTK, which stood for Billy The Kid. My mother would neither intervene in the taunts nor make much effort to stop him if he punched or pushed me, so it seemed that he was conditioned to believe this behavior toward me was acceptable. It wasn't until he hit adolescence, when my mother had far less influence over him, that his attitude toward me began to change. In fact, he often seemed downright remorseful and guilty, but, as most of us did in the family, he rarely spoke of such feelings.

I was often trapped inside my house figuratively and literally in ways that shaped my ungracious attitude toward my own body. For most of my life, I was extremely self-conscious of my body and tended to criticize the very same things that were the object of my mother's derision. For this corporeal preoccupation, I should not be surprised. I have always had a fear of parts of my body being exposed, especially my stomach, which was made bigger and pudgier than I ever wanted as a girl. This fear of exposure reached its height in high school and college when I realized that although I had become physically active with various boyfriends, I was never comfortable looking at my own body or having my body the object of another's gaze. Being looked at by a man usually made me anxious because I'd fear what he'd see and how he'd criticize my stomach like my mother instead of trying to just relax. The desire to hide the less-loved parts of our bodies is certainly not an atypical obsession for women; most of us are raised to think that we are not good enough and that we shouldn't reveal all parts of ourselves. But for me, the exposure of any part of my belly came with a kind of desexualized anxiety—it was about being vulnerable to another's negative body scan. Our female bodies are inscribed with social meaning and my body also came with a peculiar inheritance of self-hatred and anxiety.

It was another sweltering muggy day. We lived in a colonial style home in the suburbs of Greenlawn, Long Island. Laurie, John, and Billy lived next door and were always a source of fascination for me. Laurie was a pretty girl the same age as my brother, and was always dressed in cute clothes and had perfect long pony tails that flowed from the sides of her head like waterfalls. They often had beautiful ribbons in them and I wanted some too. But my hair was always cut short like a boy's and I simply didn't have anything that could grow into even stubby pigtails. Mom always razor-cut my hair in the bathroom sink because, as she reminded me, "your hair is too coarse and hard to take care of."

John was my brother's best friend and because he was two years older and nicer to me than my own brother, I had developed a big crush on him as only a preschool girl can. Billy was a teenager in high school and was in a league of his own. He'd come and go and barely noticed me because I simply didn't exist for him. He had better things to do. Joey was the same age as me and lived next door on the other side of my house, as did Ted who had a pinched face and sharp features that were dramatically different from his younger brother whose soft brown eyes reminded me of cows' eyes. And they had a teenaged sister named Deanna who was an anomaly to me. She had such ease in her body, she was beautiful, and she would often wear a bikini in the summer. Even at that young age I envied her body and wanted to look like her. But I didn't, I still had a baby's body and a soft round one at that, and the shame associated with my body was set like a clock rather early on.

I was playing in the sprinkler with the neighbors when my mom called me back into the house. I always came when called so I hustled back to the house but was dripping water in the entry way. She didn't appreciate that I had wet feet and warned that I would track wet marks all over the floor throughout the house.

"Take off your bathing suit and stay there and dry off!" she demanded.

I obediently peeled off my wet suit, but I didn't even have a towel. I was simply trapped in the entryway, naked and waiting to dry. A wooden kitchen chair suddenly appeared and blocked my way into the privacy of the kitchen.

"Do not go beyond that chair," I was ordered.

I knew that one didn't question the rules around my house unless one was my brother, so I stayed in that entryway and didn't go near that chair. To me, it was worse than barbed wire; crossing past it meant misbehavior which meant certain punishment. I stood there not knowing what to do when the cackles of Deanna and Ted came through the screen door. I turned around and looked out the door and could see them laughing and pointing at me.

"Oh my God, look at her!" they shouted as if it were the funniest thing they had ever seen. I was a vulnerable, naked little girl at the mercy of my mother's peculiar child-rearing skills and the neighbor kids' mirth. I was stuck between the neighbors' jeering gaze and the chair blocking my way to safety. My mom knew that the neighbors could see me, especially because it was one of the rare times that I verbally pleaded with her to let me free. But she ignored my cries and there I stood frozen in humiliation.

The shame and degradation of that event, the fear of being seen naked by others who would laugh at my body and in my own mind inevitably criticize it, marked how I treated my body as I grew from a girl to a woman. Rather than occupying this woman's body for its strength and individuality, I would cover it up and try my best to hide it by refusing to wear shorts outside unless I was jogging. I also hated wearing a two-piece swimsuit on the beach. The few times that I tried would bring about enough self-consciousness and anxiety that I would either leave the towel wrapped around my midsection as protection or I would suck in my stomach and barely move.

"What are you afraid of? Is it that you're afraid of people seeing the true you?" asked Mr. Blackburn, the therapist I sought out in college.

This was the first time that I ever said out loud what had happened to me as a little girl and I introduced it only after going through a series of disclaimers that my memory was a bit fuzzy and that maybe it was just a bad dream. After two sessions with the kind, attentive, mustached therapist, I managed to accept that my current shame with my body was traceable to those kinds of events at such a tender age. But afterwards, I stopped going to see Mr. Blackburn because I was simply too ashamed that I had revealed such intimate stories about myself and while I knew that he could help me, I couldn't bear the remorse I'd feel after letting someone into the cavernous belly of abuse that I carried around with me. If I stayed silent, then I could pretend that it hadn't happened.

I had developed a case of body dysmorphia that plagued my view of myself as I seemed to hone in on hating my stomach, the overfed stomach that I grew to detest as a child. It had expanded through force. As a teen and young adult, I grew to hate it because it was the most obvious expression and site of oppression. In my mind, it was the visual proof of abuse that my mother meted out on me every day. I was required to eat

and grow beyond my natural self and my stomach served as a constant reminder that I could barely manage to discern and decide for myself when
I was full, when I was hungry, and when I had simply had enough.

My mother's gaze on my body was never the admiring gaze she cast on
my brother Mike's body when she would remark on how big he was growing, how strong he was becoming, how cute his face was. It was not even
the same gaze she gave to her own body when she admired her slim sil-
houette or perfectly made-up face in the mirror. Her gaze upon my body
spoke a different language, a silent language that said I was not pretty like
she was, not thin like she was. I had become competition because I was a
girl and while she sometimes allowed me to indulge that girlishness inside
me by taking me shopping for cute clothes, as I grew older any efforts to
beautify myself were met with a flash of rage. I was allowed to have some
attractive clothing, but not that many. Not because we couldn't afford the
clothes, but because she did not feel I was deserving of them.

In the fifth grade, she did buy me those cool Mork and Mindy sus-
penders with the rainbow straps and *nanu-nanu* handshake pin that were
so in-fashion in the early 80s. I also got to have one of those cool Members
Only nylon bomber jackets that all the trendy kids wore. Although mine
was a flat beige color and likely my brother's cast off, it certainly had the
name brand that I desired, so I wore it to school most days and tried to
embellish its colorless color with a flash of bright legwarmers that had
some sparkle to them.

I stood in front of my mirror admiring the way that my pink Gloria
Vanderbilt jeans fit over my maturing seventh grade body. Although I
usually felt unattractive and slightly overweight, there was some kind of
magic in these upscale pants that made me feel taller and leaner. Perhaps it
was simply the designer label that transformed the way I looked at myself.
I turned around to see the back of the pants and how they fit over my
backside—"not too bad," I registered with pride. They were hot pink with
that fancy swan logo stitched into the front little pocket whose function
to this day evades me. I was so proud because I finally had something that
seemed like it would be in fashion in junior high. Who wouldn't notice
the fancy V with the extra wings on top sewn into the back pockets?
I wore them often but not so much that people would remember how
many times a week I wore them, because girls then and now can be vicious
about that sort of thing. I would usually wear them with my favorite white

sweatshirt with the blocks of turquoise and red stitched across my chest and furbished with gold brushed grommets. These were the pants that could do me no wrong. But my private reverie was soon broken.

"Who told you that you could you could sew your pants!" Her shouts preceded her as she ran up the stairs with another pair of my jeans in her hands. I had attempted to peg the jeans at the ankles to fit with the latest fashions. I knew that I wouldn't be able to buy pegged jeans, so I cleverly figured out how to do it myself without cutting any of the material. I simply turned the pants inside out and sewed a line up the inside leg so that it tapered at the bottom. I didn't cut the jeans; I knew better than to take scissors to them. But to my mother, I had somehow violated some unspoken code that forbade me from making efforts to look pretty, fashionable, or slim. She barged through the door wielding shears in her hand and began to shred up my jeans. Starting with the unfinished pegged jeans, she shredded them so fast at the legs that she looked like an axe murderer in a horror film who just keeps cutting despite the fact that his victim is already dead. Then came the next worst thing—"take off those pants and give them to me!" she shouted. I felt the anxiety and fear growing in my chest and swallowed any rage that I had as she then took those scissors to my beloved Gloria Vanderbilts. The pants that made me feel attractive, thin, and finally on trend, were now being ripped to shreds with little chance of sewing them back together. I watched, immobilized by fear and horror as she gathered together all my pants on the floor and began attacking them with scissors. She cut through those pants like a banshee righting some unseen wrong. She was terrifyingly silent and unreachable in her pants-murdering trance. I was terrified into silence and remained quiet, barely breathing as she finally exorcised whatever noxious spirit lived in my pants. When she had finished her destruction, she seemed to vanish down the stairs, leaving me breathless and crying over the loss of Gloria.

My mother had a way with scissors and she wielded them as weapons destined to attack my confidence and desire to look good. But by then, my mother had at last let me grow my hair long. I finally felt like I looked somewhat pretty although I was not allowed to wash my hair whenever I wanted. We certainly were not under any austerity measures and forced to take baths in used water filled only three inches in the tub, but the rules for me were clear. My brother showered every day at will, but I could only wash my hair when my mother gave me permission. So in order for me to get to school without greasy hair, I would wake up before anyone else in the house and quietly turn the on the faucet in my bathroom to a bare leak. Sticking my head under the faucet, I would slowly massage the shampoo into my hair and do my best to rinse it out and not wake her up. I would then sneak back to my room and dry my hair on the lowest setting of my hair dryer so that she would not notice that my hair was clean.

Hair for women is such a powerful symbol and long hair is the seeming proof of one's femininity. To have one's hair cut symbolizes a loss of power and identity especially when not chosen by the one donning such locks. I lost some of my power of beauty in junior high when I had grown out my hair past my shoulders. It was long, but it was stick-straight, and I wanted to see if it would curl like Pearl Liu's wavy locks. Pearl was Chinese American, and she always came to school with curly hair. She was also prettier than I was and had far more friends than I did. I was quite lonely and usually stayed to myself because I was extremely shy, but somehow, I thought that if I looked like Pearl, I'd have more friends.

My mom was out shopping at the Korean grocery, which usually took half an hour just to drive to, so I knew that I'd have a lot of time. Inside her fancy brocaded bathroom I went. I sat on her velvet-cushioned stool that was painted into an antique gold. The stool was a leftover from the previous owners of the home, but it certainly lent the room a sense of lushness and wealth. I uncurled the chord from the curling iron and flicked on the switch and waited for it to heat up hot enough to curl my Asian hair. While I sat waiting, I snooped around my mother's artillery of anti-aging creams, lipsticks, eye shadows, and blushes. I was like a princess in her palace getting ready for the ball.

The iron was hot to the touch, but I endured the harsh heat on my fingers as I made curls because I wanted to look like Pearl. She represented to me that Asian American girls could fit in, they could assimilate, and they could be popular if they had the right hair. And I wanted it. I curled and curled and curled. Soon, I had locks almost as pretty as Pearl's although my curls were amateur and looked like there were a few crimps here and there. The curls were not loose and gentle like Pearl's; they looked a bit stiff, but I didn't care. I looked close enough to her and I was satisfied.

I left the bathroom and headed back to the den as my hair bounced along the way. I was pleased with myself and imagined how cool I would look when I got on the bus in the morning. As the afternoon went on, the curls began to unravel, surrendering to the weight and gravity of Asian American hair. They were losing their swirls and soon I was left with nearly stick-straight hair again. But for that brief moment, I believed there was hope for me at school. I could look as pretty as the other

Asian American girl in my grade who seemed friendly to everyone and liked by all.

While in my hair-changing fantasy, however, I failed to cover my tracks in the bathroom. I put all the creams and lipsticks back where they were, but like some amateur thief I had left behind a glaring clue—I did not turn the iron off. My mother came home, headed into her bathroom and knew exactly what I had done. No daughter of hers was going to mess around with her stuff and try to make herself pretty by curling her hair.

"*Byungshin-ah!* Where are you? Get over here!" she screamed as she came after me with the curling iron, still hot with proof of my beauty crime. She yanked the smoking gun out of the wall and pushed it at me as her voice lowered and she used that scary voice again. "How dare you use my curling iron. Who do you think you are?" she seethed. She grabbed my hair with its barely-there curls and touched the iron to my neck. I was terrified it would burn and leave a scar, but thankfully it retained only residual heat. After touching me with the iron, she let my hair go and I thought that it was over. But the worst was coming.

She ran to the kitchen and got the scissors and grabbed my hair again. As she pulled the hair from my head, she hacked it off with the scissors. She was blinded with anger and didn't care that nothing was even and that it looked like I had cut my hair myself with my eyes closed. She had provided the ultimate humiliation for a young woman in love with her long hair. However, I had at this point gone into the safety of my own mind, long gone and protected from my mother's ability to truly harm me. I hid like that turtle and sunk into silence as she hacked away the power of my beauty.

As soon as the last long locks fell to the floor, she threw down the scissors and went into the kitchen. I was left staring down at the barely curled heaps of long black hair that were once my source of pride. But now it was no longer attached to my head and it was no longer imbued with beauty. It was a symbol of betrayal—there would be no chance of every looking like Pearl Liu. Instead, I looked like a mangled version of myself. My hair now resembled a fitful short bob that served as a cautionary tale for what happened to girls who tried to make themselves pretty. It was so ugly in fact that when my father, who made few comments about my physical appearance, came home from work he asked why I had cut it off.

This time I simply said quietly, "Mom did it." I wanted him to ask for more details and get mad at my mother for making me so ugly, but he said nothing as he got up and left the room. My tears had dried and my eyes were only a little swollen from crying, but the jagged line of my hair was so bad that even my brother refrained from laughing. I was so ugly I rendered my father and brother speechless.

Getting on the school bus the next day was a lesson in endurance in the face of abject and utter embarrassment. I got on that bus and walked to the middle of the seats with everyone's eyes on me. In addition to being a racial minority in a predominantly white school, I was now defaced by my own mother. And I had to lie about it and remain silent about what had really happened. I was waiting for someone to keep asking me what really happened but amazingly everyone bought the barely plausible story that I told—"yeah, I tried to cut it myself, but it didn't work out."

I somehow got through the laughter and jeers that middle school students can hurl. When I got home, my mother took me to her fancy hairdresser John at the Vidal Sassoon hair salon where she spent hours perfecting her own coif. I sat in the chair as John pushed the lever to raise my seat so he could fix the haircut. It was basically unfixable but as he wielded his sheers and cut with his deft fingers in order to make my hair look like just a bad choice, he laughed and asked me, "Who cut your hair? Who did this to you?"

I was emboldened suddenly. Maybe it was because handsome fancy John was cutting my hair at the upscale salon that I began to feel strong. I looked around to see where my mother was. Since she had her nose in a magazine, I murmured in the slightest voice, "My mom cut it."

That revelation and truth-telling was a short-lived victory, however. When we got back in the car to go home, the shouts and threats began. "How could you humiliate me like that in front of the salon? You should have kept your mouth shut!"

I assumed that her anger would lead to an immediate and harsh punishment, but it seemed that she, too, knew that my hair was atrocious and even she felt bad about it.

Or maybe my moment of honesty in the salon had truly scared her. Maybe she understood that she had gone too far, and I was growing too bold. Maybe she was frightened that my silent acquiescence was coming to an end, and I was growing ready to speak the truth to her maternal power.

Body Scan

I AM WALKING EVER SO SLOWLY as I feel the cool cement under my right heel. I pause to focus all of my awareness on the slight forward move of the heel onto the arch and then the ball of my foot. The weight from the ball of my foot then falls naturally to my toes which begin to curl to grip the ground. I am spending an awful lot of time trying to remember to feel all the sensations in my body as I practice walking meditation. My focus is so intense that I feel like I might topple over and as if I am a newborn colt learning to walk.

Asha reminds us, "Stay with the experience. You have no place you have to go, no destination. Just observe how the floor feels under your toes. What's the texture? Where do you feel the first step?"

I know that I am supposed to hone all my senses on the touch of my body to the earth and, in turn, feel sustained by it, but I find myself distracted by the appearance of my toes. *I should have painted my toenails,* I think as I peer over to my walking meditation partner who has a beautiful French manicure on her toenails. I stop myself mid-thought as Asha's words seem to pop up into my head, "Remember not to put a story on top of the experience. Our minds like to tell stories and they are not always very flattering."

A gentle smile creeps onto my face, *how does she know just the right thing to say?* I wonder.

During his teachings to monks and nuns in the groves where he often gave public talks, the Buddha exhorted his students to focus diligently on their bodies as objects of meditation so that they could learn to let go of their desires and disappointments with the outside world. Here on the meditation retreat, Asha encourages us to do the same—use the body as an object of meditation to gain awareness of what's happening inside of ourselves rather than what is going on in the outside world and then reacting or suddenly creating stories about ourselves and our supposed shortcomings.

Once I find my mind wandering to my unpainted toes, a phenomenon that certainly didn't bother me twenty minutes before, I rededicate myself to my mindful walking when suddenly I find myself walking barefoot down a dry patch of dirt next to two other women. At first, I feel self-conscious that maybe they will also find my feet unattractive, but then as I begin to ease the negative story-telling about my so-called naked toes, I look up and soften my gaze and behold the beauty of these women. I am struck by the realization that all of the peoples' bodies around me are beautiful and that what makes them beautiful is their distinctiveness—tall, short, big, small. I settle back into walking meditation and try once again to cultivate awareness and maybe even find the beauty in my own body.

Observing my body has never been an act of mindfulness, nor has it ever brought me freedom from desire or discontent as the Buddha would have his disciples believe. In fact, for most of my life the act of scanning my body has been entirely ensnarled with negative judgments that inevitably fueled desire—the desire to change the way my body looked and felt. I had learned by an early age to view every feature of my body negatively—and to thus view myself negatively, as if the body I inhabited was a reflection of my worth. To this day, I occasionally catch myself glancing in the mirror in the morning to give myself a scan, but I know that it is not the kind the Buddha had in mind. The Buddha wanted monks and nuns to learn to detach themselves from desires for sexual pleasure, eating too many tasty foods, and their own vanity, by seeing their own bodies as objects—containers that held together a panoply of blood, guts, bones, joints, and muscles. When they sat in meditation, they mentally visualized and counted the bones in the body and were encouraged to explore their own bodies as a way of coming to know that they are nothing more than sacks. Therefore, why get so attached to their supposed outer beauty when in fact, they are simply a combination of different elements that change all the time? If one sits in contemplation, one might in fact find that the object of adoration (perhaps another's body) is really not much different from their own—a combination of different elements that are ultimately impermanent and indeed subject to change.

Although I know that the Buddha offered such meditation practices to overcome desire for the body, it has always had a curiously opposite effect on me—I do not intend for body scan meditation to create a sense of detachment from my body. Instead, I scan my body to help me learn how to occupy it. And I do it to learn how to divest myself from decades of negative judgment from external sources like my mother, popular culture, and of course myself. My daily ritual body scan, which I sometimes do more than once a day, is not quite what the Buddha had in mind. My usual scan goes something like this—wake up in the morning and touch the belly. How does it feel? Why is it so soft? Next, take a look at it in the mirror—lift up shirt and see if it is bloated or if perhaps it is flatter today. The next ritual step includes talking myself out of stepping on a scale, but alas, I do it anyway. Next comes the judgment about what the numbers on the scale say. Rarely are the numbers neutral. They are always somehow an indictment of my self-worth and value. On a good day when the scale says what I want it to, I can swiftly dress my body and send it out the door to work, to the barre studio, and perhaps to yoga. On a bad day—well, that usually sends me straight into a mild panic of having failed to somehow live up to a standard that was set in place by a mother and a culture that seems rather far away. And yet, it still has a hold on me.

It is usually when my pants feel a little tight or when the scale seems to register numerical values that I automatically equate with being good or bad that I scan this body of mine—the belly is too soft. Why didn't I do crunches and more core work before I had children? Then the legs—why did I do so much ballet and run so many miles when I was young—I should have known I'd develop muscular calves. And why did I take up competitive swimming and canoeing in high school? I should have known that those sports activities would form my body into something bigger than the ideal Korean American woman—small boned, petite, thin without muscles. Then I remembered that I took up sports and exercise as a way of disciplining my body and to avoid the kind of body that my mother seemed hell-bent on imposing on me—decidedly unfit. It seemed unfair to me then that I tried so hard to work out and be attractive only to end up with such strong and seemingly un-Korean legs.

In Buddhism, this negative self-talk is called mental chatter. Zen Buddhists will sit sometimes for hours on end in meditation to quiet its relentless feed. But even though the Buddha talked about detachment from the body and Buddhists today always discuss the value of letting go of judgments, this Buddhist professor still manages to forget that the negative self-talk comes from karmic seeds planted long ago by my mother, who herself was embedded in a culture that limited what women could do and what they could look like. Those cultural attributes for Korean women still exist today, only now the encounter with Western beauty ideals makes it even harder to be an "ideal Korean woman." The ideal Korean woman of today is supposed to be tall, have double eyelids, large breasts, and stick-thin bodies with no muscle tone, something I see every day on my sixteen-year-old daughter's computer, as she struggles against these images herself.

Today's Korean women's body ideals are projected most prominently in the Korean pop industry where young girls with the right surgically altered look are selected to join girl K-pop groups where they sing and dance in unison both provocatively and innocently. They are both cute and sexy; Korean and Western; tall and thin; beautiful and charming. The Korean pop industry dictates that the girls get breast enhancement surgery, eyelid surgery to remove the epicanthal fold, rhinoplasty to change the shape of their noses, and sometimes cheekbone enhancement. They are expected to subject their bodies to these modifications in order to become a synthesis of all things deemed beautiful for Korean women—ideals of Western beauty—big eyes, long legs, and big breasts. In other words, the message to young Korean girls today is to be as Korean as you can and as Western as you are not naturally-born to be. Plastic surgery can make up for the gap and the industry is booming in South Korea. It is also not only the women who are ensnared in this body image machine—today more and more Korean men are expected to have sharp jawlines, dyed hair, six pack abs, and at the same time, an almost feminine face with a soft pout, doe eyes, and lots of eyeliner.

I worry about the effects of such a glamour industry on my own daughter whose half-Korean body resembles the ideal of what Korean pop stars and ordinary wealthy Korean girls pay thousands of dollars to attain. How much can she fight the urge to be like them, especially when she notices that she already kind of looks like them? As she grows and her body changes, will she have the inner strength to push back against the urge to discipline her body to remain in that mold? How much control will I have in this battle? And how can I help her when I still struggle myself? And then I remember, I am not my mother and I have not raised my daughters to hate their bodies. I have tried my best to do the very opposite, but the forces of culture are so strong. And my daughters always remind me that they too are strong—strong enough to recognize cultural pressures, strong enough to love their bodies, and wise enough to push back against my own fears that they will inherit my particular body image struggles.

I am the mother of young women. I am often struck with gratitude at how they seem to have a general sense of wellbeing and confidence about their bodies. The younger one is a dancer with beautiful strong legs; the older has the legs of her father—long runner legs that hold up the rest of her stunning self. I look at them and marvel that I haven't completely messed them up, at least not yet. But I know that that I try my very best not to make them feel bad about their bodies so that I don't repeat the sins of my mother. I remind them every day that I love them no matter what and that they are the loves of my life. Whenever I hear anything negative they might say about themselves, I offer immediate antidotal words of truth that speak back to those misperceptions.

"My thighs are big," my younger one says to me one day as she sits in the car in shorts.

I have to suppress the fear that she might end up thinking negative thoughts like me and remind myself that I have raised her differently. Instead, I say as I gaze into her eyes, "Your legs are dancer legs and they are beautiful strong and muscular like all good dancers." I glance in the rearview mirror and see her face relax.

I continue, "They are beautiful legs and you are so lucky to have them! They help propel you up in the air." I offer the antidotal commentary as a way of nipping the other negativity in the bud.

I still worry that she will carry this negative misperception in her head, but she turns to me, says, "Alright, Mom," grins, hops out of the car with her backpack on her back, and skips away; all the while my own heart is skipping a beat in the hopes that my response was enough.

But as any mother will tell you, one should never get overly confident in one's mothering skills because no matter how hard we try to protect our kids, we will inevitably screw up.

Two years ago, I read about a couple in Tennessee whose five-year-old daughter, Alexa, died after they forced her to drink two liters of grape soda as punishment for merely taking a sip or two of her stepmother's drink. A five-year-old girl killed by her parents because she drank a few sips. She was forced to drink so much liquid that her poor body shut down and her brain swelled. She was force-fed to the point of death for doing nothing more than taking a few sips. That the two could collaborate in the death of their child brought me to tears. But there was something more to my tears. It was the shock of memory. Hearing this story brought me right back to the times when as a child I was forced to sit at the dining table eating whatever my mother forced me to eat. Alexa died at the same age I was when I was force-fed.

Korean American families rarely bear witness to abuse and nobody ever wants to talk about it. But abuse is common, and all too often it is daughters who bear the worst of it. That is because the love for first sons is a fairly common Asian practice. While Mike was the firstborn son in

1967, it turns out that he was not the first son my parents had conceived.

"Well, your mom lost a son before your brother was born so when Mike came, your mom was very relieved and attached," my darling aunt secretly confessed to me, as if to offer some insight into why my mother was so hard on me. "But why isn't she attached to me?" I asked her quietly and my aunt didn't know how to answer. She gave me a look of love because my mom didn't let me have much affection. I wanted to hug my aunt, but I couldn't.

I tried as a child to understand what that meant but I would often get hung up on the term miscarriage and miscarried. Who was miscarried and where did they go? It must have been really awful because wherever that baby boy went, it certainly made my mom crazy over my brother.

But it turns out that there was more to the story than I ever knew. There's a picture of my parents in the early sixties that has always intrigued me—she's wearing a trench coat tightly cinched around the waist and her eyes are obscured by large black-framed sunglasses that I would love to get my hands on. Dad's wearing a white polyester ribbed turtleneck and checkered slacks and a bright smile. They are young hipsters in their early twenties and I always get a kick out of seeing them wearing the American fashion of the time. It strikes my fancy to see my relatives dressed so trendy because somehow, I thought that in their youth they would look more traditional, fresher off the boat. I forget, though, that my parents were very young adults and that things like dress and how they looked were as important to them as it would be to anyone else living in New York at the time. What also surprises me is that when I see my mother's face, there's a youthful sassiness reflected in her pose. By the time I was born, that youth and sassiness must have died, for I never once saw it in her face.

There are photos of her on the beach wearing a fitted sweater and some cool plaid cropped pants and she is looking rather softer than I can ever remember. She's laughing on the beach, hands clasped behind her back as she seems to be leaning into the camera, maybe to give a kiss to my father. What happened to that smile and that lightheartedness? She was young, bright, full of possibility, and came to the U.S. as twenty-year-old college student on scholarship. She married my dad, lived in a predominantly white country, and apparently wanted to do something more than immediately birth kids. But I could never figure out what she wanted to do. No one ever really talked about it—before having children she worked as a cook in a yacht club, a secretary, and a bookkeeper, but she never talked about these as career goals. Maybe it was art that she wanted to pursue—I remember sketch books in the house and she did play the piano and guitar, but to this day I do not know what her ideal career was or what her subsumed fantasy life might have been. Did she have a different picture of what she wanted to be? Was this the cause of some of that pressure she seemed to diffuse on me? She never said.

Her unrealized American dream entangled me in its disappointment as she set out to limit my success as a student and worked her hardest to keep me fat, unattractive, and silent. I was her worst nightmare of a body image and perhaps if she could keep an image of that specter in the form of my heavy, unattractive body, she'd be safe. Her hair, her body, and her face would always be manageable in her mind if she could just unleash that fear and have it manifest in me. I was less like her daughter and more like her most undesired body double that kept her safe, thin, and pretty.

Hearing Alexa's story brought me back to the countless times my mother would secretly add extra salt and butter in my food with the hopes that I would get fatter while she got thinner. She was still diligently popping her diuretics and laxatives, and at this point it seems that she added the little yellow helper (Valium) to the mix. Either way, by adding extra salt into my food while purging her own body of salt, she re-enacted her earlier practice of piling food up on my plate and forcing me to eat while denying herself food. I remember watching her at the stove, her back turned to us as she surreptitiously opened the cabinet where the salt was, poured it into her hand and then dumped it into my bowl, and only my bowl. I watched her do this time and again and became complicit in her deception because I was afraid to do otherwise. The fear was not unfounded. Her rage was swift, severe, and easy to hide.

Her secret tampering continued until I was in junior high school, when I finally had the courage to admit to my brother what she had been doing for years. It took until my food was completely inedible for me to begin to advocate for myself. Mike was sitting in front of the television eating his lunch while I tried desperately to swallow the mind-bogglingly salty soup my mother had thrust into my hands. By this point, I was already so afraid to stick up for myself that I watched her flip up the metal lid of the big blue cylinder that contained the salt, pour a copious amount in the palm of her hand, and then brush her hands over my bowl in what would become a nearly toxic bowl of saline soup. I did take a sip of the soup and forced myself to swallow it before putting it in front of my brother's face. Before he could say anything, I quietly muttered, "Just taste this." I must have had a very serious look on my face because he didn't say a word, stuck the spoon in the bowl and took a big sip. He immediately spit the soup back into the bowl with an accompanying "what the hell is this?!" falling from his mouth.

I looked at him and said in a reserved matter-of-fact way, "She always does this to my food. Butter too." Mike then took the bowl back to the kitchen right away, where my mother was still cooking, and demanded, "What the hell are you doing to her? Why is there so much salt in this?!" While he accused her of deliberately tampering with my food, my mother took it all in stride and nonchalantly remarked, "What? Oh, that must have been a mistake," and turned right back to the cutting board to chop her vegetables. I was so fearful of her retaliation against me and simultaneously so relieved that Mike had finally come to my defense. Nothing else was ever said of this incident, but it never happened again. My mother knew that Mike was now defending me and her usual tricks to fatten me up were out in the open; rather than force-feed me salt and butter, she later changed her tactics to something more emotional and less traceable. She simply resorted to ignoring me through silences that were often broken by an absolutely terrifying verbal outburst, akin to walking through a fun-house and having someone jump out from a dark curtain to startle you. I, of course, never asked for such surprises. I never did shout back though. Instead, I did what many others in such threatening circumstances do, I stayed silent and the fear, anger, and sadness lodged itself deep in the viscera of my body.

My Korean immigrant mother with the beautiful eyes and lovely figure deprived herself of food, took laxatives every day, and spent hours in the bathroom throughout my childhood. I recall her weighing herself each year and hearing her note that the numbers on the scale were moving down with each step on the scale. Gradually, she simply stopped eating.

Sometimes I wonder why a certain number on the scale seems so high for my body and another random number seems just right. Yet for my body, the effort to be at that just right number means that I have to run that much more and eat that much less, which I don't want to do. My body likes to be at a different place and yet I aim for that elusive number. And now I know why. That number is one of the numbers I remember my mother noting out loud. Anything above that was fat.

The legacy of her force-feeding me follows me sometimes when I am invited out to lunch or visit someone for dinner. I have a shift inside my body when I see the food come to the table, an immediate discomfort that says, "But I don't want that." I fight the urge to change the plans to meet for coffee instead. I don't wish to change plans because I reject the hand that feeds me. Instead, I get anxious over the idea that I might not be able to control what I want to eat and the internal struggles over food that I suffer when my life seems particularly stressful on the outside. But I do eat. I have learned the value of nourishment even if I can't yet always moderate. I do try to be mindful about why I am the way I am and try to offer some soothing to that brutalized child inside myself who never learned how to have an appropriate self-enhancing relationship to food. And I eat lovely delicious things that I enjoy baking—I make a mean brownie and flourless chocolate cake. I make beautiful raw kale salads mixed with pumpkin seeds, brown rice, tofu and spices. I make them, and I eat them sometimes for breakfast because I can and because I want to. But sometimes I eat them with a heavy heart knowing deep down that I will regret what passes through my mouth because I fear that I will become that fat girl that I was groomed to be. I fear that I will become that little girl chased around the neighborhood by my brother and his friends teasing me for being overweight. I become gloomy when I think that I will continue to be that little girl forced to eat more than she could. I fear that I might become that little girl again who ate so much she threw up and had to endure her mother lying about it and telling people that I made myself throw up. I fear that I will become that little girl forced to endure lies and hold my tongue out of fear of violent retribution.

Recently I visited a therapist who told me straight up, "Your childhood was extremely brutal," and that word is both hard to swallow and one that comes as a relief because it seems so extreme. And yet it characterizes the experience so completely. The brutality of my own childhood sometimes makes me wonder what my mother's childhood must have been like. I also see the ways that I often wall up emotionally and crawl back into my mental tortoise shell in the midst of stress, the way I have backed out of arguments verbally only to voice my outrage in my head. The ways that I present so well because I don't know how to fall apart in public because I have worked so hard to keep myself together all these years.

Yes, I have a doctorate from Harvard. Yes, I was once married to a doctor. Yes, I have two healthy, beautiful, smart and well-adjusted girls. Yes, I have a great job that I appreciate most of the time. Yes, I am physically healthy and do my best to keep in shape. I understand all that, but just because we look so polished on the outside doesn't mean that our insides are so neat and tidy. Over time I have come to realize that the costs of appearing so effortlessly put together is not worth the façade of perfection.

And I have realized that perhaps it is time to let down the guard just a little bit so that I can learn to live this life as it is and appreciate myself as I am, broken bits and all.

The Buddha taught his disciples the practice of meditation known as a body scan in order to develop our awareness of the sensations in our body and our mind's propensity to place judgments on those sensations. During the five-day silent retreat, Dee Dee teaches us to explore how we feel in our bodies in the present moment. "Our bodies often carry the stress, trauma, and burdens that filter in when we are not aware, for we all suffer and carry somatic stress and trauma," she says and I begin to perk up from my slumping posture. "Because we tend to neglect the body, we should pay attention to it through careful and deep listening," she continues in her soft, calm voice as she guides us in the practice of sitting, paying attention, and turning our senses inward. I get Dee Dee's general point about not paying attention to the body, but I often fail because I do the opposite of what the Buddha taught—I continue to do a body scan every day, not to explore how it feels but rather how it looks.

And if I don't think it looks right, then I feel bad.

I woke up this morning and the first thing my mind jumped on was judgment and frustration with myself because I had mindlessly plowed through several little bags of Halloween M&Ms, cookies, chips, and basically anything sweet that came in a small wrapper. I did that thing where I keep eating the junk and saying that I will start again tomorrow. I know that my mindless eating is simply making me feel bad about my body, but I don't listen. I go to sleep and wake up with dread over my inability to treat this body well. And so begins the body scan—especially the scan of my stomach. I never pay too much attention to any other parts of my body. I focus on the core of my body, as if it is the core of my self. Negative thoughts have begun to proliferate as each judgment of my failure to be disciplined falls into place. I had better stop eating so much sugar and crap because I am going to have to go to yoga today and then see my fiancé tomorrow and I simply can't look fat or puffy when I do that! What will they think of me? The anxiety mounts as I body scan first with my mind's eye to imagine what my belly looks like. I can feel the tightness of my body begin and know that it will take effort to release this panicking feeling. Immediately my mind jumps to all the plans I have this week that include eating with other people in public and at home. The body scan begins as it does every day when I look at my body. I scan, and I judge—puffy, overly soft, weak. The judgment has already begun—failure, unattractive, fat, undisciplined. How will I get myself back together? Does Dee Dee ever go through this self-abuse or has meditation cured her from this constant burning desire to be better through denial? Is my mind tricking me, though, that denial is a bad thing? Can I trust my mind to do the right thing by me or will I seduce myself again, like I did last night, into thinking this mindless eating is an act of self-agency? How can it be when I wake up disappointed in myself like I just binge drank and now have the shame of a hangover and some illicit activity to carry along with me. As I feel myself beginning to whirl off into endless spirals of self-criticism and flagellation over what I have or have not done, I am suddenly brought back to Jaya's reminder about the importance of returning to the breath and how the breath is really the greatest gift we have in the present moment. I am also reminded that this body of mine may have been the object of violence and hatred in the past, but that I can return to it, I can experience self-love and compassion in this very body, and I can be seen and heard in it and through it.

"It is very important to feel your emotions and remember that emotions like loneliness and disappointment can't be filled with external things. Try to identify them. They are often the result of mental hindrances like doubt and restlessness."

I remember Asha's sage-like words during the retreat and wonder if this is how she addresses suffering. Her body is not perfect according to the standards of beauty we have in the U.S., but is she free from the suffering of not being thin and tall? Does being a Buddhist meditation teacher allow her to transcend these feelings that I cling to and that have come to me every morning just as I am waking up? These emotions and judgments are like a toddler who arrives every morning to startle me awake. And I just want to go back to sleep.

"By sitting and shining a light on your emotions, you are building the capacity to be with, acknowledge, and then let go of clinging to them. Practicing the middle path does not mean to ignore your emotions. They need to be seen, felt, and acknowledged."

But, I think as I rest in the retreat center and even now as I write these words, emotions are painful and I don't want to face them. I have a life-long practice of not letting myself acknowledge painful feelings. I already know that they make me feel inadequate and that a bad morning of a body scan can stay with me for the rest of the day. Sure, I know that these feelings are a warning light to stop, and hopefully not eat the same junk I did yesterday, but to really sit and feel my feelings without clinging to them seems as nearly impossible as attaining enlightenment in this very body at this very moment in time. I am afraid that if I do a body scan and explore and sit with my emotions, I might just fall apart. I haven't sat on my meditation cushion in a long time now and maybe it's because I am afraid of what I might find there.

I found some of my notes written to myself on little pieces of paper after each dharma talk during the retreat: *One of my breakthroughs today in meditation was the realization that if I am constantly planning for the future in my head, then perhaps the insight is that it comes from fear, doubt, restlessness, and worry.* Well, that's pretty insightful, isn't it? If I sit in meditation, practice a body scan to explore how my body feels, then I will be able to see its tendency toward *papañca*, or mental proliferation, and the storytelling that I lay over the experience that I am having in my body. Then I can also figure out whether I am being assailed by the five hindrances of the mind: desire, ill will, sloth or torpor, restlessness and worry, and doubt.

Dee Dee tells us that *vedana*, or feeling tones, can move us to create and engage in the storytelling more. I have lots of stories that I tell myself about myself—is there really a way to stop with the negative storyline? Dee Dee then recounts a story of a Cherokee grandfather who tells his grandson that there are two wolves who lay inside him—one wolf is nurturing, gentle and peaceful and the other is harsh, fierce, and greedy. The grandson asks, "Who wins?"

And the grandfather answers, "The one that I feed."

Which feeling-tones do I feed? Which ones do I let proliferate? How can it stop? And then she says something that I have read about for years but have not really listened to—mindfulness. Mindfulness is like watering seeds of wholesome intention and pulling up mind weeds.

"Mind weeds are like the three distortions or misperceptions the Buddha taught. One: things must always be pleasant to be good. Two: all things should be permanent; we don't want change. And Three: we think it's all personal."

Dee Dee's words remind me again to explore what feeling tone or *vedana* I am adding onto my experiences of bodily sensations. Are these sensations in my body pleasant, unpleasant, or neutral? And what conceptual overlay of stories or *papañca* will I place over the *vedana*? In other words, if my body is feeling anxious and unsettled, will I tell myself again that it is because I am not good enough, not disciplined enough, and not perfect enough? How is it that I can have an advanced degree in Buddhist Studies and still not learn the lessons? This shouldn't be rocket science and I know all the tools to practice meditation. But as the Buddha says, it is far better to do than just to think or mentally proliferate. I need to remind the academic in me to stop thinking all the time. Just sit and be with the body even when I don't want to, even when the body feels terrible and wants me to discipline it for feeling out of control.

I know that I need to stop telling myself stories about my body's supposed inadequacies. And yet, my knowledge does not affect my actions. I continue to tell myself my body is not adequate, and therefore, neither am I.

Dee Dee continues her dharma talk and reminds us of the importance of acknowledging and facing painful moments and realizing that past traumas are in fact imprinted in our mind-body processes. "You cannot ignore this stuff. Eventually, it will come back to bite you in the butt, just like karma. You have to shine awareness on these experiences without judgment but let them be seen so that they can be freed from your body."

I try to acknowledge, feel, and shed the light of awareness on my memories and painful experiences just as a lighthouse illuminates things in the sea, but it's pretty murky in there.

Her Body as a Skin Sack

"No fair! That's my side!" I screamed at my brother who jumped into my parents' bed on Sunday morning. We weren't fighting over what side of the bed we got to lie in. Our fight for prime real estate was my mother's body. In particular, we were arguing over which side of my mother's collar bones would be our swimming pools to play in. I can't remember who decided to call the deep dips in her collarbones "pools," but when my dad wasn't traveling in Asia and the weekend rolled around, it was a pretty good bet that we'd be able to wake up and charge down the hallway, fling the door open, and hurl our bodies on top of my parents as they slowly woke up. And I wanted to swim in the pool on the right side of her neck. I used to walk my fingers up to the ledge of her collarbone and imagine that I could swan dive right in and go for a leisurely swim. When my dad was around, the game was usually on and I was allowed to play. As a kindergartener, I was both terrified of my mom and desperate for her positive attention so I dashed at the chance to be on her right side at least for a short part of the morning. Her body fascinated me because it had hollowed-out places that could collect and hold water like miniature bird baths—one for each of her children.

Her body was not like mine. I was soft and pudgy to her rail thinness, but she still allowed us into her bed to play so her body must not have been that emaciated yet. She was also beautiful to me with her soft brown hair and milk chocolate brown eyes whose pupils were rimmed in the slightest shade of blue. Unlike my coarse black hair that she often kept in a razor-cut pixie much to my dismay, her hair was soft, long, wavy and several shades lighter than the other moms I saw every Sunday at Korean church. And at five years old I had a burning desire to be held, wanted, and welcomed into bed by my mother, probably much like my daughter Haley still wants to hop into my bed today as a thirteen-year-old. If the rules of parenting meant that I had to suck up the bad times when my dad wasn't home, but was allowed to have my place on the divots wedged in her thin shoulders from a lack of fat, then it was worth it. For a brief moment in time, my mother and her body were willing to sustain me and I would fight tooth and nail against my brother to be let in and choose my coveted spot. It did not occur to me to even think about why my mom had swimming pools in her body that other mothers didn't have or even that maybe she derived some kind of pride over being so skinny that her kids could use her boney body like a playground. But over time, I began to notice that the more I was force-fed and the bigger I got, the smaller my mother's body became until it eventually elicited looks of concern and even disgust by strangers and friends alike.

Her body is not so unlike mine is today—like her, I have birthed two children and the reminders of those momentous actions of pushing life out of my body are indelibly inscribed on my stomach. The shame of those lines that can mark a woman as old, no longer sexually attractive or viable, is usually dampened by the memories of babies emerging out of my body, babies that give me a new lease on maternal relationships. While I inherited my mother's troubling bodily anxieties, the little beings that grew in my body shifted the sense of shame I felt that my stomach was getting bigger as each pregnancy progressed. I couldn't do what my mother did and restrict myself to only a few slight meals a day out of fear that I would become obese and out of control. Instead, my pregnancies were marked with a new-found hope that I might be able to appreciate and occupy my body as an expectant mother. So I ate three meals a day plus snacks and allowed my body to grow into a container of safety for my girls—I cut out the caffeine and let my control over my diet loosen up some because somehow I knew that the rules would change with mother-hood. It was almost culturally expected that I would go from fit married woman to soft mom-jean-wearing woman. This notion was constantly reinforced by my Korean relatives who would pressure a woman to remain thin and attractive through marriage at least until becoming a mother. After birthing children, it was as if a mother's need to remain beautiful no longer included the need to be thin. The rules changed because she had fulfilled her cultural destiny. But I was Korean American and resided somewhere between the Korean and the American cultural ideals and ex-pectations laid upon women's bodies. Korean culture told me that I now existed for and through my children. I was supposed to fatten up and no longer worry so much about my own body's size. But the American side of the equation demanded a different set of ideals for women who give birth—that I lose the baby weight as soon as possible and somehow emerge a full woman—a mother *and* thin.

Perhaps my mom also struggled with the social pressure to contain her body even after it gave birth because she was living in America now. She was 29 when she gave birth to me and I can mark her progress from newly-minted mother twice over whose round cheeks and soft face denoted "new mother" to that of an increasingly diminishing woman who seemed to push past even the American cultural ideal of female beauty. She had simply become too thin, and was on the verge of falling apart as more and more fat seemed just to peel off her body. As I grew older in elementary school, junior high, and high school, and struggled to learn how to care for my own body and attempt to feel when I had had enough to eat, she became smaller and smaller in her physical frame and in her social world. Rather than occupying her body, she seemed to want to vacate it until it became what the Buddha referred to as a kind of skin sack. But unlike the Buddha's exhortations to his disciples to let go of their attachment to their bodies by meditating on their bodies as simply skin sacks or containers holding in a wet mess of blood and guts, my mother's body was becoming a skin sack whose scaffolding revealed itself more and more as the years went by. The Buddha's monks meditated on their own bodies as containers of bones, marrow, and sinew in order to look for some essential self that was ultimately proven to not exist, but their views of the body did not include self-starvation. Instead, the Buddha taught his disciples to find the middle way between extremes and eat neither too much nor too little. One should eat to sustain the body and no more. My mom was no Buddhist, though, and she managed to take the extreme route and starve herself into oblivion. She no longer took up much physical space, but she made up for it by figuring out how to suck the energy out of a room through her deafening silence.

It is common knowledge that mothers and daughters are bound together in inextricable ways, and one such way is through the comparative project of comparing each other's bodies, for daughters are the material recipients of their mothers. Men are still advised to look to a woman's mother if they want to have a sense of what the woman will look like in the future. And a man was usually encouraged to select a woman whose mother was thin and beautiful as a partner. But I was raised to look as differently from my mother as humanly possible. I grew soft and round through constant rounds of forced-feedings and she deprived herself of food through starvation and laxatives in order to take up less and less space. I grew while she shrank, and it was when I entered junior high and high school that I began to realize that she force-fed me so that I could become her scapegoat and fat surrogate. She fed me the things that she wouldn't give herself but not out of any heroic gesture of saving the child before oneself. Instead, I became the instantiation of fatness that she loathed, and in turn she seemed to loathe me. I was the goose to her farmer, the goose fattened up by excessive amounts of butter, salt, and sheer masses of food so that I was the round daughter with a squashy belly to her ever-dwindling concave stomach.

The chocolate lay unwrapped in its silver foil on the kitchen table barely at eye level—for a six-year-old child anyway. To this day, I wonder who could possibly leave good chocolate lying around uneaten? My mother, that's who. There it was, just barely out of my arm's reach but by stepping on my tiptoes I managed to reach my fingers as far as I could to grab that unfinished chocolate bar. It was very small, with even tinier scored squares, and a bit darker than the Hershey's bar that I was used to, but it was mine. I was so excited by my discovery that I quickly shoved it in my mouth before anyone else could take away my coveted chocolate. I was so hasty in my theft that I barely tasted the chocolate, for it hardly had time to melt into my mouth to release its fruity flavor. Little did I know the karmic price that I would pay for that chocolate and the complicated relationship that chocolate and I would have later in my life. For in those teeny tiny squares was a substance powerful enough to send me straight to the pediatrician who told me in his gentle but stern doctor's voice, "Sharon, you cannot eat things if you do not know what they are."

But I did. They were chocolate weren't they? And who doesn't like chocolate? But chocolate they were not.

I had gotten into my mother's stash of laxatives, the ones that she routinely ate that sent her sneaking off to the bathroom after every meal. Although she later replaced the chocolate flavored laxative squares for the ubiquitous pink laxative pills that I found in just about every one of her purses after she died, what I discovered and quaffed off the table was pure chocolate purgative. To this day I don't understand why anyone would ruin the delightful flavor of chocolate by giving it such a punishing aftermath for the person who ate it, but I do know that laxatives were the preferred form of chocolate for my mother who enjoyed several squares, if not a whole bar, each day.

The fading physical form of my mother had much to do with the dwindling box of laxatives that supplied her with a somewhat tasty treat (although I knew even then that the chocolate tasted a bit funny but, as I am oft to do today, I declare to myself that chocolate is chocolate even if doesn't taste great). So thinking I had found a small foil-wrapped treasure to savor, I ate the squares. But a few hours later, my pleasure took a violent turn after I was struck with a serious case of the runs and belly aching and ended up at the doctor's office with my mother fibbing that she didn't know how I got into the laxatives in the first place. I remembered though. The fake chocolate was laying out on the table with its foil already opened and ready for consumption.

Where was she when I discovered this deceptive treat? She was sitting on the toilet where she usually was after we ate. At this point, most of our sit-down dinners would lead to her pushing her small portions of food around her plate as she complained that her stomach wasn't feeling good and that her digestion was off. We knew better than to inquire further because her health was also declining from her failing kidneys and we were too afraid to ask.

Finding Strength in the Body

I HAD MY FIRST TASTE of independence when I was 13 years old. From late June through August, I escaped New York and my mother to a small Canadian lake 250 miles north of Toronto. It did not matter that I was not a competitive athlete like most of the girls at this swim camp, which had been started by a former director of the U.S. Swimming Hall of Fame. I would happily take my designation as a "non-comp" swimmer in order to take my steamer trunk to the airport in Toronto on my own and then aboard the camp bus that would take me to a full summer's freedom far from my mother's icy gaze.

I'm not exactly sure what had prompted the camp getaways, but I suspect it had something to do with my parents' marriage. Things at home must have gotten pretty bad because my dad had jumped at the chance to send me and my fifteen-year old brother away that summer. All we knew was that my brother's friend, Roger, went to the camp and Roger came from a "good" home (which is to say, a moneyed home). So without even researching the place, Dad paid the bills and off we went. While the boys' camp didn't really appeal to my brother, from that year forward I begged to go every summer. It was an escape and it was the first time that I had lived with a group of girls away from my parents. I was hooked and wanted more and more each year.

By the time I had reached the summer before eighth grade, however, my mom's mood had gotten more and more uneven and unpredictable. It was hard to know what would be waiting for me when I got home from school, but on the day I came home and she put the chef's knife she was using to cut onions against my neck, I knew that I needed something to save me. My dad also began to talk to me about my mother's behavior and even admitted to me that their marriage was suffering.

"Your mom wants a divorce, so we might separate," he said to me in the car one afternoon. I didn't know how to respond, so I said nothing, and for a few long moments we drove in silence.

"I know that she's been so hard on you and I don't know if I can take it anymore," he finally said.

I had been waiting a lifetime to hear those words of recognition and affirmation about my mom's abuse. If I were another kid growing up with a more loving mother I might have felt differently, but all I felt was relieved and hopeful. "When will you get divorced? Who will I live with? Can I live with you?" These were likely the first words out of my mouth and I certainly know that they were the first to pop into my head. There was a chance of leaving my mother behind and my dad would finally punish my mother for what she had been doing to me this whole time.

Over the next seven weeks of my first summer at camp, I became more and more excited about the prospect of living with my dad. My mother had become nearly impossible to be around, what with her cold silences that would last for days, her erratic moodiness where she would simply wander the house in a daze like a lost and angry ghost as she played music on the stereo at nearly deafening levels and set on repeat. To this day, I cannot bear to hear the Dire Straits' *Brothers in Arms* album without cringing, especially when Mark Knopfler begins the album, "So Far Away," singing the lyrics, "Here I am again in this old town…" The album originally belonged to my brother, but my mother had for unknown reasons taken an obsession to it and would blast it in the living room, dancing slowly to it, lost in her own little world. Maybe the song reminded her of how far away from Seoul she had come or, for me, how far away from reality she seemed to have gone. In her two-toned velour bathrobe zipped to the very top of her neck, she looked like an invalid wandering about an asylum and I gave her a wide berth. She seemed to get more and more moody and unpredictable. She even began to retaliate against my brother who had started hanging out more with girls after school, drinking with friends, and even smoking pot.

"That Stacey! She is a bad influence on your brother! He's not doing his homework and what's he doing with her anyway?!" she shouted as she began one afternoon to hurl his clothing out the second-floor window of the house. Much like she'd attacked my own clothing like some crazed killer in a slasher film, my mother had suddenly let loose a fireball of energy that far outweighed her slight body. She feverishly tossed his books, football cleats, shoulder pads, and whatever else was on his bedroom floor to the ground below. While I was afraid to get in her way, I must admit to a kind of voyeuristic pleasure at finally not being the one on the receiving end of my mother's rage. This time I was safe so long as I stayed out of her line of vision. So I stayed quiet watching it all happen and didn't say a word.

My silence masked the deep relief I felt in my body because I was finally not the object of her mood. I felt like I could take a full breath as I began to ease back into my own body, feeling its solidity as my feet rested firmly on the ground.

But since it was my brother's stuff that got cast outside on the front lawn as if he were a deadbeat tenant evicted over not paying rent, and not me, the devil child she scorned, my mom seemed to wake up sooner than usual from her seeming possession to see what she had accomplished. All my brother's, and by extension our own, dirty laundry was literally on display for all the neighbors to see. That was an outcome she clearly had not intended.

"Help me clean that mess up!" she commanded me as she fixed her hair, put on her shoes, and hurried out the front door to hide the mess.

My brother came home after school as we were hauling in the final remains of his stuff. "What the hell are you doing?" he asked me with a look of shock on his face. He must have thought that I was the one responsible for throwing out his things.

"Mom was mad at you so she chucked all your stuff out the window," I replied with a slight smile on my face. It was simply too delicious to hide my relief from being spared her latest tirade and I was glad that my brother finally got in trouble. Yet my delight at his torment did not distance us; instead, it somehow brought us closer together because he had just been the object of a maternal rage that seemed to burn inside her most of the time. The drinking, drugs, and now girls, were the tipping point that had pushed my mom over the edge and she finally targeted her anger at him, and that changed everything.

My brother's transition into high school came with a greater sense of independence for him—he had taken up weightlifting as he dedicated himself to bulking up his otherwise thin frame. Every day he'd eat extra protein and work out—maybe he wanted to be as physically big as his friends or maybe he wanted to impress the girls. He was a Korean American young man going to a predominantly white school and had only white friends. In that regard he was always at a disadvantage because Asian American men were, and are, often invisible in these social circles. So with every gym workout, he'd try to put on more mass and become, in turn, more visible. The beginning of high school also brought on more opportunities for my brother to blow off steam over the pressures of growing up in an immigrant home. I was thrilled that every once in a while he'd include me too, for when he did, I felt like I had someone to bond with inside my home. I'd participate in smoking pot, drinking, and even doing whippets of nitrous oxide from small metal canisters he'd buy at the local head shop. We would put each canister inside a dispenser and suck that gas in as if it were oxygen we desperately needed. We'd immediately be hit with a head rush that felt like it was shifting our brains with each inhalation. We'd laugh hysterically, rolling on the ground, and bonding the only way we ever had up to that point. The bond between us was further sealed when, like conspirators to a crime, we had to gather up all those spent whippets and attempt to throw them away without my mom noticing.

"Mike! What is this? What are these things and why you have them?" Mom is walking toward us with a plastic bag clanking with each step.

Uh-oh. She found them, I thought, terrified of what she would do.

But she seemed to sidestep me and go straight for my brother who at this point looked derisively at my mom and simply responded with a matter-of-fact curt response, "whippets."

While I doubt she really knew the extent to which they scrambled our brains temporarily, she did know that they were drugs and kids don't do drugs. So off they went into the trash compactor along with my brother's football. Mike played football and mom was going to punish him for doing drugs by trying to squash his football in the compactor. To this day, the image of my mother throwing that football into the trash compactor and hitting the switch to try to compress it along with the whippet canisters and kitchen trash makes me laugh out loud. First, because of the absurdity of the act, and second, because my brother could finally do some wrong.

My home life was increasingly more emotionally volatile and my mom's thinness became more and more obvious. When she wasn't raging at me, she was locked away in the bathroom after most meals. Meal times were mostly spent with me overeating, partially out of fear and not knowing how to gauge when I was full, my brother eating however much he wanted, and mom barely touching her food. Her kidney disease that had been triggered by her tuberculosis from her youth seemed like it had finally caught up with her and she would always claim that her stomach was bothering her or she'd offer the usual, "my digestion isn't right" excuse as she pushed the food around on her plate.

While she became thinner and thinner by refusing to eat, I started to learn at camp that a woman didn't always need to hate her body or try to make it smaller and smaller like my mother's. Instead, over the summer I learned how to kayak, swim, and run, and I realized for the first time that some women could, and did, appreciate their bodies for their strength and athleticism. I wondered if I could do the same.

Every morning I woke up to the clanging of the 7:20 earlybird bell, rolled out of my creaky bunk bed and made my way into a swimsuit and slowly strolled my way down to the dock with a towel, goggles, swim cap, and my sneakers. Canadian mornings were so cold that I could see my breath as I stood there, frigid, waiting to dive in. I felt strong and capable in my body since I knew that I'd be able to make it the other side of the lake. My body was still a little heavier than I wanted it to be, but it least my back had muscles and I was starting to develop lines in my calves from running. And besides, I wasn't as big as some of the other swimmers at camp. The moment the camp director blew the whistle for us to jump in the water and swim around the lake to another dock half a mile away, there would be a pause that seemed like it lasted a good ten minutes.

"Swimmers! Stay in line with the canoes as you breathe! Focus your eyes on the meeting point of the orange and green sides of the canoes with every stroke so you won't have to stop or stick your head out of the water to see where you're going!" the counselors would shout through the megaphone.

It was freezing cold and my toes were curled over the end of the wooden dock as I peered down in the water trying to muster up the courage to dive in. All the competitive swimmers who swam on high-level school teams, junior national teams, and accomplished major feats like swimming the English Channel or even just swam around Lake Ontario, had already taken off. I could see the wash from their feet kicking under the water and the smoothness of their strokes as they kept a laser focus on the middle of each canoe.

I, on the other hand, was no elite competitive swimmer like those girls whose bodies had six-pack muscles rippling under their speedos. I was a fourteen-year-old girl who somehow managed to return for a second summer at a camp whose motto was "We don't sew beads on belts." This was a camp for athletes and in due time, I would later become one too. But it would be another two summers before I would become a war canoer and cast the stroke for the boat that won the Canadian Nationals. For now, however, I leaned over the edge of the water waiting for gravity to drop me in the water with little effort on my own. I was shivering and did not want to feel the cold splash of that lake water at such an early hour before the sun was ready to give off heat.

"Just pee in the water, it will make you warm for a little while," says my friend Karen who is also standing next to me. We are both going to swim the half mile around the corner of the island and get out at a dock where our sneakers have been deposited by the lead canoes who are the spotters for the swimmers. Once we get there, we will hop out of the water, shove our wet feet into our sneakers and run a mile back to the camp where we will change into our required white t-shirts and blue shorts before heading up the dining hall for a warm breakfast and a half hour of singing camp songs. In anticipation of my favorite breakfast, Johnny Cakes or corn muffins baked into rectangles and cut into squares that I would slather with butter and maple syrup, I jumped in the lake and tread water for a good thirty seconds while I tried to pee to make myself warm.

"It worked!" I shiver-shouted at Karen. As soon as I realized I was wading in my own urine, I took off for the thirty-minute swim in the cold dark water, praying for that moment when my freezing body would thaw from all the exertion.

All-girls summer camp on a scenic lake in Northern Canada gave me some of the best laughs of my life. For seven weeks each summer I could escape my house and the mentally cramped feeling of being cooped up under the control of my mother. It was here that I learned that women could be physically strong and proud of their bodies and that women simply had to eat a lot of calories in order to keep up with the round-the-clock sports activities we did each day. It was also at camp where I learned to push myself physically beyond what I thought I could handle, run farther and faster than I ever had, and realized that I could train my body to help release some of the stress and anxiety I had carried inside me for years. Living in wooden cabins without electricity, sleeping in bunkbeds with upwards of 14 girls and two camp counselors, and using toilets in outhouses that had only waist-height stalls without any doors certainly introduced me to many different kinds of female bodies. And it introduced me to attitudes toward bodies that were so different from what I had encountered before. These were an eclectic mix of girls from all over the world whose parents sent them to summer camp for athletic training and for an opportunity to bond and create life-long and transformative friendships.

After spending seven weeks away at camp, I returned home to little fanfare. My mother barely noticed my return and certainly did not register anything suggesting she might be excited that I was back. What I did notice though is that after an entire summer away swimming, running, canoeing, never watching television, barely talking on the phone, and deciding for myself how much I wanted to eat, my body was beginning to change. I was developing strong back muscles from paddling and kayaking workouts every night after dinner, and my thighs and calves were developing visible muscles when I walked.

I also returned home towing several medals in hand—my summer camp annually competed in Canadian canoeing regattas and we had just brought home a silver medal at Canadian nationals for my age-group boat. For seven grueling weeks, I had woken up and jumped reluctantly into that chilly lake to swim a mile, participated in camp activities like soccer, tennis, swimming competitions, running races, passed out for an hour and a half during the much-looked-forward-to rest hour, and paddled around a lake each evening, pushing my body to near exhaustion.

At the same time as I was disciplining my body to push itself beyond what I thought possible, I was also learning how to train my mind to move beyond what it thought it could. There is nothing quite like paddling a war canoe down a 500-meter race course stacked with fourteen other women in it, all wanting to win. The sensation of nearly losing my breath and wanting to throw up from exertion as I paddled faster and faster and matched the stroke of the women in front of me required me to let go of my mind's continual efforts to make me want to simply give up. But I never did give up because I had tasted the great satisfaction that came from pushing past perceived limitations and winning. My body began to respond to its new exercise regime and my mind learned that physical discipline has its rewards—it makes for a stronger body and more confidence. But I hadn't known until then that it was okay for a woman to want to train her body to develop muscles and be physically strong. More than anything, however, the new-found discipline gave me a glimpse into what it meant to have the ability to tamp down emotional stress by pushing through the pain. And that insight became a life-long skill that only now am I coming to realize might not always be the best medicine.

This recognition of what my mind could make my body do was a newly-discovered one, for all I had learned from my mother was that by not eating and by taking laxatives, one could discipline the body to push through hunger and become rail thin and women at the country club would envy that thin body. I watched as she got smaller and smaller while she forced me to eat so that I would get bigger and bigger, but once I'd return home, her control over me began to wane. I was stronger and had found my independence from her. She could no longer threaten me with physical abuse to make me eat, and whatever satisfaction she got from force-feeding me began to dissipate because I was no longer under her surveillance when I was away at school and no longer compliant when I was home. I was learning to occupy my body, and it was the strong body that I wanted, not the fattened one she wanted for me.

As I grew healthier and more independent, however, her body grew unhealthier. Nevertheless, while her growing frailty and my emerging strength made it more difficult for her to threaten me with beatings or stuff me like a fatted goose, she learned to wield another deadly weapon that would hurt me—her complete and utter silence. Whenever I returned home, she did not acknowledge me, barely looked at me, and spoke to me with one- or two-word sentences. If she could no longer physically bend me to her will through force-feeding and physical abuse, then she could certainly turn the knob higher on the emotional abuse through her silence, rendering me nearly invisible in my own home. She would often tighten up her mouth into that familiar flat line denoting her anger that my body had started to become my own.

In contrast, my dad was thrilled when I returned home an athlete with medals. His ready and enthusiastic, "Congratulations, that's amazing. Now what *exactly* did you win that medal for?" certainly felt great. I loved the validation that came from my father for a job well done. It was expected that I would be successful, but that expectation certainly did not diminish the feeling of pride when he noticed. My father's recognition that I was successful and doing better than anyone in my family thought I would was always important to me, not only for the sense of pride I felt, but because I also knew that my successes were in some way an acknowledgement that my childhood hadn't completely ruined me. And so I worked exceptionally hard for my father because I knew even as a teenager that his guilt over the way my mother treated me could be assuaged with the evidence of my success. It was a two-way street, for by escaping each summer to Canada, he gave me the opportunity to remake myself away from my mother's debilitating gaze.

Still, even as I write these words, I struggle to remember the sound and tone of her voice. There was so much silence in my household that memories of those later years have been muted in my mind. But what I do remember is walking in the room, showing her my medals, and telling her about the Canadian national medals that I won, and she responding with her usual heavy silence. It was like shouting into a vacuum. The silence that screamed to me her complete disdain took my breath away.

My father never failed to puff up in pride over my accomplishments, however, in much the same way that I do with my daughters today when they run races, give dance performances, or get good grades. Yet whenever he did so, my mother's face would tighten. Her eyes would narrow, her voice would shrink to a whisper, and she'd look at me and simply say, "don't brag." When she wasn't warning me against showing any kind of conceit in myself, she would grow rigid and barely register my existence. Her refusal to speak to me meant that I simply was not there or was not good enough to elicit any kind of recognizable response. I felt invisible in her presence and the more I achieved the less I felt I was even there.

Although I had returned home a national champion (and I know that her response would not have changed even if I won a gold medal because I did that later, too), I certainly didn't feel like one. I felt stronger and more confident and more in control of what I ate, yet the home that had once been mine felt even more unsafe. I was trapped in a near sound-proof house where I walked around on eggshells wondering if and when my mom's silence would simply explode into a fit of rage. I counted the days until I could once again fly the coop and return to camp. Stella was a year older than me and was probably the only other person at camp who wasn't a competitive swimmer. We both hailed from New York, but she was world-wise and bold compared to my somewhat shy Korean American self. Stella was brazen, gritty, brilliant, and far more sophisticated than most of the girls at camp. She taught me how to put a tampon in for the first time, would often extol the virtues of Duran Duran, and was the only person to this day to refer to a man, Simon Le Bon (lead singer of Duran Duran) as a "paragon of male perfection." This smart, sassy New Yorker who couldn't care less if she ran fast or swam the whole lake or not also introduced me to my first boyfriend—an eighteen-year-old French dreamboat named Remi Le Beau. Remi and Stephan from the British Isles were paired with me and Stella for the summer. We saw them at each girls' and boys' camp get-together where they would walk us to our canoes that we would paddle to our own camp. And it was here that I got my first kiss from a man who had beautiful, long blond curls and a sweet smile. We barely said a word to each other because he spoke French and, well, I didn't. But it didn't matter, it was 1983, I was fourteen years old and I had held hands with and kissed an older Frenchman. Through Stella, I was suddenly cool.

But even more than that, it was through Stella that I learned that you could actually live away from home and go to school. "It's so cool.

You live in dorms, have a roommate, and basically do whatever you want. You should try it," she'd say while she regaled me with all the interactions she had had with the cute boys at boarding school. She was a year older than me and had just finished her sophomore year, and I wanted in. All I could think about was having a new life on my own. I'd be a cool teenager without parents and free from my mom. I had already spent two summers away and knew that there had to be another way to live on my own. The very next day I got on the phone and called my dad at work.

"Dad, I have an idea and I think it'll be really great. I want to go to boarding school and get away from home. It will be a good change for me."

My dad paused a few seconds and without a beat responded, "Alright, let's see what it's about." It took only a few weeks after I got home to take the admissions test for boarding schools and I went with my dad to about six different boarding schools for interviews. Each one gave me an even greater longing to be one of those cool independent kids who had a life away from home. It was a chance to start afresh and, for my dad, it was the one thing that he knew that he could do for me to save my life. I needed freedom and I needed a safe home, and boarding school was the culturally legitimate way. I couldn't run away, I couldn't live alone, but my dad could pay for me to go to boarding school. It was a win-win situation. He'd be the savior sending me away from my mom and be the successful immigrant who could afford a fancy boarding school tuition. And I would win because I'd be able to grow up with less of my mother's reach. It was an exciting year of applying to schools and a miserable year of silence as my mother all but ignored my interests in boarding school and refused to speak to me during the entire application process. Each night after driving home from boarding school interviews, I would reluctantly enter my house and be met with dead silence. It was as if I did not exist. I was going to escape and she'd be home alone with her fury.

When the thick envelope accepting me into Chadwick Hall finally arrived, I tore it open and shook with relief and excitement. "I made it into Chadwick Hall!" I shouted. I knew that escape was near. I glanced over at my mother who had been watching my reactions and tried to catch her eye for some kind of acknowledgment. There was barely a flicker in her eye, just stone-cold silence. She said nothing.

Decades after graduation, my father recalled my decision to go to boarding school to be the best one he had ever made for me. While I recall the conversation quite differently, it felt so good to finally have my father acknowledge the abuse and finally to verbally apologize for not doing more to intervene. He felt trapped, he admitted, since any time he did try to confront my mother, she would emotionally lash out and, as he put it, "I worried about how she would treat you later." Whether or not this reason was the actual reason why my father did not intervene more in my childhood didn't matter to me; for the time being, this was enough of an apology for me and one that acknowledged how rough it was to grow up my mother's daughter. There is something incredibly powerful that happens when someone else admits to the truths that you have always known but were afraid to admit.

Paul

THE FIERY SHADES of red, orange, and rust foliage that adorn the cover of just about every New England boarding school catalogue had just begun to creep over the remaining bits of green that the leaves desperately clung to. The leaves were dying, but before they let go of their tight grip on the trees, they would explode with a final technicolor hurrah before blanketing the new school that would become my new home away from home. As the leaves prepared to drop from their branches, I, too, was ready for a drop. I was about to be dropped off at a fancy little boarding school in Connecticut where I would be a sophomore and I could barely contain my excitement over leaving my home.

My parents and I have just driven the two-and-a-half hours from Long Island in near silence outside of my dad's occasional request for map directions to the little town of Chadwick. "Welcome to Chadwick Hall," says just about every official-looking student holding a clipboard I pass while unloading my suitcases, bedding, books, and my beloved stereo that will soon belt out all the 80s tunes that witnessed my turn from adolescent into full teenager—Echo and the Bunnymen, the Smiths, the Cure, and New Order. I was attracted to these British bands because they were so full of angst and so was I. These same bands now appear on my daughters' retro playlists on Spotify and somehow mark me as a vestige of a kind of cool musical era. With most of the girls looking like they had just come off an L.L. Bean catalogue with their crisp white shirts and plaid skirts, I already knew that I wouldn't quite fit in, but that was of little worry to me.

After officially registering me in my boarding school, I walked the hallways of Foley dormitory and met my first roommate, Lena from California. As I unpacked my belongings and set up my bed, I realized that I had zero understanding of what the word "preppy" was and that it signified a culture that I had no experience with—White Anglo-Saxon

Protestant, or WASP. All I saw was that there was a lot of blond hair, lots of conservative clothes, lots of what I came to later know as seersucker coats and the ubiquitous Geiger jacket that seemed to be the dressy coat of choice for many of the girls at Chadwick Hall. This was a curious world that I had chosen for myself and I felt like I was at some kind of living zoo of strange people and fancy families that I had never seen before. These were not the kind of folks that I had seen all over Long Island with big teased hair, tight acid-wash jeans, and gobs of eyeliner. These were buttoned-up parents and their well-coiffed, smiling children who represented a world that I really didn't understand at the time—it was a world of white privilege. But I couldn't care less in that moment. I just wanted to live far away and feel safe. It didn't matter to me yet that I was once again a racial minority in a largely white school. I would gladly choose being a misfit to being mistreated at home, for I had a taste of freedom and independence from my mother and knew that I wanted more.

"Sharon?" says Paul.

"Yes," I said into the phone receiver that I am cradling between both my hands.

"Don't let those punks get you down. Do you have any idea how smart you are? Your writing is amazing. Don't worry about these jokers," he counseled.

Paul was in his first year in law school in Boston and I was in my first year at boarding school. I was telling my favorite cousin about some of the kids at Chadwick Hall and how weird it was to be in this strange world of plaids and argyle sweaters that were worn not out of irony but as a cultural uniform. I didn't understand the cultural logic of white privilege at the time nor the notion that moneyed kids were the ones who populated boarding schools in New England. I was an anomaly for Korean Americans because few immigrant parents sent their own children to boarding school. I was not a trust fund baby. I didn't come from a long lineage of waspy money that was passed down through inheritance. I was an Asian American growing up in a predominantly white culture who had begged to escape my home through the only way that Korean Americans would understand—educational opportunity—even if it came at the cost of my dad having to shell out private school tuition and having to explain to my family and his friends why I wasn't living at home. I was thrilled and relieved to leave my mom behind but I really had no idea what I was getting myself into. Boarding school was an alien land to me, but I needed to figure out how to fit in and somehow make friends.

Paul seemed to get it, just like he always did. He was seven years older than me and was handsome, smart, and the kind of guy who could walk into any bar and make friends with just about anyone. This was probably both an innate skill and one that he cultivated out of necessity. Even when regaling me with stories of various awkward social encounters or when a joke fell flat, he'd sigh, "Alas, I am not relating to the masses."

Like me, Paul grew up on Long Island. He had become a high school football player. He eventually went to college and still managed to date his Swedish American high school girlfriend. In the 80s, Paul was the only Asian American male I knew who could date a white girl. Most Asian American boys were considered too nerdy, weak, and different, to be wanted by anyone other than an Asian American girl, but Paul was unlike many of my other cousins or really any of the other Korean American boys I knew. He had the kind of looks that transcended the boundaries of race and a coolness that made you want to be around him. He had lots of white male friends which meant to me that he somehow made it out.

We'd visit his family at least once a month and spend most Thanksgiving, Christmas, and New Year's holidays together. I was always so taken with "the guys" who'd come into the house and treat his parents with casual and genuine familiarity. "Hey, Mrs. Kim! How are you?" they'd say to my aunt as they walked right into the house to wait for Paul.

Paul's best friend Steve was such an unusual yet intriguing guy to me—he had long wavy brown hair, a little mustache, and didn't seem to notice that my cousin wasn't white; but if he did, Paul's Korean-ness was not something strange. In fact, Steve would come into the house after football, dressed in his flannel shirt and gray sweatpants, and gladly eat any of the 'exotic' Korean foods that my aunt would offer him—*kimbap* (Korean style sushi), *chap chae* (glass noodles), white rice, *kalbi* (marinated grilled beef), and *kimchi*. To Steve, Korean food was simply another kind of cuisine that he didn't have access to in his Euro-American home and not something he considered too smelly or weird for his American palate. And my aunt was so sweet that it would be near impossible not to consider her a second mom.

Unlike most Korean families, my aunt and uncle were at ease with American culture and, amazingly, they were okay with Paul's choice of white friends and, even more unusual, his choice of a tall, willowy blonde girlfriend. Linnea was as Swedish as Paul was Korean—someone who was raised with a strong sense of identity who held on to her cultural roots primarily through food. Unlike the other Korean mothers who would be reduced to near hysterics at the idea of their sons dating non-Koreans, my aunt adored Linnea and treated her like a future daughter-in-law, but not the Korean kind. Korean daughters-in-law were often treated cruelly by their mothers-in-law and many a popular soap opera dramatized this antagonistic relationship where the mother was nothing without the eldest son and the wife nothing without the son-turned-husband. Even today, Korean soap operas tap into this unfortunate Confucian legacy where women were not considered fulfilled until they married, left the home, and produced male heirs. These tensions still play out on television as a kind of cultural catharsis that caters to a new bride locked into a new marital family presided over by the manipulative mother-in-law who is saccharinely sweet in front of her son, but manages to render the daughter-in-law's life a mess behind the scenes.

My aunt Ji Soo simply was not like that. It was as if she was an ideal American mom living in a Korean woman's body. She treated Linnea with such sweetness that it made me almost jealous. First, because I wished that I had beautiful curly blonde hair like she did and because I wished that my mom was as nice to me as my aunt was to Linnea. Aunt Ji Soo would invite my cousin's girlfriend straight into the home and engage her in conversation; she even talked to Linnea's family! That sort of behavior was not the norm for Korean American families—white girlfriends and boyfriends were barely, if at all, tolerated and certainly not treated as if they were part of the family. They were considered interlopers whom eventually their sons and daughters would have to give up in order to marry a Korean and maintain our identities. But for some reason, my aunt and uncle were cut from a different cloth. Even my uncle Tae welcomed Linnea—maybe he found her as beautiful and loving as I did. He could often be found in the backyard of their small home in Long Island with a Budweiser and tongs in hand, manning the grill and feeding all of Paul's and his brother's big football-playing American friends. Hotdogs, hamburgers, and Korean grilled beef sizzled side by side on my uncle's grill, creating a different kind of melting pot where differences were not washed away but held together one next to the other, each equally savored.

For all his cultural successes and smarts, what made Paul special to me was that he paid attention and listened to my struggles with my mom. He was the only one in my family I trusted to confide in and the only family member brave enough to confront my mother for the way she treated me.

"Nina, what on earth are you doing? How can you treat her this way? What's wrong with you?!" he'd challenge her. My mom's American name was not Nina, it was Evelyn, but he called her Nina because as a little boy, he couldn't pronounce the Korean word for 'older sister,' *noona*, which younger boys always called older female sisters and cousins.

I began confiding in Paul in the seventh grade about some of the things my mom used to do, like force-feeding me, calling me ugly, hitting me, and locking me out of the house when I was younger. There wasn't anyone else that I was willing to rely on at the time, and Paul was the only person who actually did more than smile kindly at me as if to say *I know what is happening but there is nothing that I can do about it.* Maybe it was because Paul was going to be a lawyer sticking up for people that he came to my rescue and took on my mother in ways that no one else could. And my mom hated him for it. He was her beloved nephew who everyone adored and he was angry at her and called her out for her abuse.

Because he was so well-loved and confident he seemed almost more of a threat to my mom than anyone else. If he were someone less adored, less popular, and less charismatic, perhaps my mom would not have worried so much about his criticisms of her. But she was enraged by his care for me and she went from being one of his closest relatives to a near stranger who was forced to tolerate him in silence. My mother's silence was one of the strongest weapons she wielded against anyone who crossed whatever invisible lines and boundaries she set up. If she was angry, she'd say practically nothing with her tight-closed mouth, but she would erect a wall of silence that would make anyone almost breathless from its force. She had an inimitable power to render anyone nonexistent in her presence as if they had simply never appeared before her. She rendered this magic to great success around most of my family members who dared to mention her abuse, but Paul was somehow impervious to her social poison. He let her punishing silence roll right off his back and would push back against her treatment of me at the time when I needed it the most—middle school into high school—when she became more and more hostile, and more and more house-bound due to her eating disorders, kidney disease, and increasing instability. Paul was my confidant and probably the best male role model who was both a protector *and* someone whom I could trust with all my other more ordinary teenage girl angst. I considered him a closer older brother than my own and an advocate—plus he was smart, good-looking, and paid attention to *me*. I was always so amazed that he considered me worthy enough of his time and attention, so much so that we'd have regular long phone calls between Boston and Connecticut every few weeks where I could check in and share my latest dilemmas, most of which were around trying to fit in as an Asian American in a largely white, upper-crusty, tight-lipped culture at boarding school.

There were very few Asians and Asian Americans in my boarding school—there was Mona from China and no one seemed to notice her. She always looked so serious and severe and she probably didn't like me anyway because I dressed in all black and teased my hair every day. I was a Korean American wannabe cleaned-up version of post-punk. Mona buttoned her shirts to the very top button which she tucked tightly into her pleated skirts and had a bob whose sharp corners threatened to stab her in the chin when she walked. She had coarse black hair like I did but rather than try to retrain that hair to do the unthinkable—stand straight up like Ian McCulloch of Echo and the Bunny Men, she accepted who she was. But of course she did. She was from China and was not Chinese American. She could be authentic, just as she was.

There were few other Asian Americans except for Jennifer Chang and, like me, she was Korean American. But unlike me, she somehow managed to fit in as one of the popular preppy girls. We were friendly toward one another because she lived a few doors down from me in the dorm and she was really pretty nice. It was always a curiosity to me, though, how she had managed to assimilate into the school's waspy culture—she wasn't blonde, white, or even particularly attractive for that manner. But then again, she managed to dress the part. Jen played on the field hockey team and wore pleated skirts that came to her knees and white Peter Pan collared shirts with blue wool cardigans. She also wore penny loafers—buffed, shiny brown leather loafers with a penny stuck into some weird little slot cut into to the top presumably to stick a penny into, of all things.

Man, waspy people are really weird, I thought to myself. *There is no way the girls from Bayview High School would ever be caught dead wearing those flat hideous shoes.* The girls at my former high school were wearing high heels with pegged jeans to school and had enough blue eyeliner rimming their eyes that it looked like war paint. They were ready to take on the world of boys and mean girls and wore their makeup and their shoes like weapons to subdue the boys and conquer the girls. Those kids had lots of money like the boarding school kids, but I also didn't fit into the suburban high school that I went to either. Still, somehow I had managed to find a few of the other misfits like me—kids who were cool but not in the right way.

Here at boarding school, however, it didn't matter that you were upper middle-class and your parents could afford to send you to an expensive school and dress you in expensive clothes. At boarding school what made a kid popular was a kind of cultural cachet that came from having trust funds and lots of money for a long time in the family. Old money. At boarding school, there were no alternative groups, no welcomed misfits, no variation in costume. Boys and girls wore those penny loafers, along with blue blazers with gold buttons which was practically the uniform for all the male students.

The girls had uniforms too—plain skirts and plain buttoned shirts. Plain colored pants, with tucked-in button shirts. And jeans on Wednesdays. I played with pushing the boundaries of those rules every day because I must have realized that I didn't fit in culturally like Jen Chang and I didn't want to dress in those hideous outfits that always made me feel completely boring and sexless. And besides, even though Jen played on the field hockey team and fit in with the girls, she never landed the guys.

She was a goody-two-shoes who became a dorm prefect, a student invested with way too many opportunities to bust the students like me who were always standing on the toilets in bathroom stalls smoking into the vents in the ceilings or hitching rides into Manhattan as soon as the dorm masters went to bed. We'd come sneaking home from the village, hanging out on St. Mark's street at the break of dawn, hopping silently and swiftly out of Charlie the pizza guy's van (Charlie who was our friend Maura's in-town boyfriend). While I was finding every possible way to be rebellious and push the boundaries at high school, Jen was studying and making her way toward a probable future as a doctor.

I myself was making my way to more and more rebellion by trying to break every rule in the handbook—which I largely accomplished. But even then, I was a bit of an overachiever. What made Jen different in a way that made me somehow feel better about myself was that while she behaved herself, I had managed to find my first blond-haired, blue-eyed preppy boy from Boston—William. He didn't even go by Bill or Billy. Nope, he went by his full name William even had a roman numeral after his name. William Carlton, III. Wow, there were three generations in this male bloodline with the exact same name. Although I found this waspy practice thoroughly bizarre, I didn't care because I had suddenly started dating a beautiful blond boy. It didn't occur to me then, however, that if you wanted to date someone, the boy should probably be nice to you and acknowledge your presence with a bit more than a nod on the stairs as you made the shuffle between classes.

I didn't care that we didn't have any emotional connection or that William didn't really like me; I just wanted some kind of proof that I fit in, even if having a cold, icy, blue-eyed boyfriend was my temporary ticket. *See Jen? You might fit in with the popular girls but you couldn't ever get a guy like William,* I'd think, looking for any kind of victory over the only other girl in school who probably understood how hard it was to be Asian American in a tony white New England boarding school.

Boarding school also gave me the freedom to learn how to eat to my own satisfaction rather than out of fear and guilt, but I still had no way of gauging how much was enough or too much. The fact that I could go to the dining hall three times a day and choose what I wanted to eat and how much I wanted to eat was an entirely new experience to me. And admittedly, I went overboard because I just didn't have any internal cues that could let me know that I didn't need to eat an entire pint of ice cream or a full plate of fried mozzarella sticks. Food was both a comfort and a lesson in freedom—or so I thought. For despite the fact that I ate as much as I wanted to, I also knew that my body was still bigger than I wanted it to be and that I was still drowning out anxiety by stuffing down my feelings with chips, popcorn, cookies, and pizza which seemed to be on endless supply.

"You really should be a writer. Don't listen to anything your mom says, you are really smart. You are amazing, funny, and cool. I think you're great," Paul tells me.

"Thanks" I say, beaming into the phone. The black phone receiver has gotten that familiar warm feeling from speaking into it for over half an hour. My face is feeling warm, as well, because Paul thinks I am smart and cool. I have shut the booth on the first floor of Foley Dorm and have my legs squished up against the panels. For forty-five minutes or so every few weeks, Paul pays focused attention to me, listening to all my worries when he could be talking to anyone else. He cultivated a faith in me that I was in fact more interesting, smarter, and even prettier than I felt in boarding school and at home. Maybe I wasn't relating to the masses—yet. I was perhaps more mature than my classmates, or so he made me feel. It wasn't me who was the problem; it was the rest of the people like my mom and my dumb boyfriends who couldn't see that I was cool and was going to make something of myself. There's nothing like a man you adore and idealize to encourage you to rethink your own insecurities. Paul was that man for me and I had come to rely on his loving protection to help me navigate life with my mom and as an awkward teenager who was like a fish out of water in boarding school. I was starting to come into my own and find my way to a social group of those few other kids who didn't seem to fit that preppy mold and together we created a small haven of alternative kids dressing in all black, engaged in the arts, and all the while working on getting the good grades. We loved to break rules, but we also loved to distinguish ourselves by making it onto the Honors list and dominating the high honors list at Chadwick Hall, lists that were publicized after every term and somehow made the sting of being outsiders a lot less painful.

We had a compensatory kind of thrill where we knew that even though we weren't blonde, beautiful, and old-moneyed, we were smart as hell and no one could take that away from us.

And then one day I got a call from my dad. His voice was so serious, I thought something had happened to my mom.

"I have terrible news," my dad said. "Paul died. He was not taking his epilepsy medication and had a seizure. He was alone and passed away."

My dad knew that I would be devastated and tried so hard to remain calm for me as he shared this news. The comfortable familiarity of the phone booth that had once been an intimate little nook where I could share my life with Paul had suddenly became a suffocating claustrophobic closet that threatened to lock me in.

Paul had taken on my mother and for that he paid the price of her silence. But unlike anyone else in my family, he was brave enough to pay that price. And now he was gone. Forever.

Shift

AFTER LOSING PAUL in my first year of boarding school, I returned for my junior year and began gravitating more and more toward the intellectually gifted among my friends. We all managed to take J.B. Smith's AP English class on the top floor of one of the boys' campus classrooms. It was the perfect little seminar room that you would find in any movie about boarding school—about a dozen students sat around an old oak table while an English teacher who was semi-bald with a short smattering of gray hair around the edges of his face pushed us to think critically about Shakespeare, T.S. Eliot, and of course, F. Scott Fitzgerald. Mr. Smith was in his sixties and wore wool tweed coats, polka-dotted bowties, and oxford shirts that protruded just slightly over his aging belly. He had round-rimmed glasses that rested at the edge of his nose, which he would push up with his index finger as he slowly paced the room calling us out not by our first names but by our last names.

"Ms. Suh, what mood does Eliot wish to evoke from his reader here?" he'd call out without even looking up from his book. It was here in J.B. Smith's class that I began to fall in love with not only literature but the act of reading and writing itself. Being in an AP English class with the smartest of the smart in boarding school suddenly gave me a sense of belonging and affirmation that I did in fact have a brain and that I would be judged for my intelligence and not so much for my body.

Perhaps it was the way that he hung on every word we tried to stammer out of our mouths or the excitement I got when I hit on an idea, but whatever it was, it was in his class that I learned to put my ideas to paper without fear—and to do so in pen because something magical happened when I wrote out an essay in my best handwriting. It was as if my fingers knew that my mind had something important to contribute and I would need the extra time to capture my thoughts in the best possible form. Writing in pen was like setting out the fancy dinner plates over Christmas dinner or the best towels when guests came over. I wanted to have the best possible visually written form for the content that I was growing more and more confident I could express. I soon took to waking up at five a.m., way before anyone else in the dorms, so that I could enjoy the quiet of being awake while everyone else slumbered. I would fill my electric kettle and settle into a cup of orange Suisse Mocha coffee from a can and begin writing away until the rest of my classmates began to stir. To this day, the ritual activity of waking up at five a.m., drinking coffee, and starting to write is what sets my day right.

Boarding schools are college preparatory machines that you enter wide-eyed and shaky because you are leaving your home and family to survive with a bunch of other privileged teenagers. And each one seems hell-bent on demonstrating their superiority over you. For the boys, the rituals of hazing generally took the form of physical harassment of the underclassmen and finding ways to humiliate them whether through homoerotic violence or just plain beating. Twenty-eight years after we graduated I was having drinks with one of my old Chadwick Hall friends, Martin, when he told me that the threat of rape by an upper classman was ever on the minds of artsy boys like him. Martin was a beautiful but quiet young man whose parents were well-known artists in New York; he came to Chadwick Hall after his parents split up, and he was literally dropped off at boarding school without much fanfare and left to his own devices. Every day of his first year, he'd basically walk the gauntlet in the boys' dining hall wondering who would call him a fag, who would try to humiliate him by tripping him, throwing food at him, or whatever other ways that only the well-bred boys of the privileged upper class could devise. It seemed that boys either had to join in the harassment of those they could sniff out as slightly more sensitive than they were so that they could distance themselves as far as possible from any association of softness, or they themselves would be the objects of such harassment.

Maybe it was because as a kid I was always on the receiving end of social torment on the bus and playground, but for some reason, it was these gentler boys who drew me in during high school. These were the boys that I wanted to be with. They were generally cuter, with their hair just a touch longer than the rest of their tightly-shorn classmates. And they carried themselves like young poets who had too much soul to fit into the world of social conformity that prep schools inspire. I found alliance with, and eventually dated, a few of these boys. We probably gravitated toward one another as a way to create a sub-community of safety in the larger sea of striped oxford shirts with loose ties hanging off the collars, khaki pants, and blue blazers that seemed to colonize the picture-perfect landscape of the boys' and girls' campuses.

Eventually, after a fortune in tuition, the education machine takes the still-unformed teenager and spits out an articulate, well-heeled, college-acceptable young adult ready to take on the world in a Brooks Brothers suit—at least what all the admissions folks wanted you to believe about their schools in New England. All the fancy prep schools, including my own, made it their mission not only to take the children of wealthy Americans and raise them into semi-mature young adults, but also to make sure that, come hell or high water, those kids would make it into a college. After all, their success as a prep school depended on their college placement success.

"Oh, this school had two students going to Stanford, one to Harvard, and one to Yale," or so the conversation would go among the parents who were about to send their offspring off for the next three or four years, to be dressed like little men and women in business casual. What the parents probably didn't know and what the school administrators worked hard to both cover up and penalize, was the fact that teenagers without parental guidance would always run amok, partying excessively regardless of the degree of their inherited privilege. In fact, it seemed that the wealthy jocks, who were usually given some preppy abbreviated name of one of their forefathers like Brock, Tad, or Skip, were often the worst offenders—heavy drinkers who in my generation probably were the ones who got away with the worst crimes—like date rape and other forms of violence toward women. And for every Tad, Skip, and Brock was a female equivalent in nomenclature—Muffy, Molly, and Kitty. These were the girls who were deemed the near-equal to the boys in preppy culture, but not quite equal because gender equality still hadn't made it to the upper crust.

This was the mid-1980s when the concept of rape culture did not exist and if date rape did occur, it was still regarded as the woman's fault. The young woman would usually be labeled a slut and somehow loose, and invariably it seemed that her family didn't have the same financial pedigree as the young man's family.

"She was drunk and totally asking for it. Besides, she's a slut," would be the common explanation amongst the fellow students if word got out about a sexual assault. "And boys will be boys," was still the prevailing narrative used to excuse male sexual violence. Nobody ever talked about sexual abuse at school, or really any kind of abuse at home, because preppy culture generally kept its mouth shut over dirty laundry. To this day I suspect that this is where the term "lock jaw" came about to refer to all the people who refused to discuss the scandals that were happening both on campus and it our own homes. Like Korean Americans, preppy culture kept its dirty laundry under wraps. We could talk about social fissures like divorce to little fanfare, but not abuse or scandal.

Whenever a scandal did take place at school, it was usually the women who suffered the most—when Lizzie got pregnant in high school, the whole school talked about her and knew that she had to have an abortion. Lizzie became a pariah of sorts, not because she had sex, but because somehow her transgression of pregnancy rendered her a slut. Of course, Pete, her cute blond-haired boyfriend with his cute European ties and rumpled blazers never got called out for his irresponsibility. If anything, he came away unscathed and a bit of a hero amongst a certain class of boys who were excited by the fact that he had sex at such a young age. It seemed at Chadwick Hall, and certainly at many boarding schools even today, the boys never got in trouble. It was always the girls who seemed to take the hit for the transgressions they both engaged in—Sarah the beautiful girlfriend of Jamie, the even-better-looking and wealthier boyfriend, got kicked out of school for drinking with Jamie. Jamie, however, got to stay in school and graduate on to an Ivy league school while Sarah had to go back home to Florida and finish out at a local public high school.

And so the wealthy young scions of old money and heirs to their lock-jawed grandparents would churn through the college prep machine, their way guaranteed by their athletic prowess, their conventional American good looks, and greased with trust funds. These boys scared the hell out of me, not only because they exuded a waspy male privilege to an extent that I had never witnessed in the predominantly Jewish suburbs of Long Island, but because they also managed to look right past and through me.

As an Asian American young woman dressed all in black, I was neither the right race nor class to be deemed worthy of being seen in their eyes. I was relieved to not be the object of gaze and sexual conquest by the boys who rowed crew or spent their time on the ice-hockey rink and bragged about it later in the locker room. Even now, decades later, a man can boast of sexually assaulting women, call it locker room talk, and be elected president—as if it's all just harmless, boyish behavior.

But the invisibility of being an Asian American woman—and one told by her own mother that she was unattractive and unacceptable—certainly made me feel less than desirable. When I look back on those high school years and the culture of boarding school, it occurs to me that they served as a kind of container that bred a social, racial, and gendered elitism that at least managed to avoid the construction of Asian American women as docile, hypersexual China dolls. Stereotypes of Asian women as sexual objects to be toyed with and eventually discarded certainly proliferated in Hollywood films and other forms of popular culture with the adventures of Fu Manchu's evil and sexually dangerous daughter, and of course all those prostitutes with hearts of gold. But somehow, at least on the surface, preppy culture didn't much acknowledge the existence of those stereotypes, perhaps because such images of Asian women rubbed up against the race and class-based investments of wealthy well-bred white privilege. It seemed that we were invisible at best and for me that invisibility was echoed in my home.

There was another consequence to our invisibility, one that felt more intimate and hurtful. In the hallowed halls of the New England boarding schools in the mid-1980s, interracial romances were not yet normalized. Even when I went to college, I learned rather quickly that I would not be widely accepted into the family of my boyfriend, Ben—who also happened to have a Roman numeral appended to his last name. Because of that roman numeral, his social world included the upper echelons of waspy New York society that included a blue-blooded mother who made it quite clear that her son would not be marrying an Asian American woman like me. I had always found it rather incongruous that his preppy, conservative mom, who lived in a four-story brown-stone apartment, resided in the New York that seemed so fashion-forward and liberal to me. He was a great guy but one who would eventually settle down to marry a nice white woman who traced her heritage back to Scotland as did Ben. He married in a kilt.

Although I was out of my social league in high school, I did find my identity through a combination of alternative music, anti-preppy outfits, and art class with Mr. Mettier. Jean-Paul Mettier embodied everything I thought that a French artist should be—he had wild gray hair, an introverted demeanor, and welcomed all the misfits into his print-making studio with an unspoken respect. Perhaps it was because he knew that my friends and I did not quite fit into the prep school environment with our teased hair, dark eyeliner, and generally somber moods. We had a reputation for being iconoclastic and pushing against the force of privileged social conformity and he was the artist offering us shelter in the art studio. I wasn't a particularly gifted artist like my friend, Phil, who later became a famous landscape painter, but going into the studio a few days a week gave me the opportunity to pursue art-making as a kind of ritual act that removed me from the pressures of living away from home in a foreign environment. It gave me a glimpse of what it meant to recreate the self through art-making. I was a teenager and teenagers by nature are full of angst, uncertain of who they are, and paradoxically fiercely loyal to who they want people to think they are. Print-making took deliberate practice, vision, planning, honing of skills, and a certain amount of chance, and so it was a perfect opportunity to reimagine myself through my work. It also became a ritual activity that I later learned in my religious studies courses in college and graduate school was a way of making meaning out of life when things fall apart. My love of print-making, painting, and pen-and-ink drawing followed me to college where I would spend hours each day drawing in my dorm room as a way of redirecting my energies toward something other than my social life, partying, and studying. It was a quiet, creative activity that allowed my mind to rest on something internal to myself rather than constantly feeding my social self on campus. During art-making, I could drown out all the noise around me and indulge in the pleasured discipline of creativity. It never mattered to me that I wouldn't be an artist for a living—what mattered was that I got to work on my art and myself simultaneously so that I could find meaning in what had already taken place in my childhood with my mother. Through print-making and drawing, I could imagine myself anew.

Around this time, I was also involuntarily, but later happily, inducted into a group known as the "Moonpigs." I only learned about this peculiar social moniker after it was yelled at me while walking down the hallowed halls of the boardwalk by Tristan, the overly-large rower uncomfortably stuffed into his blue blazer. As I walked with my younger classmate Ryan, who like me had spikey hair and wore all black, Tristan stopped, pointed to me and turned to his friends yelling, "Look, there goes a Moonpig!" I had no idea what this term meant but I knew that it signified difference, and not a very acceptable one at that. I was used to racial difference but this name was something entirely new and I never really understand its etymology except that it referred to my group of female friends who did not quite fit the mold of the preppy girls and to the boys who were simply not masculine enough according to some boarding school code.

They were boarding school oddities like me, not because of their race but because of their class—their families were not part of the wealthy upper crust of New England and so while they fit in in terms of race, they were excluded from the wealthy container of privilege that seemed to comprise most of the school's culture. Of course, we never talked about it because for the elite boarding school types, one never talked about money; it was simply uncouth. However, even if we didn't talk about it, we always knew who had money because we'd see all the kids coming back from break all tan with their trips to Bermuda, and they all vacationed on the Cape in the summers. After holding our breath a bit until we got out of the gauntlet of the boardwalk, Ryan and I looked at each other and cracked up; he was relieved not to get punched, pushed, or threatened as he oft was subjected to, and I was just glad to have someone who I adored as a friend near my side as we witnessed this new classification. Eventually, we engaged in that great practice of resistance and subversion by adopting this bizarre name for our own group of bright, artistic, non-preppy friends and created our own social sub-group that provided us with a safe haven amidst the otherwise daunting world of New England white boarding school culture where old money was the ticket to success.

Despite the pressures of social conformity in the boarding school culture, I relished the new-found freedom away from my mother's gaze to figure out who I wanted to be. And part of my identity included learning to make good grades. I wanted to be artsy *and* intellectual like my gorgeous friend Maura, whose brilliance always landed her at the top of the leader board on the Chadwick Hall high honors list when it was rolled out at the end of every academic term. Maura had a kind of unusual European beauty that made her stand out from the rest of us. At the mere age of seventeen, she had a voice that was oddly sexy for her age and seemed to be filtered through several glasses of bourbon (and of course, French cigarettes). She hailed from the mid-West and so was a bit of an oddity for her sophistication, but I was mesmerized by her corn-fed roots that were miraculously supplanted by this preternatural cool that must have been magically imported from Paris.

Like me, Maura was prone to wearing dark clothing—she always wore a dark grey cardigan that was fraying just the right amount around the edges of her sleeves, which she rolled up to expose her exceptionally pale, thin arms. She was tall and lanky and somehow seemed like she could also be from the 1930s with her long limbs, slim build, and perfect bob. Despite the ubiquitous bob that seemed to sit atop most of the girls in boarding school, Maura's bob stood out because of what lay beneath it—a face that was both reserved and wild. She had slightly dark circles under her eyes and would occasionally line her mouth in a darker shade of red that would make her look effortlessly chic. Her casual-couldn't-be-bothered-with-the-fact-that-it-was-fraying sweater covered her slim shoulders like a coat on a hanger and she wore one of the many black, thrift-shop dresses I would comb the East Village searching for on holidays. I envied her look—tall, thin, long skinny legs that always looked good in any length skirt (at the knee, mid-calf, short), pale, serious, and damn smart. I, on the other hand, felt short at my 5' 3.5" status, with what I perceived to be squat legs resembling radishes (as the Koreans liked to say about women who had shapely thick legs like squash), and unattractive with my moon-shaped face (another negative term given to Korean women's rounded faces). In other words, my Asian American features and my lack of white skin tone made me feel less than my white friends—and envious as hell.

If ever there was a woman destined for the Ivy Leagues it was Maura, and we all knew it. Because we knew that she would be the one statistic from our school chart that ended up at Harvard or Yale, my friends and I would always let her get away with her occasional moments of non-coolness where she'd cut me down to size and suddenly render me vulnerable as if I wasn't good enough for the pack. One afternoon, we were getting ready to head into town for lunch at the pizza place where her boyfriend Charlie worked. I tried to look cool and nonchalant like Maura and put on my vintage cardigan sweater, scored from the Village in New York over Christmas break. I was feeling fashionable and hip because the sweater had antique buttons and beading from the 1920s and it made me feel slim. Maura, however, didn't have the same opinion. She opened her mouth and cut me down to size immediately asking slyly "Oh, where'd that sweater come from? It's... unusual."

Unusual was not the look I was going for, I wanted her approval and hoped that she would notice that I was cool enough to select a great sweater that she herself would want to wear, but I had failed. Rather than assuming that we simply had different taste, I took the comment as an indication that I was not up to par and worried whether or not she would still hang out with me. I hadn't yet realized that clothes do not make the woman.

While I considered Maura the female icon of hip smarts and beauty that I wished I possessed, Randall was the male counterpart and, true to prep school form, ended up going to Yale. He was part of my group of friends and was destined to be an intellectual. He already dressed the part. He wore horn-rimmed glasses, tweed jackets from thrift stores in the coolest blends of browns and greens, a rumpled white Oxford shirt with its own fraying collar to Maura's fraying sleeves, and he could talk as eloquently as Maura. Randall enchanted me because he already looked like a young college professor and I had decided by the middle of my junior year that I wanted to be an intellectual and maybe one day I'd want to be a professor.

It was at Chadwick Hall that I began to think that being smart might be my ticket to success. Of course, I didn't really have a choice about success, anyway, at least not in my dad's eyes, but it also became a way for me to fight back against my mother's silence and glares. She was more interested in hearing about my failures, and these I was sure to tell her about as I struggled to find some acceptance in her eyes. She never even got upset with me for the things that most Korean parents would be furious to discover, like when my best friend Trina and I got caught smoking by the dorm prefect and we were forced to stay an extra two days before Thanksgiving break to clean out the horse stalls. My dad was absolutely livid when he picked me up from the Port Authority bus station, his mouth drawn in a very straight and somber line, his lips pursed as he leveled a severe warning that if I ever did anything that stupid and humiliating again, I would face serious consequences.

I already knew that I had embarrassed him, but he reminded me again when he said with utter disappointment, "I cannot believe that any daughter of mine would be stupid enough to smoke and that you also got caught and left at school."

I half expected the same from my mother but when I returned home and my father told her what had happened, she barely registered any emotion on her face. She simply looked at me, her face blank, and said, "go eat dinner." I shouldn't have been surprised by her lack of concern over smoking because only a few weeks earlier she had surprised me by driving up unannounced to Chadwick Hall and took me out to lunch.

"What are you doing here?" I asked her somewhat suspiciously. I was relieved to have some company and feel like my mother loved me enough to come for a spontaneous visit, but this trip was out of the ordinary.

"Oh, I just felt like a car trip. Let's go shopping and get some lunch," she responded. I was certainly not going to look a gift horse in the mouth, especially since all I ever wanted to do was do the things that I thought mothers and daughters did—shop together and laugh over meals and manicures. No matter the reason, I jumped at the chance and off we went in her black BMW down to the quaint town of Chadwick Hall where she bought me pants and a few sweaters from the local thrift shop.

"Why do you want to wear used clothes?" she asked me, since Koreans did not appreciate the concept of vintage clothing, but after my continual explanations that the clothing was really funky, she relented. Next we went to lunch, my arms heavy with shopping bags full of clothes. We sat down and ordered pizzas and salads. To my great surprise, my mother picked up her fork and knife and proclaimed, "I'm starved. Let's eat!" The shocking thing to me was that she managed to eat the whole plate of food without so much as a complaint about her stomach aching or being too full to eat.

I watched in amazement as my mother relished a meal like I had never seen before. I was even more incredulous when I asked her if I could smoke a cigarette and she replied, "Sure why not?"

To this day, I have no idea why I was audacious enough even to ask to smoke because it was clearly against the school rules and everyone knew smoking was bad for us. I wasn't so far away from the anti-smoking campaigns that warned us that "These are your lungs. And these are your lungs from smoking" alongside a horrifying image of the burned-out withered lungs of a smoker. Maybe I was emboldened because she was doing something she never did—eat a meal with enjoyment. I was a teenager and teenagers are said to push boundaries. So I pushed and I had succeeded. I smoked nonchalantly as some of the other Chadwick Hall students looked over at me in shock. I didn't care, I was proud to have a mother who let me smoke and break the rules. I felt like a renegade.

My mother dropped me off with little fanfare at my dorm and simply said, "That was fun. It was good to get away."

I shut the door and waved goodbye as she sped back to New York. I had no idea what sparked this random visit, but it was a unique chance to imagine what a somewhat normal mother-daughter relationship could be. After she left, the realization that our visit was a one-time opportunity made me even more nostalgic for something that would never happen again in the same way.

I returned to school and put her behind me. I called home regularly but the comments were no more than curt words, "Hello. What do you want?" There were no other words of reprimand or any comments whatsoever about my behavior that she had witnessed at Chadwick Hall. She didn't seem to care that I broke the rules, compromised my health, or that I could get kicked out of Chadwick Hall if I violated the handbook again. I was still dumbfounded that she came to visit, ate a full meal, chatted with me like a real mother, and let me smoke. Smoking in front of one's Korean parents was simply unheard of and here I was violating both a cultural code and the Chadwick Hall school code with my very own mother. I don't think she would have cared at all if I had been drinking, smoking, or even having unprotected sex. For her, it seemed that these cultural violations were far more acceptable to her than any of the positive things I was doing. When I ended up on the honor roll for the first time, I was so excited because I had just started to really hit the books and I mentioned it over Christmas break. My dad beamed with pride shouting out, "Hey! Great Job Sharon! Keep it up!"

"Stop bragging. Nobody wants to hear about it," my mother muttered quietly. She returned to cutting up vegetables in the kitchen and it was clear that there was to be no further discussion of my grades.

Later that evening over dinner, my father looked at me and remarked, "Hey Sharon, you look you are really getting in shape. Have you lost a few pounds?" Normally my father didn't say anything about my weight, but my efforts to try to control some of my late-night eating and after-school snacking must have made an impact.

I beamed with a pride and responded, "Well, I started running again at school so maybe that's it." I didn't dare mention eating less because I saw my mother glance down at my body as if my slight weight loss was a direct insult to her. I dug into my dinner that night with a little extra gusto because I was suddenly anxious that she would retaliate. After rejecting her demand that I take a sip of her noodle soup, she scowled, scrunched up her eyebrows, and replied with a near sneer, "Since when did you start dieting? You better finish up your dinner."

The implication here was that I had directly offended her by making my body healthier. Rather than congratulating me on rededicating myself to exercise, her comments came out a threat, as if to say, "Who do think you are trying to defy me? I am the one who decides what you eat."

But by the time high school rolled around, I was living on my own for most of the time. Because I was terrified that she would somehow manage to get me to overeat or that she would somehow force-feed me, I made sure that for the rest of break, I finished all my meals. To eat in front of her was a survival strategy that allowed me to avoid the fear that came with her verbal attacks. Although I was no longer a child who could be strapped to a chair and forced to eat until I threw up, the memories of the pressure, fear, and stomach aches remained.

I also began to notice a shift at school—mealtimes began to lose some of their anxiety-producing reactions and I began to trust that other people were not trying to making me purposefully fat for their own satisfaction. I began to learn that my friends and I could socialize and bond over meals and that they were not watching me like a hawk while I ate. I had also taken to running at night after dinner with my Walkman in hand, looping around the campus for half an hour each night and taking more control of how my body looked. Because I was living away from home, I could treat my body the way I wanted to. And while I still had enough anxiety about my stomach to fast the entire day before a swim meet so my stomach would look flat in my Speedo, I also knew that if I didn't live at home, my body would eventually become fully mine.

Perhaps it was a way of rebelling against the way my mom ignored me whenever I did well in school or she heard anyone say that I was really intelligent, but while I downplayed my successes to her face, I became even more determined in high school to be as smart as Maura and Randall. My academic success would later become my armor against any mental assaults I would face from my mother. I also learned in high school that along with my alternative image, good grades and being smart were going to be part of my identity and self-making. I knew I was not smart in the preppy way that somehow included a kind of social capital I never had—no one in my family was named Buffy or Bunny and I had never even been to Cape Cod or Nantucket. Koreans simply did not vacation on any little Island on the New England Coast; they were fairly recent immigrants who arrived in the U.S. mostly in the mid-1970s and worked nearly seven days a week minus a short break for church. I wanted to the kind of smart that would get me noticed; I didn't want to be invisible.

And I wanted a way to get back at my mother because I was excelling at the one thing that she couldn't bear to see me do—get better grades than my brother. During these years, my brother lived at home and made mediocre grades while smoking pot and drinking excessively with his friends. My parents were extremely disappointed, because Koreans were never all that accepting of anything that didn't smell of high academic achievement and his B grades were not making the cut. He was bright, but my parents were afraid he was becoming a bit of a pothead. He later managed to ace the SAT, which my mom would brag about to just about anybody who'd listen, and he was admitted to a small liberal arts college in Connecticut where again he managed to disappoint my father by claiming that he wanted to become a writer.

I certainly didn't go to high school thinking that I would be particularly exceptional in any way. I was considered smart in my local public junior high school, but I was far more interested in finding a peer group and desperately working to score well on my Secondary School Aptitude Test (or what I referred as the baby SAT) so that I could leave my house and move far away to another state. Going to prep school was a hard and fast lesson, first in feeling stupid and out of place, and second in learning to work hard enough day after day so that I could one day be on that high honors list like Maura and Randall. The consequence was that no matter how hard I worked, or how much I achieved, I never felt that I'd done enough or deserved the recognition and honors I received. I always felt, deep down, that I wasn't as good as Maura, and I wasn't real professor material. Like so many women, I found excuses for my academic successes—I was just lucky.

It was not until my forties, however, that I ever came across the term coined to describe this sense of insecurity over our accomplishments—Imposter syndrome, the idea that somehow I managed to succeed despite the fact that I must have been a fraud because I certainly couldn't achieve the accomplishments on my own. Imposter syndrome did, however, serve me well at Chadwick Hall because the more I hung out with the smart group of misfits for whom literature, art, and music were more important than the athletic successes of the other kids at school, the more I discovered an identity that didn't depend on the way I looked. I was neither tall nor thin like Maura, was not nearly as beautiful as my roommate Libby, but I could work on developing my intellect to distinguish myself from many of my peers. I might be a little awkward, a little overweight, and a little too Asian American for this boarding school in Connecticut, but I began to believe that I could make my own way by developing a reputation for being smart, pushing myself to achieve academic success, and continue to discipline my mind and body—and that was the Korean way.

Finding the Buddha

"ALL (MENTAL) STATES have mind as their forerunner, mind is their chief, and they are mind-made. If one speaks or acts with a defiled mind, then suffering follows one even as the wheel follows the hoof of the draught-ox," recited Mrs. White from the *Dhammapada*, or *The Path of Virtue*, one of the most famous of the Buddhist texts. "So you see, the Buddha understood that most of our suffering comes from our own minds and how we perceive or misperceive reality. We perceive impermanent things to be permanent and so we suffer greatly when we cling to things and even to ideas about how we think things should be," she continued.

Mrs. White was rocking my world, for never before had I thought that maybe the ideas I had about my own body were not based in reality, maybe they were just mental projections. Could it be that the thoughts that seem to come without invitation like, *I need to diet; my stomach is too fat today; my legs are too muscular; I need to be thinner*, were indeed just thoughts without a corresponding reality? Could it also be the case that this body of mine was also subjected to change all the time? If our bodies were constantly changing, then maybe I only needed to learn how to appreciate it in the moment.

"Although he taught over 2,500 years ago, the Buddha's words still make sense today—so why waste your mental energy worrying about things that don't have much basis in reality?" Mrs. White asked.

I had no idea that the Buddha whom I so often saw in restaurants with a big smile and generous belly could offer such powerful insights and encourage us to rethink how we view ourselves. I just thought he was a deity like all other deified people in the world's religions. But that day in class, he took on a different image—he became a wise teacher who understood suffering, its origins, and its solutions and made me feel like my own problems could be solved by my own efforts.

Just a few moments earlier I was sitting in my history class listening to Mr. White lecture about Japanese history and culture but I was barely paying attention. My thoughts had strayed to how much I had eaten for breakfast and whether or not I should limit what I ate later in the day so I would feel thinner in my bathing suit at swim practice.

My attentions returned to the class, however, when Mr. White introduced his wife, Chieko. She was a young Japanese woman dressed for the occasion in a smart little white suit (the humorous correspondence of her name and the color of her suit remains with me today) to teach us about religion in Japan, beginning with Buddhism.

I will never forget the way my ears perked up as Mrs. White began to talk about how the Buddha was born a prince and later became a wandering ascetic. She spoke in a kind voice as she taught how the prince's wanderings led him to reflect on the nature of reality, and especially, the ways that we cling to phenomena that are always changing. As I listened closely, she continued with a glimmer in her eye, as if she knew that these words would fall just right on the ears of high schoolers.

"The Buddha or the Awakened One taught his early group of monks and nuns that the body is made of ever-changing elements and you are never the same person twice. You only think that you are and when you cling to that idea of permanence, you create suffering for yourself and for others."

Wait a minute, I thought. *Does this mean that I don't always have to be the same person? That change is okay? That maybe I won't always look or feel as bad as I do sometimes?* As I reflected on the possibility that I wasn't locked into the personality and body I was stuck with, but that I could continually transform, Buddhism became a more relevant and personal topic to explore.

A ray of light began to emerge in my mind when I learned that I was not permanent, but that I am like a river that is never the same each time you step into it. In other words, I could transform who I was by transforming how I thought about myself.

"Events are happening, things are happening all the time. You yourself are not a permanent entity, you are a process and everything, the Buddha taught, arises and passes but there is nothing permanently there. Things like the self are happening but they are not a noun. They are a verb," Mrs. White explained.

Wow, I am not a noun, but I am a verb. I do not have to be defined by my past, but can continually evolve, I thought. This was the first I was hearing about this groundbreaking idea and yet it made perfect sense. It was as if Mrs. White was delivering the Buddha's message from his mind directly to my own. I never knew that there was an actual pathway and process of discovering that suffering exists and that there are clearly defined tools for dismantling it. I was a teenager and full of suffering, but had not yet heard of a such a helpful alternative. There was something so powerful to the Buddha's simple response when asked by a guest if he was a god. He replied, "I teach suffering and the end of suffering."

I wonder if I can be a Buddhist. Should I be a Buddhist? What do I need to do? Sign me up immediately! I thought as I jotted down all the things that Mrs. White said. I could barely keep up, but I kept at it because I knew intuitively that there was a kernel of truth, a gem of resilience bound up in these words. The word that appeared in my own mind later in the day when I read through my notes was *hopefulness*. I had gleaned from the morning's lecture that there was indeed a way to end suffering and that if I learned to imagine myself as a process rather than what my mother said I was or was not, I might grow to feel more confident and begin to accept my body more readily.

Mrs. White had come to give a guest lecture on Buddhism in Japan and began with an introduction to Buddhist philosophy that morning. But she didn't just offer me an objective lesson in one of the world's great religious figures, she gave me a possible antidote to years of feeling bad about myself and my body. *Maybe the Buddha can help me come to terms with my childhood and learn to feel peaceful and content in my own body*, I considered. I put my hands on my belly, the one I imagined sometimes looked like the Buddha's round belly, and smiled—he had a giant stomach and given the smile on his face, he looked pretty content.

When Mrs. White explained that the Buddha understood there was suffering in the world and through his compassion for all sentient beings, he offered a set of teachings that were aimed at uprooting that suffering, I knew that I wanted to learn more about the Buddha, the way that Buddhists lived, and the practices needed for having a little more gentleness toward myself.

Mrs. White had a serene smile on her face as she taught us that hour and I imagined that Buddhists must be very relaxed people. While I listened to her explain that all beings suffer, I felt seen for the first time, as if someone could actually understand the suffering I experienced but rarely talked about. I settled down into my desk chair and relaxed a bit as I began to feel that my experiences were not unique after all, because if all beings suffered then I was not alone. I wrote down all Mrs. White's notes from the blackboard and as I learned more about Buddhism, I began to develop a plan for how to uproot my suffering, with a deep sense of relief that the

Buddha and Mrs. White had something to offer my particular experience of *dukkha* or suffering.

I held onto that tenth-grade history notebook for a good ten years because it held within it the code to transforming suffering into liberation and wisdom through what the Buddha taught as the Four Noble Truths—First, In life there is suffering; Second, The cause of suffering is desire or thirst; Third, There is a way to end suffering that leads to liberation or peace; and Fourth, The way to end suffering is through the Noble Eight-fold Path (right view, right intention, right speech, right action, right livelihood, right effort, right mindfulness, and right concentration). I also remember my fascination in learning that the Buddha was considered a universal physician because he offered a diagnosis about the truth of suffering; the etiology or origins of suffering in desire; the prognosis that if we uproot desire, we can experience peace; and finally, the prescription or the pathway to letting go of suffering. But as I later discovered and continually forget, to know something intellectually compared to knowing it experientially are two entirely different things. It is far easier to know that my suffering comes from clinging to images and ideas that are not based in actual reality, but it is far more challenging to live those truths on a daily basis. Even today as I teach my students about the Buddha's words, I am also reminding myself of their power and potential so long as I take the time to practice and experience them

I continued to read books on Buddhism outside of my classes and by my senior year, I began the ritual of applying to colleges. After researching as many small liberal arts colleges as I could on the East coast, I ended up applying to about six schools. My first choice was Bard College. Bard was an alternative universe of smart, artsy students that I gravitated toward. When I walked through that campus for my tour, I had that immediate sense that I would fit in, but I could tell that my dad was not having it. "Sharon, I cannot support you going to this school," he declared as we walked around campus. I was beaming with excitement because I felt as if I had finally come home, finally found the place where I belonged.

"But, Dad…" I began, before he cut me off.

"I can't see it doing anything for your future. It's too different." He shook his head over and over, disturbed at the thought that he had come to America and worked non-stop to send his daughter to boarding school so that she could get into a great college and get a great job. And here he was looking at what he must have thought were very privileged, lazy wild-looking kids who seemed more interested in drawing pictures than solving complex mathematical equations. The accountant in him pre-vailed as he spoke the words I knew I had to heed: "You're not going here."

With great disappointment, when I received my acceptance to Bard I declined and enrolled in the same college as my brother in Connecticut. I was ready to join the class of 1991 along with several other of my prep school classmates. I would soon meet several other recent graduates from other fancy boarding schools in New England and begin my freshman year moving into a single dorm room in Larch Hall in the Fall of 1987.

Taking a quick look around the beautiful New England campus with its stunning Episcopal chapel and ample green rolling hills along the quad, I knew that I was starting school in yet another preppy, waspy environment. But at least this time I was prepared. Besides, I could finally take a class in Buddhism and begin to study in earnest the thing that seem to make the most sense out of all my experiences to date. Because I had gone to boarding school and learned how to party and live away from my parents, I was more prepared to hit the books hard and had already learned that I could both drink at night and wake up in the morning to go to class. So as I honed my social skills at parties searching for my own community, I also began in earnest to follow my new passion in studying Buddhism. Lucky for me, my first class in Buddhist Thought and Practice in college was of-fered by a former Tibetan monk, Professor Rodriguez, who opened up an entire world of possibility when he lectured during the first day of class.

"There are several ways to be a Buddhist. You can be a religious Buddhist born into it or even become a monastic like me. But you can also be a philosophical Buddhist which means that you see the world through a Buddhist lens."

At that moment, something clicked deep inside me because I had already begun to interpret my suffering through what the Buddha taught. I decided in that class that I would become a philosophical Buddhist.

A Hungry Ghost

"HUNGRY GHOSTS are beings that have throats the size of pinholes and huge bellies. They are always hungry and never satisfied. They are the epitome of craving," Professor Ferguson lectured in the auditorium as she drew a figure of a ghost on the blackboard with a protruding belly and spindly arms and legs. "These hungry ghosts are part of the cycle of rebirth and they are all around us. We just can't see them," she continued. "Some Buddhists believe they literally exist and some see them as symbols of suffering beings who can never get enough."

I shifted self-consciously in my chair and wondered if she was talking about me. I was very good at feeling hungry but not so much at feeling full despite feeding myself plenty of pizza, bagels, beer, and ice cream in college. Instead, I fed the hungry craving ghost in myself. As I gazed at the rail-thin hungry ghosts she projected onto the board, their arms and legs as frail as mosquito legs, I thought of my mother as a hungry ghost herself, never satisfied, always hungry for something she could not or would not name.

Buddhism is definitely getting interesting, I thought as I also imagined myself teaching a class like my professor. She was a warm and compassionate woman who looked like she had just stepped off a plane from India, with her long dark hair, black kohl eyeliner tastefully smudged around her eyes, intricate silver jewelry dangling from her ears and neck, and her woven satchel that she used to carry all of her books. Although she was a middle-aged white woman who travelled to India and Nepal, she never seemed like she was trying to be someone she was not. Instead, she seemed like an incarnation of a Buddhist or Hindu deity in human form—besides, she also had studied Buddhism in graduate school for years, read several ancient languages, and knew her stuff. She was neither imposter nor cultural appropriator. She was a scholar who travelled to India and Nepal for research and introduced me to a topic so practical and so unreal at the same time—a world of hungry ghosts, enlightened beings, monks and nuns, and meditation. I was immediately taken with her and wanted to be just like her when I graduated. I wanted to teach in the front of a classroom, intellectually lighting up minds like mine and offering teachings that could provide some practical relief.

I put my hands on my stomach that had started to gurgle during class and wondered if I, too, was like a hungry ghost constantly craving, always wanting to fill myself up, but never satiated. I began to wonder what would happen if I kept on eating whatever I wanted. Would I get out of control? Would I become the fat person my mother always wanted me to be? As I sat writing notes and staring at the images of the hungry ghosts projected on the screen, all I could hear was the Rolling Stones' lyrics to that song I was singing and dancing to the night before when out carousing with friends and beer. "I can't get no satisfaction 'cause I try and I try and I try and I try. I can't get no, I can't get no…"

Clomping around arm and arm with my male and female friends nearly shouting the lyrics to this song, I was having a blast drunk on cheap beer, but wondered deep down if there wasn't some deeper truth to this song besides not being able to get enough pot to smoke or booze to drink. It was in the early morning fog of the residual hangover that I began to see there was perhaps some Buddhist truth to what Mick Jagger had been belting out over the stereo in the house where I had been partying the night before.

Back in class, I was intrigued and afraid of the painted images of the ghosts' world in the Buddhist wheel of life, or *samsara*. They're in their own little plane of existence; they wander about suffering with normal sized mouths but have throats the size of pinholes and whatever food they are able to scrounge together immediately sears their already compromised throats. They are, as I tell my own students decades since I first learned of them, the epitome of what the singer K.D. Lang croons about in her song, *Constant Craving*. The students laugh when I realize that they are far too young to really know who K.D. Lang is, but at the same time, I can see in their eyes a recognition that they, too, suffer from a constant thirst and desire for things that will never ultimately satisfy us. As the Buddha taught his disciples 2500 years ago, as Professor Ferguson taught me over a quarter of a century ago, and as I teach my students now, we are never satisfied with what we have and we always want more. Thirst is the cause of so much suffering precisely because we think we can fill ourselves up to the point of satiety, but, according to the Buddha, we can't because all things are impermanent.

The impermanence of all things and the ever-elusive concept of satiety is one that I had developed rather acutely in college, for I was no longer under the regular rhythms of boarding school meals where we got most of our food three times a day. I was in college now and largely independent, since I could eat when I wanted and what I wanted without any authority figure telling me what to do. It was up to me to learn how to feed myself, and while I did so without being forced by anyone, I still hadn't figured out how to feel full and satisfied. Sometimes the food that I ate seemed to sear my throat like a hungry ghost. And while I dabbled here and there with purging in the dorm bathroom after bingeing on pizza and ice cream, I couldn't bear the feeling of forcing myself to throw up. Forcing myself to purge seemed so violent, and I had tried it enough times to know that rather than make me feel better about losing what I had stuffed into my mouth, I simply felt and looked awful. All it took was my friend Jemma asking, "Are you okay? You look like you've been crying," after coming out of the bathroom for me to realize that if I purged, people would know because it was written all over my face. It was hard enough learning how not to overeat and stuff down feelings; the shame of being caught purging made my face hot and I turned several shades redder.

"Yeah, I'm fine. Just having a bad day," I lied as I wiped the tears off my face. Forcing myself to throw up had a way of making me look even worse than I had originally felt. There had to be a better way to deal with feeling better about my body and in my skin, and throwing up wasn't going to help me. I wondered if my mom was also a hungry ghost who never let any food in her mouth because it would hurt too much. What I did know was that I did not want to end up like her; while I still struggled with my body image and often felt like I had the same protruding bellies like the ones I saw in class on those desperate ghosts, I was sure that I wanted to distance myself as much as I could from my mother. So I stopped purging and stayed far away from the laxatives she popped like candy.

Many of my college days included drinking too much beer and cheap red wine from an enormous jug with an ironically small little handle at the top (made more for a Barbie doll hand to carry), and late-night eating in the Den, the small underground café open afterhours. If living at home meant being excessively force-fed by my mother, college offered the opposite—an opportunity to engage in an overindulgent lifestyle without parents and dorm masters watching over my behavior. So I smoked regularly, overate, drank too much, and engaged in my fair share of casual relationships.

I don't think that I was all that different from many of my friends because we did many of these things together; the only things that felt different about me was that I seemed to suffer in silence over my indulgences far more than my girlfriends did. And I knew that I had to get up in the morning after spending most of the night partying so that I could make it to my favorite classes. There was no way I was going to give up late night drinking and escaping my problems through inebriation, and there was no way I was going to give up on taking in as much knowledge that I could so that I could earn my A grades and get myself closer to the goal of being a professor. I wanted it all, but I also knew that I couldn't have it all.

I had become that hungry ghost looking for love, but what I did not realize at the time was that while I was looking for love and attention from outside sources, what I really could have used was some self-love, the kind of love that came from myself toward myself rather than outward signs of validation. Of course, these kinds of lessons fall on deaf ears in young college-aged females but it appeared that some of my friends had at least a little bit of self-love because they never seemed to beat themselves up or obsess over their nightly overindulgences. It was as if they already knew how to be kind to themselves and to have a little self-compassion when they overdid it. For me, however, there seemed to be little room for self-acceptance, kindness, or compassion when I felt like I screwed up. If I overate and found myself eating mindlessly while studying, or failing by lunchtime when I had set an intention in the morning to fast all day, I took it hard and berated myself all day for it.

"In Buddhist monasteries, it is common practice for monks and nuns to set aside a grain of rice to transform into nourishing particles to feed to the hungry ghosts so that they can get some sense of nourishment," Professor Ferguson, explained as she walked around the front of the class. "It is a practice of compassion," she concluded. The concept of feeding the hungry ghosts a morsel of rice out of compassion, rather than reject them altogether, struck me profoundly.

Professor Ferguson was one of the few women faculty in the Religious Studies Department. She was about the age I am now and also a mother, and I felt her eyes lay warmly on mine as we caught each other's eye. I felt as if she could see right through me, and as if this entire lecture was aimed at me alone and the kind of suffering I was feeling at that time—I wanted to be perfect, thin, and beautiful but didn't seem to ever be able to feel those things because I felt they were ever out of my reach. It didn't occur to me at the time that most of the feelings of inadequacy that I had were ones that I had generated for myself. I didn't yet understand that if I learned to let go of those desires and understand that they were themselves simply fictions, then I might have a little freedom. At best, maybe I could treat that hungry ghost in myself with a little more compassion like those monks and nuns in Japan who would give an offering of rice to those pathetic craving creatures in *samsara*. Those Buddhist lessons would, however, take a little longer to germinate because college was not yet the time for the ideas to manifest. I was far from being an adult capable of both seeing clearly the nature and source of a problem and putting into practice some of the Buddhist solutions that I had been learning about in class. If anything, I am still working on them today, as they are a life-long practice. The difference is that now I have more faith in my capacity to retrain how I see myself, my body, and my need for perfection. I have seen the value in locating the origin of my desire to control how much I eat, how much I weigh, and how often I exercise. And when I am looking clearly into these problems, I can see that they are based on false perceptions that keep me from being fully present in my body in this very moment.

As I expanded my intellectual interests, met new friends, and struggled to figure out who I wanted to be, my mother's social world and body seemed to shrink in tandem. Going home over winter vacation, I noticed that she spent less time on the telephone and even my parents' closest friends, Mr. and Mrs. Shin, had stopped coming over for dinner on the weekends. I had grown up seeing the Shins most weekends and babysat their two young daughters, but when I asked my dad about what had happened to them, he casually replied, "Well, Mrs. Shin became a Jehovah's Witness and is always proselytizing so we don't see her much anymore."

When I pressed him for details, he finally said, "Well, there isn't much more to say about it and besides, your mom doesn't want to see them anymore." The way my father quickly changed the subject indicated that the conversation was finished and I dared not ask my mother what had happened to them.

The Shins were not the only people my mother stopped speaking to—gone were the visits with the Cho family whose father went to middle school with my father in Korea. Also gone from their social lives was my father's best friend from elementary school, Mr. Kim, who was married to the ever-glamorous former Miss Korea contestant. They used to come to our house during all their visits to New York when they weren't working in Seoul or vacationing in Paris. They were the friends I missed seeing the most, because they were such jetsetters and because they had taken such good care of me when I went to Seoul for a brief study abroad in my junior year.

When I asked my father another time about the Kims, he was circumspect again and replied, "Well, they're really busy now with their kids and don't have much time to visit."

I knew, however, that there must be something more to the story because I knew my father visited with them while he travelled and during his business dinners out. Whatever was happening to their social life, it was clear that my mother was at the center of it. She had alienated everyone and had begun to spend more and more of her time alone. Yet to this day I have no idea how she spent that time in solitude since she wasn't much of a reader and no longer spent any time chatting on the phone. She just stopped talking directly to her friends and family, while seeming to have no problem spending a lot of time and energy talking about people.

Just as I had been her nemesis when I was small, she always had a target or a perceived enemy who occupied much of her mental energy. For the longest time she had focused her energies on me, but after I moved out of the house, I noticed more and more stories she'd relate about people who worked with my dad. "That Mrs. Randolph, she's no good! She is always gossiping and forgetting things and shouldn't be working for my husband. I don't trust her. She does a terrible job and is spreading lies about me," my mother claimed until finally my father had to let his secretary go.

During college, I also saw the subsequent firing of Mr. Wang, my dad's right-hand man in his company who, according to my mother, was "a lousy, sneaky man always trying to take credit for himself and cheat your father out his money." Then there was Al Jones, my dad's comptroller in his expanded jewelry and import business who, according to my mother, was "a stuck up, disrespectful cheat always talking behind your dad's back and making up stories to cover up his own mistakes."

She always managed to find someone trying to pull the wool over my dad's eyes, someone who'd be gossiping and spreading lies about her, or someone just plain out to get her. My father never seemed to outright contradict her nor take her too seriously because most of his co-workers managed to stay on the payroll. His response was instead, to thank my mom for looking out for the business and suggest, "Honey, maybe you should take some time off from helping me out in the office. I appreciate your help these past few weeks, but you need to take better care of your health since you're not feeling that well." Even he appeared to be afraid of what her emotional reactions might be when he asked her to stop meddling in his office affairs. She had become a work liability and my dad needed to maintain the peace at the office.

Like a microscope lens focusing on ever-more minute details, as the years passed my mother's life shrank to the petri-sized dish of the dark apartment between Lexington and Park Avenues where she lived with my dad in Manhattan after my brother and I had moved out. While I studied, partied, and developed new insights about myself through my classes in Buddhism, I had noticed that things worsened for my mother—she was thinner than I had ever seen her. One evening when we sat down for dinner at her favorite Italian restaurant two blocks away, she didn't eat a thing.

"Aren't you hungry at all? You haven't eaten much today and you need to eat to get healthy," my dad asked her.

In reply, she mumbled in a barely audible voice, "I already ate," as she pushed her pasta from one side of the plate to the other. She knew how to look like she was eating and when my dad pressed even more, she took a small bite and immediately declared, "I don't have any appetite."

She had lost not just her appetite for food, but her appetite for friends, for family, and for joy. Thinking back to all the ways she had hurt me, humiliated me, and injured me, I was coming to realize that I was no longer angry with her. I felt sorry for her. She had willed herself to disappear into solitude and silence, as those around her continued to live. Perhaps I was developing compassion for her like the monks and nuns did for the hungry ghosts. I learned through Professor Ferguson that when they chanted the sacred words of the Buddha, their rice would transform into nourishing particles for the hungry ghosts. They did this before each meal out of compassion for the pathetic ghosts. *Maybe I can learn to feel sorry for my mother and have compassion, too*, I thought when I first learned of this ritual. Learning how to have compassion for her was not going to be easy though. I still harbored a lot of anger and hurt.

While I was learning the importance of taking care of one's body, and that the Buddha admonished his disciples to practice the middle way between extremes, even with regard, my mother had taken her eating to an even greater extreme. She was wasting away, refusing to eat her meals. I watched during an entire break as she played with the food on her plate rather than eat it. Like a stubborn child who doesn't want to eat what her mother has placed before her, my mother controlled what she would and would not put into her mouth as if it were some type of victory over those of us who watched her starve.

When I asked her if she wanted to go out for a walk to Central Park or go shopping after dinner at the Italian restaurant we frequented, she remained silent. We slowly walked the two blocks home, my mother clutching my father's arm to prop herself up. Once inside the apartment, she quickly retreated to the bathroom and locked herself in it for nearly an hour. Whatever she was doing in there, she certainly wasn't taking a bath.

"Are you doing okay?" my father inquired.

After hearing her curt response, "I'm fine," we just glanced at each other without saying the obvious—she was popping laxatives hoping to purge her body of the smallest bites of pasta she just ate.

As I entered my junior and senior years, whenever I came back home for break, I'd find my mother cooped up in the tiny little TV room, where I would sleep whenever I visited. It was a dreadful room, its walls papered in a frightening brown snake-skin pattern, a remnant from the previous tenants. Inexplicably, my parents never changed that wallpaper, and I never did become accustomed to it.

Over one spring break, I walked into the apartment and, finding nobody home to greet me after my long absence, I peeked into the room. There she sat, propped up on the bed barely uttering a sound.

"You're home," she seethed, unhappy with my intrusion. She continued to stare into the television, watching the home shopping network on cable, as if I wasn't there. By that point, she had gotten so thin that she seemed no more than a sheath of skin overlaid on bone.

I was on edge standing in the doorway, waiting to be welcomed by my mother who may or may not have been getting ready to pounce like a snake on its trespassing victim—me. Despite her shrinking size, she was still as emotionally volatile and completely unpredictable as she was when I was a child. No matter how great her silence or how immobile her shrinking body, I never knew if she was going to be relatively passive about my visits or unleash some unexpected, unprovoked rage. She was too small and weak physically to harm me, but I couldn't shake the fear that one day she'd strike out at me like a cobra and come at me when I least expected it.

To this day, I have a terrible snake phobia that emerged in childhood, as well as inheritance of that wallpaper. My mother also had her own fear of snakes, that I learned of in a story often told throughout my childhood. When I was an infant she had encountered a black snake in the basement of our Brooklyn apartment. She was so terrified that she rang my dad who ran home from work, captured the snake and, to his remorse, wrapped it in newspaper and burned it alive. Even just writing about this event sends shivers down my spine; the image is that horrific.

Growing into a young adult had changed me, yet in so many ways I carried much of the mental weight of my past. I still feared my mother, but unlike in my childhood, when I knew the rules—I knew I wasn't to play with my brother's toys, I knew I wasn't to get into her hair products or alter my own wardrobe—once I had left her home and matured outside her control, if there was a line I wasn't supposed to cross, I certainly didn't know what it was. Yet that line still felt ever-present. She never warned me about it, but intuitively I knew that she could clearly see it. Sometimes it seemed that by the mere act of breathing in her direction, I would somehow cross that boundary that would trigger her rage. I could never figure out what the things were that I was doing wrong so I could never prevent them.

But they continued, less violent perhaps, but palpable in their fury.

On one return home, I had just set down my bags and said "Hi, Mom," when it hit.

"Throw out all the trash!" Her command and the cold glare of her eye made it clear my return home was again unwelcomed. I was the dutiful daughter who had arrived to serve a purpose, nothing more, no questions asked, no complaints registered. She demanded, I complied.

Another time, enjoying a delicious dinner of Korean food but having learned the limits to my hunger, I set my fork down and announced I couldn't eat another bite.

"Don't waste that food!" she hissed. She nodded forcefully at the plate, her face fixed in fury.

I obediently complied and we didn't share another word for the rest of the evening, or, for the most part, the rest of my visit.

Whenever I did make an effort to connect with her, through idle pleasantries, if my efforts didn't meet her stone-cold silence, I risked her rage. One time all I had done was go to the TV room to ask her where something was, and her response flew through the air like a monstrous blow.

"Leave me alone and shut the door!"

I closed the door and left her alone in the snakeskin room.

While I imagined my friends at college enjoying vacations and loving family time with their parents, I usually spent most of my vacation time either running in Central Park or meeting up with friends. When completely desperate for relief over extended holidays I would work at my dad's company as a receptionist since he could always use the help.

But back at home I tried to be as helpful as I could when I was in my parents' apartment; it no longer felt like home. I learned to be exceptionally tidy, for any glass left in the sink unwashed would send her over the edge shouting at me, "Who do you think you are? Take care of that mess right this minute!"

Even today, dishes left unwashed in the sink make me a bit uneasy so they usually don't last in there for more than five minutes, and if they do, it is because I am trying my best to let go of some of the those tightly-bound rules that I adhere to even decades after her death. But just as she did back then, she can still sometimes appear out of nowhere like a ghost or specter in the room and decrease the temperature for me just a hair so that I feel a slight wave or shiver of anxiety when the house is messy.

"What's your mom like? Can we meet her?" my friends would often ask in college; or, "Hey, can I stop by when I'm in New York to meet your family?" whatever current boyfriend might inquire. I never disclosed the truth about my home life; instead, I always made up some sort of excuse about them being on vacation. If we were close enough, I might simply say, "No, trust me. You do not want to meet my mom." I would offer these warnings mostly out of self-protection because I was always nervous that my friends would ditch me if they found out about my past or my mother humiliated me in some way in front of them. She had done it once before with Bill, my boyfriend from freshman year, and I was not interested in experiencing anything close to that kind of dismissal and embarrassment again.

Male Gaze

BILL WAS MY FIRST SERIOUS BOYFRIEND in college and I met him while wandering the halls of my dorm. He'd be hanging out in his room with the door open, listening to an intriguing band that I had never heard of—he always managed to surprise me with his unusual taste in bands and he would always say hi to me when I passed by. I was shy, and would barely look up, offer a small "hello" and off I'd go to class. But one day, I was bold enough to stop outside his room when he said hi to me. There he was, tall, tan, and handsome, wearing a tank top that displayed his muscles toned from cycling and rowing.

"Hey, how are you? I'm Bill. I've been wanting to meet you. Would you like to come in?" he asked with confidence. Thankfully, he left the door open as I began to settle into his room and breathe normally. While I found him impossibly handsome, I was less interested in his muscles; in fact, they intimidated me because I always felt like I was supposed to be the female version of his male physical body. He was tall, well-built, and handsome, and in my mind I was neither tall, willowy, nor pretty. I didn't think a man like Bill would be at all interested in me.

What attracted me to Bill was his electric smile, when he chose to show it, and his broody artistic nature. He was a fantastic artist whose line drawings of his own hands impressed me with their precision and beauty. To my freshman eyes, he was a perfect composite of artist, athlete, and intellectual. Of course, it helped that he had asked me out on a date which included going out for pasta and wine, which seemed hopelessly grown up to me. It also made a difference to me because he found me attractive. Within a week of going into his room in the early days of September, we had become a couple and would date until late Spring when we broke up for good.

One Christmas, Bill had driven over to my house bearing a gift for me—a smelly purple bottle of Poison perfume that I both loved and loathed at the same time. I loved it because it was so sweet of him to buy me something so romantic and loathed it because it stank up the house.

I loved him but I was also a bit embarrassed by the fact that he seemed a little tacky—he wore his hair in a slightly greased up one-inch-long crew cut and wore a thick gold chain around his neck. He had come to Connecticut from Atlanta, but he was far more rural than he was preppy collegiate material. Nevertheless, his athleticism, good looks, and six-foot-two frame made up for lack of wealth and social capital. Bill was a hulking presence who simply could not be ignored. He was a force to be reckoned with, yet my mother managed to cut him down to her own size and even smaller with just one of her withering glances.

"Hello Mrs. Suh, it's a pleasure to meet you. My name is Bill and I've heard so much about you," he said in his most polished tone as he extended his hand to shake my mother's.

She, of course, left his hand hanging in the air. She said nothing to him and barely registered his existence except through an even more impenetrable silence.

I was absolutely humiliated at my mother's inability to muster the graciousness to respond to my boyfriend who had driven to the house to wish me a Merry Christmas. I immediately regretted inviting him to my home and wondered if he would break up with me after he left. As I stood in shamed silence, Bill did his best to maintain his composure, glanced over at me, winked, and remained cheerful. After all, I had already prepared him for the inevitably cold reception he would get from her, but somehow I had tricked myself into thinking that maybe she could be as pleasant to my boyfriend as she was to my brother's friends who came over. However, that behavior was reserved for my brother and certainly not some near-giant that I had brought to the house. I felt great admiration for Bill at that time, because I realized that he could withstand all sorts of nonsense and that he would be able to protect me because he was not afraid of her.

Thankfully, as we stood on the driveway, my father immediately came out of the house to meet Bill, his hand already extended to give him a proper welcome, which alleviated some of the awkwardness we had both felt. Yet even my father's warmth concealed a certain chill. I could tell he greeted my new boyfriend with some reluctance because Bill was not Korean and, at over six feet tall compared to my short father, he was rather intimidating physically. My dad was forced to crane his neck up to meet this relative stranger who came to our house, dressed in a gold chain, a denim jacket, and his military-issue combat pants and boots. Bill was not the Korean boy my father had fantasized I'd be with, and his amiable face barely concealed his disappointment.

In fact, Bill was not the type of guy I was usually attracted to; I liked the artsy, long-haired boys—either they were a little bit crunchy granola and played guitar or they were alternative music aficionados less interested in expressing their hyper-masculinity and more interested in being soft-spoken, slightly shy, and somewhat introspective. Bill had none of these characteristics—first, he hardly drank and never smoked and woke up daily at 6:30 am to work out which meant that he was regimented and highly disciplined. Second, he was a jock who rowed on the first boat on the crew team. Third, he was a fraternity brother who belonged to one of the snootiest fraternities on campus—the kind that hosted Saturday night formals where the boys dressed up in tuxedos and their girlfriends came dressed in high heels, pearls, and little black dresses. What saved Bill from exceptional scrutiny in my eyes was that his tuxedo was always a little ill-fitting and a bit small since his bulky frame seemed far too uncomfortable in something with so little give and because he didn't quite fit into this elitist little social club. He never struck me as that into the preppy girls who were the female guests at the fraternity parties and he always managed to stay sober despite the ever-present partying that took place in the fanciest of social clubs on campus. Bill was a bit of a misfit; he was exceptionally smart, hard-working, and a wonderful artist. Perhaps it was this jack-of-all-trades skillset he had that made me like him all the more—or the fact that he was so giant and yet so sweet in the way that he called me "Boo." Whatever it was, there was something about him that allowed me to bypass all the things that set us apart. Either way, in freshman year, I was besotted and had my first college boyfriend.

Beyond these superficial connections, we also shared the common bond of surviving horrendous childhoods marked by trauma, and we had both disciplined ourselves to overcome them and never let others see our weaknesses. We shared the same survival tactics of academic success as a kind of salve and antidote to cover up, and perhaps one day purify, the seemingly indelible imprint of abuse we had both been stamped with. I knew I could confide in Bill in ways I never had with anyone else before, except perhaps for my cousin Paul. Trauma does that to people, it bonds them together in a delicate net of trust that holds each one hostage to the other.

As to be expected though, freshman year first relationships rarely stand the test of time and ours was over by the end of spring break. Although I was heartbroken and lonely after our breakup, I was also relieved that I no longer had to worry about feeling pretty enough to be with Bill or thin enough to be with someone who had such a perfect rower's body. I never felt comfortable revealing my body in front of him because I assumed that I would never measure up. Whenever we would be in bed, I'd immediately reach down to cover my stomach with my shirt or my hands, for it was the one spot on my body that gave me incredible anxiety. It was the belly that was the object of daily scorn from my mother; I had yet to learn that what she said to me did not reflect who I was and that just because she said something didn't mean that it was true. *What will he think if he really knows what I look like? What would anyone think if they could really see me without having to cover myself up?* These questions plagued me throughout college and it is only now in retrospect that I can see that my fears were not just based on someone judging my physical body as ugly and not good enough. I was also terrified that if people really knew about the kinds of suffering I experienced at home, then they might judge me less than worthy and have less respect for me. I had yet to recognize that I was not the child I had been years before, and that people have the capacity for compassion and not just automatic judgment.

With Bill, however, I felt once again that I wasn't tall enough, thin enough, or conventionally pretty enough to be with him and I spent most of our relationship anxious over whether or not I had put on weight and if he would notice. Since I was not immune to the so-called "freshman fifteen"—the average number of pounds a freshman puts on in the first year of college—I had put on some weight with the late-night drinking and one day he noticed.

"Boo, you should work out or stop eating so much. You seem like you're putting on weight," he remarked as we lay on his futon one afternoon. I had been trying to suck in my stomach because I noticed that my pants were a little tight around the waist and I certainly didn't need anyone else confirming that I had somehow failed at being thin and avoiding freshman year weight gain. I went silent after he said those dreaded words to me and could barely find my breath.

He tried looking into my eyes but I had turned away, red-faced and full of shame. "Are you okay? It's not a big deal. It's easy to lose," he continued. The more he talked, the more I receded into my head and felt damned. He had leveled a harsh assessment of my body and in his eyes I had failed. My stomach suddenly felt like it had grown to grotesque proportions and that no matter how hard I tried, I was doomed to walk around like that pathetic creature constantly craving, never satisfied, and always hurting.

"Are you okay? I didn't mean to hurt your feelings," he offered, but by then it was too late. I threw my sweatshirt over my offending stomach and covered up the rest of my body as best I could; he had found the weak spot in my armor and I was vulnerable.

All I could manage was a tight-lipped "I'm fine," as I raced out of that room as fast as I could. It was early morning, so the dorm was quiet since most college kids would be sleeping off hangovers on Sunday mornings. I went back to my own room one floor down, frantically searching for the box of Camel Lights that I hid in my drawers, lit up and wondered how I had let myself go so far in my eating that my perfect-bodied boyfriend would notice and judge.

I had already assumed that if I gained weight, Bill would criticize me and love me less. When we were together and passed random women on campus, he would often quip, "her ass is so big" or "she's so out of shape." Each time he made these comments, I'd go quiet because I knew that it was the worst thing anyone could ever say to me. I was always on edge and waiting for him to notice that I was the same as those women. And on that morning in bed, he had finally said it to me. Suggesting that I exercise meant that somehow, I had become unacceptable, automatically unattractive, undesirable, and unlovable.

After our relationship ended that Spring, I went back to spending more time partying and socializing with my artsy, nerdy, and alternative friends. I also started to date men who could make me feel at ease in my body, or at least as best as I could at that time. I had not yet figured out how to settle into my body and see if from the inside out rather than assuming that my identity was based on the external labels people like my mother and Bill had placed on me. I was, however, learning that not everybody was out to judge my body and that there were some people who might actually appreciate the whole of me rather than what I lacked. Even though I continued to pull all-nighters, had taken up cigarette smoking and dabbled with pot smoking, I also kept my eyes on a bigger prize. I simply couldn't afford to party my future away like it seemed many of my friends were already doing. Buddhism was going to continue to play a significant role in my life and I decided that I wanted to be a college professor. I was not willing to let my intellectual curiosity take a back seat to drinking and smoking pot. I had made it that far and I needed to ensure that I would land a place in graduate school if I wanted to be like Professor Ferguson and stay far away from home. Returning to the snake-skinned room to live was not an option. With my mind set on a definitive goal, I seem to focus just a little less on worrying about my body since it suddenly seemed less important than a life of the mind.

In my junior year I decided that I wanted an adventure and to live outside of the country, so I decided to travel back to Seoul for a nine-month study-abroad program. I had gone back and forth to Korea as a young girl a few times with my whole family, but this was the first time I would return to live on my own. I remember the shock I felt when stepping off the airplane because I was suddenly in a sea of people who looked just like me—black hair, Korean face and all. For the first time in my life, I simply blended in with everyone around me and didn't feel like an outsider. I was no longer a racial minority no matter where I went and felt incredible relief that my face and my body looked a lot like everyone else's. My homestay family hosted two other Korean students who lived in Japan and my new housemates, Soon Ja and Jae Min, and I became fast friends who studied, partied, and went sight-seeing together.

My Korean facial features and body no longer seemed an oddity; in fact, it was the opposite. There was little besides my American accent and my style of dress that marked me as different and I became keenly aware of a new-found comfort that came from being with people who resembled me. This similarity was reinforced each time I visited the public bath-house down the street from my homestay, where I would pay to bathe in hot water, since my host mother liked to keep the hot water under tight control at the house to save money. Into the bath-house I'd go each day and sit and bathe in the tubs and then sit on one of the ubiquitous plastic chairs lined up in front of mirrors hosing myself off with the handheld shower. Everywhere I looked there were women who had similar bodies to mine. Although Korean women are quite modest outside of the bath-house, such modesty was of no concern in the spa where female friends and family would sit side by side fully undressed and discuss all matters big and small without any indication of body shame, anxiety, or self-consciousness. Rather than feeling immediate shame at undressing in front of all these other strangers, I felt myself relax in a way that I never had before because the women I saw all had bodies similar to mine.

Living in Korea also solidified my desire to continue my studies in Buddhism. Each week I would walk two or three times up the mountain near my house where I would visit one of the local Buddhist temples. I would pick up a few sticks of incense and bow in front of the Buddha statues and make silent offerings to the hungry ghosts whose suffering had indeed been akin to my own. The beautiful statues, the serene faces of the nuns, and the noble but modest temple grounds made me wish that I too could live a monastic life at times, because it must have been pretty great not to worry about what to wear and what my hair looked like—I wouldn't have any as a nun. This trip back to Korea was a return home of sorts, but my grandparents were no longer living and I could not retrace any of my steps or invoke any memories from when I was a baby living with grandparents. Nonetheless, those nine months offered me an opportunity to feel the first measure of freedom from my anxiety over my body and I knew then that there might be more hope for me later.

Anyone who understood suffering and the way out, like the Buddha did, was certainly going to get my attention and my devotion. I was hooked and set my path toward that goal. Every day of my senior year, I'd don the same uniform I gave myself of a Tibetan-style cap, jeans, a white t-shirt and an old brown field jacket, and I'd make my way to the library where I had a tiny carrel that resembled a monastic hut one would find at the top of mountain in Tibet. To finish off the look of the serious Buddhist meditator and budding scholar I also cut my own hair so that I would have less things to fuss over and be attached to. While I thought I looked pretty cool, my boyfriend at the time was a little confused by my new look and certainly a little crestfallen. After the traumatic experience of my mother chopping off my hair, I had grown it out to waist length as a way of defying her, but also because I knew that it was a potent symbol of beauty. But once I'd found Buddhism, I had other things on my mind.

I had given up heavy drinking and partying and trying to find my identity through other means because I had finally found it by studying Buddhism—even my advisor and mentor, Professor Ellen Ferguson, thought so and showed it as she returned my senior thesis back to me with a big knowing smile on her face.

"No one has written a senior thesis of this length and depth before! You are definitely going to be a professor and a writer. Congratulations." To this day I remember that incredible feeling of validation that I could become what I had decided that I wanted to be. I graduated Phi Beta Kappa that year and received the annual prize in Asian Studies, and I set my plans in motion to become a Buddhist Studies professor with the same sense of fervor and focus I had given to my thesis. I wondered, too, whether my mother would ever be proud of such a plan.

Choosing Buddhism

MY IMPENDING GRADUATION from college filled my head with lofty plans of becoming a professor. I wanted to be admired for my intelligence, devote myself to the life of the mind, and indulge my love of books stacked this way and that all over the shelves of what would undoubtedly become my classic New England-style college office. Visions of being a cool professor lecturing at the front of the classroom, chalk in hand while students took furious notes, danced in my head. But I had no game plan. I had a romanticized dream about what it would look like to be a college professor, but I had not yet realized that there were some preliminary steps involved. These steps included taking an aptitude test, figuring out what exactly I wanted to study and where I wanted to apply, and then of course convincing some fancy graduate program that I really did belong there.

"How about something in Asian Studies or Korean studies? Why not do something practical like that? What are you going to do with a degree in Buddhism?" my dad pushed when I called him in a near panic before leaving school. "How will you make a living? It seems a little impractical don't you think?" He continued asking me these questions after I figured out that I wanted to be a professor just like Professor Ferguson. She had not only ignited my intellectual curiosity about Buddhism, but she also offered me practical lessons in alleviating suffering. It was her course on Women in Buddhism, though, that really made me want to pursue the academic life because I knew somehow that if I pursued a career as a professor, I could be both a teacher and a student of the religion. It seemed clear to me that she loved her job and was incredibly good at it. I don't remember when we talked specifically about my plans to become a professor, but I do remember her encouraging comments that she could see me as a scholar after reading some of my essays.

One day, after a particularly rough morning of weighing myself and discovering that the scale had inched a few pounds higher, I was full of dread and anxiety that somehow somebody might notice that I had gained weight. Although it was only three pounds, I was convinced I was fat. So after throwing on some loose sweatpants and a sweatshirt to mask my supposed hugeness, I stealthily took a seat in the back of Profesor Ferguson's classroom and began to shed the layer of self-consciousness that had been exposed. The lessons for the day on Buddhism and the body spoke directly to how I was feeling at the time.

"The Buddha taught monks and nuns that it would be possible to let go of attachment to their bodies and all of the negative thoughts or mental chatter associated with how we think about ourselves. All that we think is simply the act of thinking," she lectured in class. Her brilliance aside, all I knew was that I was feeling lousy and disappointed with myself for letting myself overeat, and I began to wonder why it was that I was so fixated on a number on the scale and how it could make or break my day.

If all that I think about myself is simply the process of thinking, then it must not signify who I am as a person, I thought. *And besides, didn't the Buddha teach that who we are as people is constantly changing? Do I really want to spend all this time filling up my mind with negative thoughts? What would happen if I stopped thinking bad things about myself? Would I feel differently?* I sat up in my chair. The idea that I could think differently about myself and therefore feel differently about and in my body was intriguing enough that I knew I was hearing something that would stick with me for a long time. I knew my father was worried about my career and that Korean immigrant children should make good use of their parents' sacrifices, but I also knew that there was no way that I was going to change my mind. The karmic seed was planted for my future direction. I had the what, and now I just needed the where.

Deciding where I wanted to go to grad school was pretty easy since there weren't that many programs in Buddhism. After reviewing the list, I decided to apply to the University of Wisconsin, Columbia, Berkeley, and Harvard. Of course, what I kept in my head and didn't speak out loud to anyone besides my father was that Harvard was my first choice. It was the most well-known school and had such a reach that I set it as the top of my list despite the fact that I didn't think I had any chance at all of getting in—Harvard was for the exceptional student and while I had graduated with distinction and won the prize for Asian Studies in college, I didn't exactly think I was a shoe-in. My father, however, knew about it and I figured that as long as I got a degree from Harvard, he wouldn't care what I majored in. And the degree I had decided on was a Ph.D.

With a Ph.D. I would automatically be considered successful despite my personal history. To both my father and me, a Ph.D. would far outweigh whatever abuse I had experienced at home because I could then look back and claim that my hardships had made me stronger and pushed me to greater accomplishments. This kind of myth of adversity was widely held in the Korean immigrant community among the men and women who sacrificed social status and financial stability in Korea when they came to the United States in pursuit of the American dream. I had a dream, too, but it wasn't about America; it was more about proving to myself that if I worked hard and pushed myself diligently, I might be able to perfect myself in the public eye so that I wouldn't feel self-conscious about my body and my relationship with my mother. I wanted to completely remake myself, and the Ph.D. seemed the ultimate goal for doing just that. I also believed at the time that Ph.D.s were the top of the academic food chain, and my mother had only reached the level of an Associate's degree. Although I didn't actively seek a Ph.D. to prove that I was better than my she was, I certainly cannot discount that the desire existed. She had gone too far in putting me down, reducing my value, and making me feel invisible. Now I wanted payback. I wanted to show her that despite all her abuse and neglect, I had won. I would excel where she had failed.

As for my mother, I didn't say much to her about my plans for graduate school because when I had mentioned my interests early in the summer, she looked at me blankly and offered nothing more than a blunt, "Oh. Fine."

There were so few words exchanged between us by that point that I stopped reporting many of my goings-on at the time, both because she didn't seem to support any of my decisions to pursue a teaching career and because I didn't want to let her take away my excitement or my confidence. Her sharp, withering stares left me feeling as if I'd been cut down to size and I just wanted to avoid her glance as much as possible. Although I was afraid of her gaze as a child and often longed to be truly seen and actively loved by her, by the time I had graduated from college, I wanted my life completely to myself. That decision meant that I would need to stay as far away from her as possible. Unfortunately, that goal was not as easy as it would seem because her health was getting worse since she had cut back even more on what she would eat. It was becoming increasingly clear that she was not just giving up food, but she was giving up her will to live.

After leaving college, I knew I didn't want to move back home to New York like many of my friends were doing while they regrouped and figured out what was next. Living with my mother was not an option, as far as I was concerned. But although grad school in Buddhist Studies was definitely in the plans, I still needed time to figure out what programs would be right for me and where. So after graduating I packed up my dorm room took a trip to Cambridge where I soon found a summer sublet from a first year law student. I hadn't been accepted to Harvard, but I figured the closer I was to it physically, the closer I was to it academically.

"Hello. My name is Sharon. I work for MassPIRG, the state's largest environmental and consumer advocacy group. I'm here to generate support for the most recent piece of recycling legislation coming up for a vote. Can I count on your support?"

Each afternoon throughout the summer of 1991 I'd be dropped off in some neighborhood in Western Massachusetts with a clipboard and address cards for former members of the Public Interest Research Group. I had recently responded to an ad in the *Boston Herald* calling for "environmental activists looking for an exciting summer opportunity!"

"What are you going to be doing in Boston?" my father had asked me on the phone as he quizzed me on where I would live and what kind of jobs I was applying for.

"Campaign jobs" is basically what I told him, and basically all I knew about MassPIRG. But the important thing to me was that they were hiring in Cambridge and, since I wanted to be in close proximity to the school, it was a start.

After canvassing for the summer, I was hired on as assistant director for one of the PIRG offices, in Amherst, and so I quickly moved to Western Massachusetts with my college boyfriend, Charles, and ran the canvasing office, trained staff, and continued to canvas door to door for the environment for a year while I applied to graduate schools in Buddhist Studies. I applied to at least five different grad school programs and was delighted when those big bulky envelopes began to arrive in the mail with news of my acceptance. Although I had gotten into a number of excellent Buddhist Studies program including the University of Wisconsin, I really wanted to get into Harvard Divinity School. I had been told that getting a Master's in Theological Studies in the Divinity School would be a great opportunity to get my foot in the door for the Ph.D. program in Buddhist Studies. So, as with the red envelopes full of money that Korean children often receive from their parents during the Lunar New Year, tearing open that fat envelope was full of promise, and I was ecstatic to find inside the news that I'd been accepted into Harvard's Divinity School.

When I called my parents to tell them the good news, I could feel my dad glowing with pride as he admitted, "When I got my graduate degree in accounting, I always dreamed that I would teach at a place like Harvard. I had a secret dream to be a professor too." When I pressed my dad about what had thwarted his plans, he replied wistfully, "Well, I had to work and make more money because I was also sending money home to my family in Korea. So I really want you to go. It was my dream and now you can do it."

I hadn't known anything at all about my father's early dreams, for he was revealing a side of himself I simply never knew about—he, too, wanted to live an academic life. He sacrificed those dreams for the sake of his family, and knowing that my dad had wanted to do the very thing that I was going to do with my own career, I knew that he was so proud of me and that I couldn't fail. I had to succeed for my own sake and also to help my dad fulfill his own dreams of being an academic.

"Mom, I got into Harvard, I am going to go in the Fall," I spoke carefully into the phone. I was hoping for an acknowledgment or congratulations but was met with an icy, "So what?"

I knew not to be surprised or to expect much by way of congratulations but I was so excited about getting in and really craved her approval. It didn't come and so when I hung up the phone, the tears came readily and wildly.

Without any hesitation, I immediately packed up my suitcases, responded to an ad for housing in the *Boston Herald* and settled into a sweet little mother-in-law apartment above my new landlords, Beth and Stu, owners of a cute, light blue craftsman-style home just a few blocks from the Porter Square T-stop. Two months later, beaming with pride and excitement, I began my Master's at Harvard Divinity School concentrating on Buddhism and Culture.

"Without acknowledging painful experiences and facing reality as it is, we risk perpetual rebirth in the endless cycles of suffering or what the Buddha called *samsara*. Escaping from *samsara* is the end goal of Buddhism, a cycle of meaninglessness," lectured my Buddhism professor in the hallowed halls of Harvard. There I was in one of the most prestigious institutions in the world, pen in hand, gazing around at all my classmates wondering if they were all smarter than me and if I would succeed. I was eating the professor's words up and looked all around the classroom listening to the radiators hiss and moan as they worked the heat through their rattling bones. All the undergraduates in the Yard looked so fresh and bright and the grad students all wore serious expressions on their faces as they walked through campus making sure that everyone knew that they were grinding on some complex question that would somehow bring humanity to its next stage of development. I felt like a kid, and a happier kid than I ever was before—walking around with my huge back-pack weighed down by Sanskrit dictionaries, Indian texts, and Buddhist volumes; I was living my version of the dream. I was amongst the intellectual elite hoping that one day I would make the cut, graduate from the Master's program, and soon be accepted into the doctoral program. But for all my confidence, I was still socially shy, and felt completely out of place. Professional academia seemed an earthly nirvana, and Harvard Square itself, with its arthouse movie theater, smoky cafés, and ancient bookstores, was everything that I wanted it to be—a little village for and about the mind. I wandered about feeling like an imposter and that my acceptance was somehow a fluke because this was a dream that had come true for me and I wasn't used to getting everything I wanted. In class I was often nervous to open my mouth, lest my cohort discover that I was not as smart as they were.

"*Samsara* is continually fed by the delusions or ignorance that we seem bound by. It is only by waking up to reality as it is and by facing the truth of our experiences that we can escape this cycle," continued Professor Heinrichs, my forty-something year-old professor with a body so thin and pale it looked like it never saw the light of day. Along with the glasses hanging miraculously from his nose without falling off despite constant edging toward the tip, and the rumpled white cotton shirt and khaki pants he always wore along with a blue wool sweater, he was the quintessential grad school professor. And I wanted to be just like him—a scholar of Buddhism who was so smart that he could wow anyone just by uttering a sentence or two in Pali, the language through which the Buddha's teachings were originally recorded. I had a deep intellectual crush, not so much on the professor himself, but on the idea of being a professor in a university dispensing wisdom and eliciting admiration from a room full of smart students.

Amidst all this, what really brought my professor's lecture alive for me was the realization that when the Buddha taught his disciples about ignorance as the root cause of suffering, he reminded them that ignorance is not only not-knowing the truth, it is also ignoring the truth.

"The truth is something that we often keep from others and from ourselves," Professor Heinrichs lectured, "but by learning to see the truth, we can liberate ourselves from our own suffering and delusions."

As he continued teaching us about the six realms of *samsara* that we could be born into based on our karma, I wrote furiously in my notebook in the lecture hall in Harvard's Sever Hall. My hand took down his words verbatim on the pages that had come to resemble my own sacred text, one that I would return to over and over as I attempted to somehow absorb my teacher's intellect through the ink. I refused to stop writing and would occasionally shake out my right hand which would cramp from excitement over what I was learning, and the fact that I was learning it in the ivory towers of Harvard.

Professor Heinrichs' lecture moved onto the Buddha's systematic approach to the existence of suffering as a fact of nature, suffering's origins in ignorance and attachment, the possibility of ending suffering, and the prescription to ending it. I was intellectually smitten. Here I was in graduate school doing an academic study of Buddhism, but I was also getting the important life lessons that I needed to help make sense of my life. How fortunate I was, I came to realize, that I could dedicate what would eventually amass to nine years of my life in graduate school to figuring out how to both see and acknowledge the truth *and* make a living out of it. I just couldn't admit to my cohort or my teachers that I was studying Buddhism for something more than becoming an intellectual and a scholar. The course work was rigorous and I seemed to be working all the time keeping myself on top of my game, but earning a Master's degree would take far more than studying and getting good grades. It would also require finding the strength to endure the death of my mother and the potential loss of my father.

A Death and a Diagnosis

"Have you heard back yet? When will you find out?" These two sentences seemed to mark the second year of any Master's program where, like hungry ghosts, all the students were craving acceptance into a prestigious Ph.D. program. For my cohort and me, there really was only one top choice—the Committee on the Study of Religion in the Graduate School of Arts and Sciences at Harvard. The competition among friends was fierce and barely suppressed behind the veneer of casual smiles we painstakingly forced onto our faces—we never wanted to acknowledge that we were vying for what were only a few positions in the department, but we all knew it. I was not sure that I would be one of the anointed, since I was not one of the beloved grad students of Professor Heinrichs— that position fell into the lap of one of my best friends, Jennifer.

"William asked me to T.A. his course! I'm so excited! William wants to do an independent study with me in Pali. William this… William that…" she gushed as my heart fell a few notches. She would probably get in and I would end up at another university, which on its own merits would probably have been excellent; however, this was the world of stiff competition where we vied for the top while also being friends with the very peers who might stand in our way.

Because I knew that the doctoral program at Harvard would be a reach despite my high marks in the MA program, I made sure to apply to several programs in Buddhist Studies and was flown out by several programs on their own dime to explore the possibilities of studying at the University of Michigan (which brought me out at the same time that the Dalai Lama was visiting and I had a chance to meet him in person!), the University of Virginia, and the University of Washington. I felt like an anointed one away from my cohort and Cambridge and definitely a desired candidate, but alas, I had already drunk the Kool-Aid and assumed that there could be no better program than Harvard simply for its name and renown. After submitting all my applications, I waited out what seemed an interminable few months and finally, a week or two after Jennifer got her acceptance letter, I got in.

"Congratulations! I'm so proud of you! You did it!" my father whooped into the telephone when I called him at work. "All your hard work finally paid off," he said with admiration. He paused briefly and took a deep breath. I could tell that he was relieved that I had made it into Harvard, on the one hand so that he could enjoy some bragging rights among his friends, but also because I knew that he saw my acceptance as proof that I hadn't been completely damaged by my mother and I had prevailed despite the conditions of my childhood.

"Yes, Dad. I made it in and I'm really excited. Let Mom know, okay?" I didn't bother telling my mother because I was not in the mood for what would have been an inevitable lack of joy in my success and most likely some comment that I was stuck up. I hung up the phone happy that I could make my father proud, and relieved that I wasn't one of students who didn't make it into the program—rejection from the doctoral program would hardly have been mitigated by an acceptance into another prestigious institution, at least in my mind. Of course, in retrospect, I know that there are several other programs that probably would have been a better fit with more financial aid and faculty guidance and support. However, I was willing to risk the mentorship of great faculty and more hands-on direction in other programs that had great reputations for a chance to be a somewhat second-tier student at the illustrious Harvard. It didn't matter to me that Jennifer and my other classmates got full rides and immediate positions as teaching assistants and I didn't. At the end of the day, I was in it for the training and the degree; like my father, I thought that a Ph.D. from Harvard would mean that ultimately, I would be fine because I had the external marks of success.

I graduated from the Divinity School without much fanfare; I was simply eager to move into the Graduate School of Arts and Sciences and quickly leave the Master's program. Although many of my classes ended up being in the classrooms of the Div school that Fall, it didn't matter to me. I graduated with a degree, and I was now onto the best next thing. But the next thing up ahead was something as wholly unexpected as it was inevitable.

"You have to hurry up and come back to New York, Mom is sick. She was coming back from Virginia visiting your aunt and she had to be taken off the plane by ambulance." My father was calling from New York Hospital where my mother had been taken immediately from the airport. Her younger sister, a doctor, had been golfing in Virginia when she was struck by lightning and severely injured. My aunt was incapacitated for a few weeks and my mother had been caring for her, or at least making an attempt to care for her. Fortunately, my aunt miraculously survived with all but her speech intact. She simply spoke a bit slower after recovering from the freak accident, but my mother wasn't as fortunate. Flying back home, she contracted a bacterial infection in her catheter port where she had been receiving portable dialysis. "She is in really bad shape and not conscious," my dad continued. "They put a tube in her so that she can breathe."

I went silent on the phone trying to figure out what to do next and while I tried to sort out my feelings, my father's next words made the decision simple.

"She might not make it. It's really serious this time. I would come home."

I got myself to Logan airport as fast as I could and planned to spend the long weekend in New York. I hoped to make it back to school on Monday so that I could still take my summer class in reading French, which was required for the Ph.D. program. I was so far emotionally removed from my mother that rather than worry for her health, I was already calculating the hours lost in study time versus time spent in the hospital with my mother. Still, I knew I had to go, so I hopped a cab from JFK as soon as I landed and went straight to the hospital, my carry-on bag loaded down with French books and my notes so that I could study while attending to my mother. I hustled into the hospital elevator, ran to find my father and brother who had already arrived from work, and saw my mother's tiny body laying underneath several thin, white cotton blankets with a breathing tube down her mouth and taped across her mouth. She would never be able to speak to me again.

Because she had had tuberculosis in her youth, she was also susceptible to renal failure, and while I was in college and grad school she had started to exhibit acute signs of illness through her perpetual exhaustion and ever-decreasing body weight. In many ways her health seemed to be a kind of chicken-and-egg game; my dad knew that while she suffered from kidney troubles due to the tuberculosis, she was also cramming her body full of laxatives and diuretics to get rid of that puffy-faced look associated with the "moon faced" roundness of Korean women and the swollen cheeks associated with renal-failure patients. To this day it is near impossible to tell whether her complete kidney failure could have been circumvented had she not overtaxed her kidneys with excessive use of diuretics. She wanted to be skinny and was willing to compromise her already-jeopardized health to get there. At that point, nobody wanted to push her on it, for she was in fact sick.

As I was growing up, however, all I really understood was that while she certainly seemed to spend an awful lot of time cooking for us in the kitchen and preparing my extra-buttery, extra-salty meals, she herself would eat like a bird and then quietly go off to the toilet, presumably to forcibly remove any food that went into her mouth. Laxatives, diuretics, and what I later discovered to be several stashes of Valium, eventually made her so small that I was embarrassed to walk around with her. She began to look like those cautionary photos of emaciated children in Africa shown on the Save the Children commercials, whose bodies were wasting away because of famine. The difference was that hers wasted away from her own doing.

While there are many things about my mother's behavior that I think my brain has forgotten out of self-protection, her verbal declarations of her weight remain clear in my mind even if I have blocked out the sound of her voice. Each year was marked by an almost embarrassed pride in the weight that she had lost—110, 108, 105, 103, 98, 96, 94, 92 pounds.

By the time she lay in the intensive care unit she weighed 82 pounds. She had gone into complete renal failure and had contracted sepsis, despite having had a kidney transplant the year before, partly because she refused to eat and continued to abuse her laxatives and diuretics. After her kidney transplant also failed, she had opted for portable dialysis and immediately had a catheter port surgically placed in her lower abdomen so that she could have the dialysis at home rather than spending several hours a week hooked up to a machine after my dad got back from work.

While I wish I could say that I had developed immediate feelings of compassion for my mother, and that her illness would remind her that she didn't have long to live and that she ought to make amends with me, she only became more and more angry as she carted her dialysis IV bags around on a portable cart. Like Ebenezer Scrooge walking around with heavy chains as he dreamt of Christmases past, present, and future, my own mother lurked around our Manhattan apartment chained to her machine, and was just as hostile and bitter as Scrooge was at the opening of Dickens's novella. When I later saw her in the critical care unit, immobile and dying, I was unsure how I felt. I had spent my childhood grieving for the loss of her love and the loss of a real mother. The woman who lay dying had given birth to me but had never mothered me. She was almost a stranger.

My mother remained in the critical care unit for weeks. I'd like to say that there was some sort of reconciliation in the hospital between us but there was none. I simply took care of her, brushing her thinned-out hair, washing her face gently with a warm cloth, brushing her teeth, and moistening her mouth with the foam swabs provided by the hospital when her mouth became too dry. She was intubated for much of that time and unable to speak from the moment she entered the hospital until she died. I spent each day that summer in the hospital room with my brother, sister-in-law, and my father.

"I can't believe that she's dying. How the hell did this happen?" my brother cried.

My sister-in-law put her arms around his shoulders, adding, "I don't know what to do. Everything will be so different without her. Jasper will grow up without his grandmother."

My aunts, uncles, and cousins had been rotating in and out of the unit to visit my mother, who by late summer had slipped into a coma. She lay completely still in that hospital bed only to suddenly begin shaking head to toe in a seizure.

"It's okay, Evelyn," my aunt whispered into her ear as she stroked the hair out of her face. "It's okay to let go, you have suffered so much in your life. You will go to a better place and to peace. Don't worry."

I immediately relaxed at the sound of my aunt's sweet, soothing voice. She was married to my mother's youngest brother, a quiet but intense man who seemed to be as full of kindness and love as my mother had been full of rage and anger. As a child, I used to marvel at how my aunt and uncle were such gentle parents and that my uncle had come from the same womb as my mother. While he shared her tendency toward quietness, his came from shyness and a low-key persona that always made me feel calm in his presence. Even as he held my mother's hand, he remained quiet, his face expressing deep pain and sorrow.

Each of my extended family members came to the hospital to visit my mother and each one also made sure to tell me how good a daughter I was to take care of my mother in the hospital. "It's so great that you can be here with her. I know that she appreciates it and she loves you," my favorite aunt, Paul's mother, reassured me. "I know that she loves you," she repeated as she looked into my eyes and cradled both of my hands in hers.

I nodded in assent, afraid to open my mouth lest I say what I was really thinking at the time—*I don't think so.*

I didn't know what to feel as she lay dying in the hospital, some of it was compassion over the pain she had physically experienced, some of it was relief that she wouldn't be hurting anymore.

It is hard to say for sure, because I also had succumbed to a kind of emotional numbness to keep myself from feeling a sense of mourning over the fact that I would never have an opportunity to vent my rage and grieve over a mother-daughter relationship that never was and never could be. I was afraid to open my mouth and give voice to what I really felt because doing so felt like risking opening Pandora's box full of anger and resentment, overwhelming all the opposing sentiments of grief that filled the hospital room. I feared that speaking my true feelings would threaten to drown out the focus on my mother and my family's opportunity to say their goodbyes, and I worried that I would silence them and force them to confront what they had known all along but seemed to forget in their grief—that she was a questionable mother and how I wished that I had one who could elicit authentic feelings of grief. There I was in the hospital room, a fraud of a daughter whose relatives were showering me with sympathy, thinking that I had felt a deep loss over her impending death. I am not sure what I felt.

I already carried memories of her deep in my bones, the memories that made my body feel like it would never be good enough, never acceptable, as if it were mere matter out of place. As a good Korean American daughter, however, I remained silent and kept my feelings to myself, for this was a time for saying goodbye and not for holding onto the past.

She died in September, shortly after I had returned to Harvard to begin my Ph.D. I returned home and cried along with the rest of my family, although to this day, it is hard for me to pinpoint what it was that I was crying for—maybe the cries were a sign of relief and the kind of cathartic event that allows a person to move forward. I can't say whether I shed tears of grief over her loss or over what could have been, because those are forged out of the bonds of deep love, and what I felt were the bonds of deep obligation that bound me to my mother. The end of her life brought no reconciliation because she couldn't speak, but I also knew that she would never admit to her abusive behavior. Therefore, any resolution was going to have to be on my own terms. I wanted to be the kind of person who would not allow my history of abuse to keep me from feeling the kind of grief that others thought I might feel, but I did not. I did feel sadness over her pain, and the mental and physical struggles she must have endured, but at that time I felt little emotional attachment that could give rise to authentic grief. If anything, I felt numb, but maintained some hope that I could repair the damage done in my relationship to myself and future relationships with others.

Following her funeral and burial, I returned with my father to the apartment and in a few days began to sort through her belongings. I felt compelled to hold onto some of her jewelry and her clothing, even the wedding ring that I wished my finger was thin enough to wear. Although I didn't yet register a palpable sense of missing her, I did have a fascination with her old clothing, especially because I was surprised that I could actually fit in them. So I took a few of her blouses, skirts, and pants back to school with me and even began to wear them to class each day. In some ways, I had stepped into my mother's life by virtue of fitting into her clothing.

It was in the midst of looking through her belongings that I happened upon the most recent purse that she carried. As I pulled it out of the closet, I heard a rattling from inside the bag and stuck my hand in it to see what I'd find. Out came two full vials of pills—the bright pink laxatives that she had used since I was a child, and what looked like a hundred little yellow pills of Valium. The Valium must have helped calm her nerves and her hunger because later I found several more discarded brown plastic medicine bottles filled with the little yellow pills with the letter V imprinted in them, and those cursed pink laxative pills. Right up to the end as she lay dying, she wasn't thin enough in her own mind. I dumped all the pills on the kitchen table and sifted through them with my fingers wondering what could cause a person to want to waste away.

Looking through the pills that testified to the painful life she'd led, I felt neither grief nor joy over her death. I simply gathered the pills in my palms and unceremoniously tossed them in the trash. I am afraid to say that even today I am not sure that I feel much more than relief that I am free to live my life far away from her rage and her debilitating gaze upon my body.

I returned to school to much sympathy from my friends, and while I knew that I was supposed to present myself as grieving, I couldn't help but feel happy to be back in school and focusing on my work. I hit the books hard, studied as much as I could by surviving on coffee and bagels at the coffee shop where I worked part-time, happy to finally be a doctoral student. Unfortunately, that happiness was somewhat short-lived. Just two months after my mother's death my father called with some terrible news.

"It seems that I have some cancerous tumors growing in my liver," he reported as calmly as he could. "It's not looking so good."

I fell to my knees and felt the wind knocked out of me.

Not my dad. Please, not my dad. Tell me this isn't happening. Please. I prayed. I sobbed into the phone, "Dad, I'm coming! I can't believe this is happening. I'll be there tonight."

Once again, I hopped a plane from Logan to New York back to the very same hospital my mother had been in two months earlier. I got there just as my dad was wheeled into surgery for a liver resection to remove the tumors. I was twenty-four and not ready to be an orphan. I told myself that I was going to do my best to get my dad in full recovery because there was no way in hell that my father was going to die so soon. I was not ready to be left alone and on my own.

I took an informal leave of absence from Harvard and finished my Fall semester classes as independent studies, since I didn't want to fall behind and start over again the next year. I already had plenty of experience studying in hospital rooms, which is what I'd done all summer, and I was ready to be a full-time caregiver to my dad as well as a full-time student.

"I'm not taking no for an answer, Dad. Forget it. I'm staying home with you until you heal from this surgery. I will not leave you alone," I declared, as my father tried to convince me from his hospital bed that he could manage without me.

"I can go home, hire a nurse, and your aunts can take care of me, Sharon. Please, don't worry about me," he tried to convince me.

I wasn't hearing any of it. I had the bonds of love that make such suggestions utterly ridiculous and unheard of—we do not leave our loved ones unattended. I was also unwilling to imagine my father dying without me and was set on getting us through what turned out to be the early stages of his miraculous remission from liver cancer.

"I couldn't live with the idea that my daughter left her Ph.D. program to take care of her father. It wasn't right," my father tried to explain as he introduced me to his fiancée on the phone.

It was February, just a few months after his diagnosis and a few short months after my mother's death. "I didn't want to get in the way of your future. So I decided that since I couldn't live alone… well, your aunts decided to look for a spouse for me," he said. "You know Korean men don't know how to live alone," he added sheepishly into the phone. "We're getting married in April at Tavern on the Green. Please come," he all but begged.

I felt myself go numb and my face reddened with embarrassment. My father was going to marry someone only seven months after my mother had died.

I didn't know what to say; I felt he deserved a chance at happiness after living with my mother for 34 years, but I was also dumbfounded that he could find someone so fast, and I worried about what my mother's family would think. I loved my father though, and knew that I couldn't live at home and take care of him and give up school, so I eventually relented and acknowledged the new wife in my father's life, a forty-seven-year-old Korean fur designer who had a college-aged son of her own.

Our first meeting seemed to set the tone for the rest of our relationship. She showed up in Cambridge with my dad, covered head to toe in a fancy white fur coat and hat looking like a veritable snow queen. She bore gifts too—skincare products. I instantly felt like I needed to fix my face. I received the fancy lotions and acted as if I knew what they were for and stammered, "Uh, thank you. These are very nice." She stared at my face intently and replied almost too quickly, "I thought these might help." She smiled, a tight-lipped turn of her lips, as if to say, *You can use all the help you can get.*

After an extremely awkward lunch, she and my father drove me to Lord and Taylor in Boston Common, and she went straight to the designer section and selected two suits that she insisted on buying for me, suits that I never would have picked out for myself. "Everyone needs to wear nice clothes to look good in public," she insisted. I looked to my father for help, but he simply nodded in agreement, "Yes Sharon. That's right. You need to dress better."

The suits were the conservative kind that she might wear and were certainly far too dressy for a grad student, but I acquiesced because I wanted to show her that my father knew how to raise a grateful daughter. The sizes she selected were too broad in the shoulders and too long in the legs, but I didn't complain. I stood in the dressing room on top of a small wooden stool with my shirt hiked above my waist as the tailor measured the waist size of the pants. She then moved to pin the hems of the pants and as she crouched down, I looked briefly in the mirror and could see my future step-mother gazing upon and assessing my body. My body immediately tensed up and my heartbeat seem to quicken, for I had been here before with that familiar gaze that made me feel like I was not good enough. When the suits arrived, perfectly tailored, I put them in the back of my closet and barely looked at them again.

Finding the Mat

I AM CROUCHED in child's pose with my forehead resting on my yoga mat as I slowly try breathing into my whole belly, a difficult endeavor since I am feeling it swelling a little more than yesterday. I hope no one else can see my stomach sticking out from under my loose shirt and then chide myself for my narcissism.

No one else cares what your belly looks like. Settle down and settle in! I tell myself as I try to shake out the stress that I feel when my body doesn't feel right. I had rushed over to class after catching a glimpse of myself in the mirror when I changed into my yoga leggings.

I am definitely looking like a middle-aged woman, or getting there soon. When did the skin on my elbows get so dry and wrinkly? I guess this is what middle age looks like, damnit. It came on so fast that I barely had time to prepare for it.

I have no idea what I could have done to prepare for the thing that is happening all the time—change and transformation. I remind myself that all things are impermanent and that I shouldn't objectify myself so much. I ponder this new-found negative thing known as elbow wrinkles to focus on, and quickly will myself out the door. I hear the negative judgmental voice inside of me, the one who wonders if I will still be loved as I grow older, and I tell that voice that I don't have time for her because I am going to be late for class and miss the very thing that will always lay my mental bodily burdens to rest.

Sorry, I do not have time for the mental proliferation today. Catch you later, I tell my harsh self. *I have a class to attend and a body to take care of. Out of my way*, I say as I leave that voice behind and shut the door on her likely shocked expression.

I know that I have moments of utter despair over my body and want to discipline, weigh, and diet her into perfection, but I am also learning that there might be another way that has nothing to do with what I do to my body. Instead, it has everything to do with how I speak to her. Speak gently and perhaps she won't fight so hard to be perfect, thin, muscular, and feminine all at the same time. That's a tall order and one forever on the horizon for someone who is rarely satisfied.

"Set your intention, whatever it may be that brought you here today," says Carla in a slow near-drawl.

I am here because I feel like shit about my body and need to let this feeling go, I think as I lay prostrate on the ground.

"Offer some gratitude to yourself and your fellow practitioners for being here and for being willing to set aside the time to look internally and settle in," Carla encourages us.

"Thanks body for eating too much and then taking it out on your brain," I mutter under my breath. This 48-year-old Korean American yogi is not feeling the love or the calm.

Carla suddenly seems to read my mind and says out loud, "Remember, this is a time for gentleness, awareness, and the development of courage to move toward liberation for mental habits and mental formations that we continue to hang on to."

How the hell does she always know the right thing to say? I am clearly hanging onto way too much negative thinking about myself. I need to let up on myself. I know that it can be done. Please body and mind, let it be soon, I silently pray. I begin to move my body onto its hands and knees and feel my hands and toes on the earth and remember that as the Buddha says, the earth is a great witness to awakening. I hope that I, too, can experience some kind of change in how I treat myself and my body, and bring awareness to how I am feeling in this very moment, so that I create the conditions to let go of my mental habit loops that tell me I look out of shape. I have been primed my whole life to judge my worth by my body, and conditioned to label it as unattractive and unacceptable. It is as if I still see myself through my mother's eyes and through the ones that I developed as a child. I am hoping that this yoga practice will allow me to see more clearly and without the judgmental add-ons.

I remember to let myself be held up by the ground which, as our teacher reminds us, "is always there to hold you up, no matter how crappy you feel." The professor in me begins to write a script in my head for my own future yoga class where I'd instruct my own students to "practice so we might imagine loosening some of the tight bonds that external forces constantly place upon us—whether family, culture, work, and school." I imagine myself telling my students and, let's face it, myself, to "take this opportunity to deepen into ourselves as we are in this present moment, and see ourselves with our own eyes rather than as external eyes might look at us."

I begin to wonder if yoga and mindfulness can really carve a space for gently holding ourselves and allowing us to see that we are just right as we are. Can yoga and mindful breathing loosen the expectations that once we meet a certain set of goals (like lose five pounds), then we can live fully? Can I be a teacher and take all that has primed me for disappointment and harsh judgment of my body and redirect it toward something good?

My mind is racing with hope and questions—when will I recognize that I have all that I need to settle into my body just as it is? Can I really develop confidence, mental flexibility and endurance to approach anew each unfolding circumstance I encounter or is this all still an abstract intellectual hypothesis? While I am not exactly a person of faith, it is part of the reason why I am face down on my red yoga mat trying to ignore the feeling of my yoga tights digging into my stomach. I am trying to stop my mind from focusing on the sensation of having a muffin top and chiding myself for eating a lot of cake the night before. *Geez, all this yoga and meditation and you are still worried about this bullshit...* my mind says to me. I laugh in response as I realize that I am right where I need to be.

It is Sunday afternoon on the last session of this weekend's yoga teacher training. I have signed up for a 200-hour yoga teacher certification training in Seattle with the hope of learning how to help myself and other women like me to learn to appreciate and settle into our bodies. After all, my philosophy has always been that the best to way to teach is to become the student. For as long as I remember, I have not listened to my body's signals—sometimes she wants me to eat and I ignore her. Sometimes she tells me to stop eating and that I will regret the brownies and chips I have stuffed mindlessly down my craw and I ignore her again. Sometimes she feels like the me that my mother used to ignore and silence while I finished every last bite of food on my plate.

Yoga, my teachers tell me, "brings awareness to sensations in the present moment and allows us to connect with something deeper than ourselves." I had enrolled in the Karuna Yoga studio in my neighborhood and the head instructor is trained in mathematics and mindfulness. Lili is near six-foot-tall, stunning, French, with long, wavy brown hair and dark brown eyes eyes. She has the long, sinewy muscles of a runner and the upper-body strength of a gymnast; every time she moves her body to teach us about a pose, it is like looking at an anatomy model where we can see just about every muscle twitch and flex. Lili speaks with a thick French accent about Indian philosophy, neuroscience, and mindfulness in a no-frills European way. She does not have that more-spiritual-than-thou intonation to her voice as a teacher. Her yoga voice is direct, maintains brevity, and is entirely her—wise, humorous, and humble. And I love it.

She is not at all the type of yoga teacher I thought would attract me, because I had in mind that my yoga teacher should be an Indian yogi whose ethnicity matched the homeland from which the tradition emerged. But perhaps one of the gifts of yoga is to let go of our preconceived ideas of ourselves and others, and learn to see the mental habits we have, and the narrative overlays and judgments that we place onto our experiences. So here I am learning about flow yoga, the body, the mind, and spirit from a French goddess and a gray-haired business-woman in recovery. I am loving every minute of this unusual mix and it is here that my intellectual, judgmental mind is invited to rest and, well, shut up. When I turn off that calculating, discerning mind, I learn to recognize sensations in my body and the mental habits I have that like to make me judge myself and others.

"See if you can learn to control that urge to place a label, name, or judgment on your experience. And try to laugh a little at yourself. If your body can't do a particular pose, then back off a little. No one cares and neither should you. What you can't do today, maybe you'll get tomorrow. And what you could do yesterday may not be accessible today. Ho hum. Get over the drama and be with yourself now and treat your body with some respect." As Lili guides us through a Sun Salutation she sounds just like all my favorite Buddhist meditation teachers, and I begin to realize that yoga and meditation are not so different—one accesses awareness through movement, the other accesses awareness by stilling the body so the mind's thoughts become more clear. I also recognize that in order for me to begin to occupy my body, I will need both the flowing postures of yoga and the mental observations of meditation to find my way back in there.

There are twenty-eight students in the class; this is an unusual cohort because it is an all-female student body and, thankfully, the range of ages and bodies in there is vast. There are the young twenty-something-year-old women looking to make a career as one of the countless beautiful yoga teachers in this city of yogis. There are young mothers in great shape with their taut muscles and post-baby flat bellies they love to flaunt in their sports bras and matching low-slung Lululemon tights. These are the women who used to intimidate me because they seem so confident in their bodies and have no problem showing them off. But then there are women like Leila, a 55-year-old woman with a soft, round body and white hair that she has dyed pink. When asked to tell us why she decided to take the training course, she laughed, pointed to her hips and exclaimed proudly, "I am here to learn to appreciate this post-menopausal body of mine. It's been through a lot and it has a lot of offer."

I immediately smile and relax around her honesty. She is like an earth mother and when it comes time to practice our *kapalabhati* breathing, which requires quickly sucking in our bellies and forcing the air out swiftly, she lifts up her shirt with ease, gently places her hands on her generous belly and commences with her practice. I am amazed that she has such confidence in her body and that she can reveal her soft underbelly in public. She inhales and exhales with quiet concentration, her belly ripples rhythmically, and in that instant she appears more beautiful to me. I am intoxicated by her willingness to let it all hang out with a gentle carefree attitude that I hope to one day cultivate. Of course, for many women such a public revelation is no big thing—but to me, it is everything.

Tara, the young woman in her thirties who looks like she is used to being looked at by women and men alike, likes to dramatically pull her shirt off each time we begin the training session. She seems accustomed to constant attention and comments about how great she looks. Even our yoga teachers refer to her when they talk about the importance of not comparing ourselves to anyone else.

"Look," Carla says. "My body is aging, it will never able to do some of the poses I teach. Hell, I will never look anything like Tara, but I don't give a shit. I feel good in my own skin."

She had me at "aging," but as soon as she compared herself to the anointed one in the room, I found myself comparing myself to Tara, as well. Of course, Tara smiles in response and manages to appear self-deprecating as she shakes her head and laughs, "No way, what are you talking about?" as if it had never occurred to her that her body was one to be envied.

It is curious and funny how my mind works—I was feeling pretty good about myself and developing my flexibility, and maybe one day I would even feel as confident as Leila. But as soon as Carla compared herself to Tara, I found myself doing the same. The negative storylines begin on my part as I begin to measure myself against a thirty-something-year-old woman. *I bet she isn't a single working mom with two teenaged girls. She probably has way more time to work out. She probably spends way more time focused on her looks and not her brain. I bet her husband helps take care of her home and everything for her. If I had her life, I'd probably look that way too!*

Lili's reminder not to waste our energy focusing on judgment brings me back to where I am and what I am doing—I sheepishly realize that I am creating a story about someone I don't even know, and I judge her based on my mental fabrication. Maybe she, too, judges herself too harshly and focuses only on her body's perceived flaws. After all, no one is immune from the pressure to have a perfect body and the message that once we achieve them, we should never "let ourselves go." I force myself to sit next to her during the next lecture on yoga energy points in the body, strike up conversation, and am quickly ignored.

Well, at least I am more friendly, I tell myself, knowing already that such a thought is also a petty and pointless comparison. The Buddha taught that we should just be honest about our views, and so I simply acknowledge the rising of jealousy and try to let it go. Tara's body is Tara's and hers for the displaying if she wishes. My body is unique with all its history and perpetual change and, as Buddhism teaches, our bodies are but a complex of processes that are inherently in flux and therefore have no essential qualities that endure.

After giving myself a mini-lecture on getting over myself, I also admit that I am amazed at her ability to take her shirt off and be seen. I have never considered doing that my entire life; the thought of an entire room full of women staring at my belly elicits an anxiety that ties knots in my stomach and tightens my throat. I do not like to be seen without my shirt on, not now and barely ever, but that certainly isn't Tara's problem or fault. I realize that I have been both admiring and critiquing her confidence. *What the hell is wrong with me? I want body acceptance and love and here's a woman who has it and now you hate her? What kind of feminist are you?* I reprimand myself as she sashays by me with a slight swagger.

"Listen to your heartbeat," Carla intones. She pounds lightly on a drum to the rhythm of a heartbeat. We are all sitting with our eyes closed in lotus position with our legs crossed. For some, meditation is a new practice and so they wiggle around trying to settle into some mental quiet. I am used to this practice and posture by now so I relax quickly into what I thought was going to be a mindfulness meditation. "Imagine you have only 24 hours to live. What regrets do you have? What things did you leave unsaid? Who have you not spoken to? What would you like to do? What would you like to let go of?" she continues.

I am jolted out of my usual practice of letting my thoughts go by without clinging to them and begin to make a list of regrets—not taking better care of how I treat myself. Not taking better care of my body. Pounding my body too hard with endless miles of running in order to discipline it into my ideal vision of what it should be (and which never came to be no matter how hard I drove myself). Not listening to my own intuition. Not standing up for myself against my mother and later, against my ex-husband. Not demanding that I be taken care of. Not being more present to myself. Not being more emotionally generous and compassionate to myself. I am pretty good at doing all of these things for my loved ones, but in the process, I have ignored myself. So I set an intention to take better care of how I think about, refer to, talk to, and treat myself.

Carla beats the drum a few more times and Lili rings the meditation bell to signify the end of the session. We are silent as we stand and each of us has a glazed, perplexed look in our eyes over all the things we regretted. "Pay attention to those regrets and now that you have your life back, what are you going to do? And more importantly, what will you stop doing?"

Tears are forming in our eyes as we remember all the unkind things said to us by our own inner critics, and then Lili makes us practice a silent meditation of gazing into each other's eyes without looking away. One by one we move from one person to the next as we awkwardly stare into each other's eyes for about 30 seconds. As we do, I begin to see the beauty, the pain, and the compassion in everyone's eyes. We all had tears in our eyes and as I looked into the eyes of 27 other women, I felt as if I were seeing them for the first time. I remembered the Buddhist meditation on loving kindness and silently wished each of them to feel safe, happy, peaceful, and free from inner and outer danger. I also told each of them silently that I saw them and I felt their gazes upon me as the radical acknowledgement that I was being seen and that I existed.

In that moment, I began to feel what the Hindus refer to as *darshan*—to truly see and be seen. I was vulnerable and excited by this amazing act of bravery and courage—and also relieved that I didn't have to stare into Tara's eyes, since she had already left.

Marriage and Motherhood

HE SAT ON THE WASHING MACHINE of his brother's apartment in Cambridge, fresh from Portland. He had long dark hair, gold wire-rim glasses, and a well-worn gray fisherman's sweater. He looked at me through dazzling blue eyes glassy from smoking pot.

"Hey, how's it going? I'm Chris. Great to meet you," he introduced himself with a slow nod to his head that seemed to move ever so slightly as if it were bobbing atop a haze of weed. He was my friend Rick's brother who was visiting for Spring break and I was immediately struck with the thought, *Wow, he's the one.*

Chris regaled us with stories of his various interviews with law schools around the country as he expertly chopped vegetables and mixed spices for the Thai dinner he was preparing, all the while sipping from what seemed to be an ever-full glass of red wine. As I watched him, I grew more and more attracted to this fellow from the Pacific Northwest who was smart enough to get into law school, cool enough to smoke pot and still sound intelligent, and even cook a fantastic Thai dinner. By the end of dinner, I walked myself home and thought, "I am going to marry that guy."

He returned to Portland, but his brief visit had made an indelible impression on me. I was not an impulsive person and rarely dated but by the end of my first year in my doctoral program, I was besotted. After corresponding through letters, the early versions of email, and hours-long phone calls from my tiny apartment at the Center for the Study of World Religions where I had been the resident assistant, I had decided for sure that we were meant to be. Unlike my usually methodical planning and careful self, I decided on the spot to purchase a ticket to Cabo San Lucas so that I could share a condo on the beach with him, and I didn't even tell my dad that I was going out of town.

"I'm headed to Mexico with Chris," I told my friend, Jennifer. "I'm going to marry this guy! But for now, we're just going as friends. Don't tell anyone. If my dad calls and leaves a message for me in the Center's office, just let him know I'm out on a short trip."

Jennifer nodded with a dubious half smile on her face that told me she was working hard to refrain from judging my rash behavior. I loved her in that moment because that was exactly what I needed. I didn't care that I was doing something totally out of character and was grateful that she had not said anything more than, "Have a great trip! Good luck. I'm so happy for you!"

I barely remember getting on the plane in Boston and the long layover mid-country. Everything was focused on meeting up with Chris in Portland for a day and then hopping a plane to Mexico the next morning. We hadn't talked about dating or even the obvious fact that we'd be sharing a room in Mexico and although I knew that I had fallen head over heels in love, I certainly wasn't going to say a word until he made the first move. "Yes, of course, I would love to go to Cabo with you… as friends of course," I lied when the topic came up on the phone.

My heart was racing and I could feel each heavy thump in my chest as I came down the gangway and looked for him in baggage claim at PDX. *What if he doesn't show up? What if I can't remember what he looks like? What if he doesn't like what he sees? What if…*

My doubts were cut short as he called out my name. "Hey! Hello! Over here! It's so great to see you," he said as he gathered me into a big warm hug. He looked even better than I remembered—his hair was lightened from being in the sun, he was no longer wearing winter clothes from head to toe, but was now in his old Birkenstocks that I began calling his Jesus shoes, a pair of shorts, and an old blue denim shirt. He wore a tiny gold hoop in his left ear that I hadn't even noticed before and had cut his ponytail into a cute surfer boy haircut. Without saying a word, we grinned at each other. He grabbed my hand as if we had been dating for months and walked me straight to his VW van and off we went to his studio apartment on Queen Anne hill. *Thank God he feels the same way*, I thought as my face began to hurt from smiling so much.

"These are my plants I've been growing lately. Check it out; I've been tracking its progress over the past two months," he explained as we stood before his window sill staring at a tiny pot of green buds. He took a hit from his bong and walked into the kitchen, reaching into the tiny freezer section of his fridge for the Chunky Monkey ice cream. He was a pot smoker and, at the time, it just added to the aura of his intrigue—brilliant, fun, and a little bit of a bad boy. I thought he was perfect.

The next morning, we got on the plane and headed to Cabo San Lucas. After a week of playing on the beach, drinking at all the college student-focused bars that shot tequila through giant flasks into the open mouths of inebriated Spring Breakers, and wallowing in a stomach bug, we decided that we were going to get married. I had discovered an impulsive side of myself through love.

"Hey! Where have you been? I've been calling the office at the Center for days now. Why didn't you call me back? I was so worried. I can't understand why you wouldn't call me back!"

My father's tone was extremely angry and I immediately felt ashamed for my lack of respect for him. I knew that I had purposefully kept him in the dark about my recent trip to Mexico because what good Korean daughter plans a trip to Mexico with a man, knowing full well that she's going to be sharing his bed? I knew I had to come clean.

"Dad, I met someone. I'm so sorry that I didn't call you. I went on a trip to Mexico," I confessed.

As soon as I heard my father's exasperated sigh which would inevitably be followed by a "You did what?!," I interjected with what I knew would be a calming salve and tonic.

"His name is Chris, and I met him through a classmate, and he's going to be a lawyer."

I could feel my father's anger shift a little on the phone. "He's a Harvard law student?" he asked.

"No, he's going to go to law school in Los Angeles and probably going to be corporate lawyer." I didn't really know what that meant, but my father did and that seemed to appease his disappointment that I would get on a plane for a week to another country and not even tell him. "Honey, she went to Mexico and met a lawyer," I could hear my father say as I imagined him covering up the phone and turning his head to tell his new wife. I knew that the law school detail would be the thing that would appease my father, since running to Mexico with a lawyer instead of a musician, or with someone without a plan (as he liked to refer to Charles, my boyfriend from college), was a far more rational and appropriate choice.

Chris and I were married a year and a half later in a country club in Long Island in front of a sea of black-haired Korean guests—most of them friends and family on my side, and a small contingent of blond and brunette family and friends of his. While most of that day was an absolute blur, what I do remember is walking down the aisle with my father, shaking as I looked up from my veil, and wondering why on earth my fiancé was wearing his old glasses instead of his contact lenses. I later learned that he was so hungover from the night before that he had dropped his contact lenses down the bathroom sink before heading over to the wedding. It was a small, but significant, sign of things to come.

After heading back to Cambridge to pack up my apartment, we flew to Los Angeles to share our first home together, an apartment in South Pasadena where I would soon learn that it was not okay to disturb him at all while he studied and that in order for him to thrive academically in school, I would have to make myself silent until he was ready to socialize and drink with our friends. It simply didn't occur to me at the time that the heavy drinking in law school would eventually become one of the biggest problems in our marriage. I was naïve to think that it was just a passing phase and that when we got on with our lives as a professional couple and as parents, he'd simply grow out of this heavy partying stage. Instead, the partying remained; I eventually resigned myself to it and convinced myself that it was as normal as he was trying to tell me and that, besides, it wouldn't last forever. But that transformation never came. Instead, we spent three years living in Los Angeles while he finished law school and I became an assistant dean at a Buddhist college, and then an executive director for a Korean American museum, and finally a researcher at his university so that he could obtain tuition benefits. All the while, I also managed to finish my qualifying exams at Harvard for the Ph.D. and completed my dissertation research. Los Angeles and our loft apartment just south of Griffith Park became home for me and I was devastated when forced to leave this newly-adopted city after Chris was offered a position in Seattle. I was desperate to remain in Los Angeles after making the move from Cambridge just three years earlier, but Chris reminded me daily that I had made some sort of agreement when we got engaged that I would move to Seattle no matter what. Memory can be an elusive thing; I still can't remember ever having agreed to uproot my life once again.

What I do remember is the familiar feeling welling up in my chest of acquiescence to something that I did not want. After weeks of arguing back and forth and even threatening to remain in Los Angeles while he moved north, I finally gave in and packed my bags. Chris had an unmovable one-track mind and wouldn't accept any diversion from his plan to return home; if I chose to remain in Los Angeles, the marriage would be over. Although I had secretly thought about the benefits of that decision, I quickly swallowed the fantasy and drove up to Seattle a few months later.

He did eventually become an attorney after we moved to Seattle where he secured a position and I eventually became a professor. But over time, as we settled into our married life, respective careers, and life as new parents, Chris became less and less available. The intense love that I once felt slowly dimmed, and the tension between us grew.

After moving up to Seattle for his job, I was immediately preoccupied with finishing my dissertation, adjusting to my pregnancy and growing the little being that became our first child. My body was changing—pregnancy was doing its job rounding me out, swelling my breasts and giving a little baby bump that I happily carried around for a walk every day between writing sessions. It was September and I had just short of nine months to write my dissertation. Once the baby was born, there would be no time for writing. So each day of my pregnancy I'd write early in the morning for a few hours and then, after a satisfying session of putting words to paper, I'd take my hour-long walk in Seattle, my new home, and wind my way back home to our tiny little apartment where I would spend a good forty minutes preparing my daily veggie burger. I'd eat the thing in about five minutes, hit the books, and do my research until Chris came home late in the day from his new job at the office.

Pregnancy offered me a respite from the constant vigilance I had maintained over gaining weight for most of my adulthood. I had internalized the belief that I had the potential to gain weight at any given moment and still felt the shame that came a few years earlier when I had asked Chris the one thing any woman should know better than to ask—"Do I look like I've put on weight?"

He didn't skip a beat and responded quickly with what any man should know better than to tell a woman—"Well, your ass does look a little bigger."

As soon as I heard those words, tears sprang to my eyes and I went silent. I had failed at disciplining my body and had done the unthinkable—I had gained weight. I suddenly felt disgusting, unworthy, and like a failure. It didn't matter to me that I was smart and successful; I had crossed over a line that I drew for myself and had lost control. And there was visible proof of my failure—a fat ass. It took a few weeks to recover from that mental blow as I brutalized myself with thoughts of my failure, my weakness, and my unattractiveness. It had never occurred to me that my body was fine as it was and that it was perhaps my husband's insensitive response that was the problem.

Be that as it may, pregnancy meant that I could hold my body to a different standard—a maternal standard that suggested I gain about 25 to 30 pounds for a healthy pregnancy. Just a few months earlier I had experienced a miscarriage early into the pregnancy and I was terrified that I wouldn't carry this baby to term. So for the first time in my life, I knew it was imperative for me to nurture my body. And I knew that I would comply because it was for the sake of my baby. My baby would need good food and some extra nourishment which only I could provide. My belly would expand not because I had failed at disciplining it, but because I had finally learned to let go of my anxiety of gaining weight. In this case, the failure to gain weight would be the problem, and I was not willing to do anything that could jeopardize the health of my child.

As my body expanded, I learned how to turn the volume down on the negative voice in my head that might whisper fear-inducing thoughts of becoming that mother who gained weight but couldn't shake it once the baby was born. I learned how to halt the voice that told me I would no longer be attractive because my belly had expanded up to the point in my ninth month that I could no longer see my toes. It was as if I intuitively knew that when it came to being a mother, the needs of the baby would always come first, even before the criticizing internal voice which liked to tell me that having a thin and perfect body was always the most important part of me. I hadn't realized that the concept of the thin and perfect body was simply a fictional storyline that I had breathed into myself as a reality. Growing a healthy baby inside my body gave lie to that myth and allowed me to embrace and appreciate the fact that my body could expand to hold a child.

We didn't see much of each other that year, since he always seemed to be in the office. The height of our virtual separation and my increasing isolation came when he was at work and I woke to a startling wetness seeping beneath me onto the bed. "Come quick! I think my water broke, I think I'm going to have the baby!" I blurted out rapidly into the phone. "When can you get here?" I assumed he would jump into his car and pick me up to take me to the hospital. After all, isn't that how it was supposed to be done?

There was brief pause on the phone followed by the words that would mark the rest of my marriage and parenting, "Look, I can't leave twork now. Why don't you drive yourself to the hospital and I'll meet you there when I can, okay?"

"What are you talking about? I'm having a baby and I can't take myself to the hospital on my own," I shouted in a panic.

His voice went steely and in a measured clip he replied, "No one else can take my place. I can't leave work. I will see you later." There was no changing his mind.

He locked into a decision and no one, not even his about-to-give-birth wife, was going to alter his plans. To this day, I look back on that incident as one of the most revealing and emblematic symbols of Chris—he was exceedingly driven in his professional life and singularly focused on success, so much so that he was willing to put off witnessing the birth of his first child and leave me alone to give birth until he was done with his shift. In many ways, I could see how much of his mother's hard determination he had inherited; she too was an attorney, and when she dug her heels in, there was no wiggle room and little concern over the impact of these decisions on those around her. While I had loved his fierce determination and ability to get things done, I had not expected this trait also to dictate how he would respond to the birth of his first child.

Throughout our marriage, Chris often referred proudly back to his heroics in the office during his first year, as a sign of his dedication to his job—after all, "who else was going to do it? I couldn't just leave!" While I saw this unwillingness to find a substitute so he could join me in the birthing room as abandonment and a source of great embarrassment, I am still not sure that he has changed his views on this decision at all—not even after being told explicitly by the marriage counselor we visited twice that he should have been there. To his credit though, he did take off time to come to the hospital to witness the birth of our second daughter two and a half years later. However, all this was to come later. Right now, I was having a baby.

We hadn't been living in Seattle very long and I didn't know anyone else I could call. There was no other option in my mind. I was going to have to drive myself to the hospital. I had become so used to taking care of myself on my own at this point, that I didn't even think to call a cab. I was humiliated as I picked up my carefully-packed suitcase and closed the door to the apartment. I drove myself to the emergency room parking and hobbled into the ER exclaiming to the late-night check-in clerk, "I think I'm having a baby."

By this time, my body had grown heavy with fatigue and I was looking forward to getting my baby out of my body, for she had begun to rest on my diaphragm and bladder, and the mere act of walking was becoming exhausting and would send my heart racing. She needed to be out, and since I had already finished, submitted, successfully defended my dissertation a month before, and landed a tenure-track job, I was ready.

With a red-hot face, I answered the nurse's questions about who was going to meet me at the hospital, and since I hadn't heard back from Chris, I phoned my mother-in-law who in a very similar manner replied, "I'm on vacation, but I'll see you in a few days. I can't wait."

At that moment, I began to doubt why on earth I was having a baby with a man who wouldn't leave work for his first child and wife in labor, and how I could have a mother-in-law who would choose vacationing in her beach home a mere two hours away rather than awaiting the arrival of her first grandchild in person.

"Okay, see you then, I guess," I said as I quickly hung up the phone. By this time, my body began to writhe in pain as the labor had begun in earnest. The nurses had checked my blood earlier and I had tested positive for a common bacteria, Group Strep B in the womb, so I needed to take Pitocin to speed up the process.

Hours later, Chris strolled into my delivery room and the first thing he said was, "Wow, that was such an intense night. I haven't even slept yet."

Shut up. Who the hell doesn't bother to come to his wife's side when she is giving birth? I muttered silently in between excruciating labor pangs that felt like someone was taking a sledgehammer to my tailbone. After a good seven hours of un-medicated, grueling pain the likes of which I had never before imagined, I gave birth to Hannah, my beautiful golden-haired girl that the nurses began calling "Blondie." She was the most amazing creature I had ever seen, and I couldn't believe that I could create something so exquisite and delicate. When they put her into my arms, I held her up to my face, sniffed her hair, looked into her seal-gray eyes and told her, "Welcome to the world, sweetheart." Chris was there, too, and as he looked at the baby, I could see tears well up in his eyes.

I was delirious from lack of sleep and worried that somehow my baby wouldn't make it through the night, but we both did, and two days later, I was packed up and ready to bring her home and start my new life as a mother. My body was exhausted, but I was so proud of it for giving birth to a healthy baby and proud of myself for allowing myself to eat whatever I needed during the pregnancy. And here was the proof that I had done well. Hannah was a good 6 pounds 13 ounces at birth with a healthy little body. *She doesn't look anything like those scrawny babies that look like old men or baby chickens*, I thought proudly. She has a delightful little round body and I had made her. For the first time in my life, my body had grown beyond itself with the progress of the pregnancy and had even developed a few stretch marks, but I didn't care. I had become a mother, a vessel to carry this baby from conception to birth and she was perfect. Therefore, my body must have been okay too.

Like most new mothers discover, breastfeeding can be a challenging experience when the baby won't latch on or when the milk doesn't come in right away. My body, though, seemed to betray me and it was a betrayal that to this day, perhaps unfairly, I attribute to my mother-in-law. A day after returning home from the hospital, I opened the door in a complete brain-slowing exhaustion. Hannah was trying to nurse every hour and my milk hadn't yet come in. Carol came into the house carrying a giant watermelon and a six-pack of beer.

"You need the watermelon for fluid. Chris, here's some beer for you. You'll need it as a new father." She then took Hannah from my hands, cradled her, and offered, "Why don't you take a nap, you should always rest when you can."

I took Carol's advice because after all, she had given birth and raised four children. A few hours later, I woke from a delicious nap only to find Hannah sucking away at a bottle of water. "What are you doing? She needs to nurse from me so that she can get the milk. She's not supposed to have a bottle!"

I was panicking because I knew that my milk would only come in with constant nursing. "Chris, what's in that bottle? Why are you feeding her water? She needs my milk," I whispered severely.

"Oh, I gave her a bottle of sugar water. She was obviously hungry and that's the only way she'd stop crying," Carol chimed in.

My mouth dropped open and I was shocked into silence. I was betrayed in my sleep—someone else had taken over my essential job of feeding my own baby.

"Oh yeah, she also drank from that bottle of formula that the nurses sent home," beamed Chris.

It felt as if they had both conspired to take away my right to feed the baby from my own body even though it might take a day or two longer for my milk to come in, and it had been done all in the hopes of keeping Hannah quiet. There was nothing that I could do other than grab Hannah and cast aside what had become the evil replacement nipple and put her back onto my own breast to suckle. Hannah was refusing, however, to work so hard at something that came so easily from a bottle.

Chris and his mother tried to convince me not to be so stubborn because my baby must have been suffering. Giving in, I let them feed her the rest of the formula while my milk failed to come in fully. The body that I had so lovingly cared for from conception to birth, the body that I had grown to love despite its weight gain and lack of muscle tone, had suddenly failed me, leaving me thrice betrayed by my husband, my mother-in-law, and my very own breasts. Betrayal usually leads to a desire for some kind of revenge and while I knew that I couldn't push back against my mother-in-law or blame her outright for circumventing my natural parenting plans, I eventually focused my revenge on my usual object of negative fancy—my body. It had given birth and suddenly I felt that it needed to be the best fit mother body that it could possibly be. I was also worried that if I didn't lose the baby weight quickly I would somehow dematerialize into invisibility—I would be subsumed under the category of mother with a misshapen body that had failed to bounce back.

It was the early 2000s, and Hollywood had begun to valorize the celebrity mother, actresses who married, gave birth, and carried their babies around with them like the newest Louis Vuitton bag. While the babies clung to their milk-engorged breasts in all the celebrity magazines in the grocery stores, it also became *de rigeur* for actresses to show off their maternity-defying abs and tight bodies. In other words, only the mothers with beautiful bodies, who made it seem as if they had never been pregnant but for their telltale breasts spilling dangerously out of the halter tops, were worthy of being seen. Mothers with ordinary post-partum bellies that did not miraculously firm up and whose biceps did not bulge with mini-muscles whenever they picked up their perfect little children were basically told that they were not worthy of being looked at. They had failed because they made babies but did not look after their bodies. "Oh my goodness, you have a beautiful baby. You don't even look like you had a baby," became the common refrain for those mothers deemed successes, and I felt like I was supposed to be one of those mothers too. After all, it was also at this time that the message of feminism was co-opted into the false claim that we women could have it all—fulfilling careers, successful marriages, beautiful children, and now, beautiful bodies.

Our bodies were now seen to be progressive because even though they made babies, they could also be disciplined into making it seem like we didn't have grueling schedules, work-life imbalance, demanding kids, and sagging bellies and breasts from nine months of gestation and childbirth. Everything on our bodies was supposed to be tight, but it seemed to me that what was most tight on me was the smile on my face whenever any-one would tell me that I didn't look like I had just given birth and that they didn't know how I could do it all. I was doing it all, and I shouldn't have had to—my feminism had failed me because rather than giving me all kinds of opportunities, I learned that there were limits to what I could achieve. Once I had the career, the husband, and the baby, I also ended up with the additional burden of trying to have a body that didn't look like it gave birth and pretending that I had a great marriage where family respon-sibilities were shared, when I quickly learned that I alone was responsible for the baby, the house and our meals—along with my demanding career. My upbringing had taught me to look good at all costs and never to ap-pear as if there were any problems, so while I was struggling as a working mother with an overly-preoccupied spouse, I made sure to always keep up appearances—including magically looking like I had never given birth. Unscathed, unmarred, untarnished motherhood is simply an oxymoron and I knew that it would take some form of magic or excess to look like I was managing magnificently as an intelligent, successful mother. The only magic potion I knew was also my poison—the desire to be thin and over-work my body. I knew it was counter to all my feminist beliefs, I knew it was more than I could handle, but I was ready to take it on anyway.

Running to Empty

RUNNING LONG DISTANCES became a way to conveniently keep myself thin while eating most of what I wanted. I knew could never stop eating, but I believed that I had to stay thin—without repeating my mother's anorexia and bulimia. So I took up running—not short spurts of a few miles, but long runs that have topped twenty-some miles in training and a number of marathons. It is common knowledge that running burns about 100 calories per mile. By running, I could continue to eat whatever I wanted without gaining any weight. I have run several races, qualifying for the Boston Marathon with almost every marathon I've run. I've placed in the top ten in my age group and won small awards in the local Seattle Marathon twice and the See Jane Run half marathon a few times. Because I was running quickly and placing in events here and there, it seemed that no one could ever give me a hard time about running so many miles and looking thin. It seemed to me that if I looked a little thin, I could quickly reply that it was because of the marathoning and since I was running so fast, I couldn't be suspected of over-exercise. At the same time, running was not just a way to keep my body thin, it became my solace, my meditation practice, and an opportunity to push my body beyond what I thought it could do.

Currently, however, I have had to set aside my running shoes because I have pushed myself too hard through the miles I've collected under my feet over the past ten years and, as my doctor recently remarked, "You've blown out your immune system. It might be time for a break." These words of advice came to me after twisting my ankle so severely that after a year of recovery I still have trouble balancing on my right foot without shaking like a leaf in the wind in my yoga class.

I once even ran twenty miles on my treadmill. There I said it. Most of the time, I keep that little fact a secret from folks who might think that I am a little obsessed with running, which I was. I ran so far and was in such a trance that I didn't realize that the machine automatically shut down at ten miles. I was zoning out as I pounded my legs on the belt mile after mile listening to one of the few books on CD, by Anita Shreve, that I found at the library, *Fortune's Rocks*, about a young girl falling in love with a far older man along the seaside in Maine. I was in for the long haul and knew that I would need something to occupy my mind while I trained my body to get used to running long distances. The Seattle Marathon was just a month away and I had been disciplining my body to get ready to run 26.2 miles for the first time, about 11 years ago when my girls were two-and-a-half and five years old. Running become a way to escape the stresses of raising kids and working full time, but it was also a way of trying to discipline my body into being fit and thin after giving birth twice.

But running is no longer my meditation, as it once was. I would often put on my running shoes to discipline my body for strength and endurance, which was also a way for me to gain and hone a mental endurance and ease. It worked for a while. I needed these skills to get through the daily grind of work, raising kids, and dealing with an increasingly troubled marriage.

When I ran, it was mostly just me asking my body to relax into its run, to learn to breathe and appreciate what it does and to thank my body for giving me the strength to continue on. Running was a mindfulness practice for me because it required that I remained in the present moment. I couldn't get ahead of myself by thinking of the next five miles. I couldn't dwell on the previous ten. I needed to remain where I was in the process and breathe into my body, my hard-working body that gave what it could when I asked of it. Surely it deserved to be treated well and offered nourishing substances to keep it healthy and strong.

"Why do you run so much? I don't know how you do it." Many people at work used to ask me what my reasons were for the long runs that I took and I often said wisely, "Oh, well, it calms my mind and helps me with stress," and it did for a while. My body ran along the beach and up and down the hills of West Seattle while my mind was cradled gently in my head. The constant movement of my body allowed my mind to rest for there was little work that needed to be done outside of scanning and determining how I happened to feel at that very moment. It was simply about putting one foot in front of the other and staying present to the road under my feet.

After several years of running long distances, entering races, and developing some mild success in my speed, however, I noticed that running started to become less of a refuge and more of a disciplinary practice, and eventually an escape from the stress of an unraveling marriage. It had gone from a source of joy to a form of numbing emotional pain. I would run so far that I was simply too tired to focus on my mental suffering. But no matter how fast or how far I ran, by the time our second daughter was born I couldn't escape the truth that my marriage was making me miserable.

At first, I thought that we were no different from other long-married couples with children and jobs, but over time, Chris began to distance himself from me even more. He worked constantly, leaving the house right after his breakfast, and even when he wasn't working on the weekends, he started spending more time with his friends, eventually shutting me out altogether. What I did not know, but would later learn, was that he had been seeking relief outside the marriage since the beginning. What I did know was that he was always working and he had retreated into drinking to numb the stress, and our marriage slowly dissolved.

When he did come straight home from work, he would immediately change his clothes, grab a beer, and head to the backyard to garden or talk on the phone. He no longer dazzled me with his intellect, nor excited me with his enthusiasm and humor. We had run out of things to talk about and whenever he did talk to me, it seemed as if I was just an object for him to dump his day's struggles onto. I had by this time also withdrawn into the familiar patterned chaos of being a mother with a job outside the home. Trying to balance teaching, writing, and raising kids seemed not only to be inevitable but also seemed to be my way of checking out of the relationship emotionally. I was simply too busy to attend to the relationship, which in retrospect seems not so unique, and something that I had chosen rather than a simple matter of circumstances.

Then one evening when I was in Chicago for a conference, I thought my luck might change for the better. Chris had randomly texted me at night declaring, "I am quitting drinking. I have already told the girls that I am not going to drink again. I also told my friends." Although a part of me was shocked and angered that he had told my girls, thus acknowledging to them that he had a drinking problem, I was also relieved.

When I returned, I suggested therapy and AA but was immediately met with a teeth-gritting, "I don't need anyone else's help. I am going to do this on my own." He was accustomed to being in charge, and thought he could kick it on his own and bare-knuckle his way through sobriety. I wasn't so sure.

My fears turned out to be well founded. Although Chris did quit for a while, it wasn't long before he secretly returned to drinking. The discovery came when he'd had a particularly angry outburst with one of our daughters, which he completely forgot about the following morning. When it dawned on me that he'd blacked out the entire event, I confronted him, and he admitted he'd been drinking again, as casually as if he'd admitted he'd returned to drinking coffee. He'd might as well have said, "Yeah, so what? What are you going to do about it?"

In that moment, tears began to fill my eyes because it became clear to me that he had been lying to me when the truth was he was just drinking on the sly. This discovery made even more sense to me when I tried to figure out the extra-high receipt from a downtown bar that I found crumpled up on the desk in the basement. It was for a bar that I hadn't heard of so I looked it up on the internet, only to find that it was a hotel bar in Seattle. "Chris, do you know what this receipt is for? It's for $165 at a bar downtown," I had asked. I foolishly thought that maybe someone had gotten hold of his credit card and used it.

"Oh, that? That was just from lunch," he casually explained.

"But," I began, confused. "Who spends that much money for lunch? Were you by yourself?"

He shifted his eyes and looked back again, "Well, I guess it was just an expensive lunch."

The lies began to fall into place for me as I realized he had been fooling me about the drinking for some time, and I felt stupid for assuming his bad moods were due to sobering up when in fact he had been partying up. I also foolishly assumed that the receipt might have been due to his buying rounds of drinks for friends; it didn't occur to me that there was most likely another person sharing his lunch with him and it certainly wasn't me. I was red in the face and humiliated that I was the last to know that my husband was back to drinking. Rather than express my anger at him, I did what I usually did when in stress—I kept quiet and went for a very long run.

I was not just angry about the secrecy and lack of intimacy that had come to characterize our marriage. I was also beginning to worry about the effects a bad marriage and his drinking were having on our children. I felt as if my life was spinning out of control and I desperately needed to control it. So I decided I was going to discipline myself even more through my diet by controlling what I ate—I became a raw vegan and did away with eating bread, rice, and other cooked forms of carbohydrates, and basically lived on fruit, vegetables, and raw seeds. I bought a fancy juicer and a food dehydrator, and made smoothies thinking that I had somehow honed in on some new plan of making myself healthier by limiting supposedly unhealthy foods.

The side benefit, or perhaps the root motivation, for all this excessive raw food eating was that I began to watch my weight quickly drop. Each day I'd wake up at 5 am, drink my coffee, and head onto the treadmill to run ten miles before I would make myself a green smoothie that I would blend in the new fancy blender. My life resembled a factory line where I would wake, run, feed my kids, sort of feed myself, head to work, teach, return home to pick up my kids, feed them, drive them to their after-school activities and once again feed myself some raw vegetable concoction. Like my mother, I was practically starving myself, but pretending that it was for my health. Perhaps I thought that if I got thin enough, my husband would at least start to put my desires and needs first, but things often do not turn out the way we want.

What did happen, however, was that the more weight I lost, the better I felt about myself because I could finally see the contours of some muscles in my abs and, cliché though its sounds, while all else was falling apart in the marriage, at least I could control my weight and feel good about myself. I had grown tired of taking care of everything in the house on my end, suppressing the fact that I had considered myself a feminist, and pretending that I had a great marriage. In reality, I was taking care of the kids by myself while dealing with a man who put his job, his friends, and his partying over us. I had been at my wits end but didn't feel like I had any options, so I controlled my body—because I could.

As I obsessively controlled my body, my confidence helped me to clarify what I wanted for my life. I was tired by Chris's ritual practice of swinging by the local wine shop after work for a tasting and sneaking in not bottles, but cases of wine. In classic alcoholic fashion, I had caught him hiding bottles of wine under the old paint cans in the garage and when I confronted him on it, he'd shrugged his shoulders and said, "Yeah, so what?" When I saw him sneaking a case of wine in through the side door of the garage, he looked at me and lied right through his teeth, "It's easier to move things through the garage this way than to open the garage." We had an electric garage door.

It became clear that I had become a "so what" in his eyes and I no longer wanted to pretend that everything was fine in our marriage when it wasn't. I was tired of literally running away from my problems and controlling my diet, and decided to take control of my happiness and my daughters' well-being instead. I worried what would happen to my children and how I could support myself over the next decade or so, but I had at last decided that I wanted to be happy.

Finally, seventeen years into our marriage, I had simply had enough. He had stayed out all night again until he passed out at a friend's house. I had spent the night calling, texting, wondering if he'd gotten into an accident, only to find a much-later message from his friend that he had passed out reading a bedtime story to someone else's child. Without acknowledging my anger, I slipped on my running shoes and headed out for a two-hour run with my girlfriend and finally whispered to her, "I think I'm going to leave my husband."

We did eventually separate and divorce, and Chris moved around the corner to a house a few blocks away. Despite the inevitable upheaval that divorce brings, and the grief, and doubts about whether or not I had made the right decision, we each seemed to make our way slowly through the detritus of a marriage gone awry. The first step for me was to take a seat.

Finding the Cushion

As an Asian American woman who has studied Buddhism for over 30 years, I have been a late-comer to the actual practice of meditation. Much of this reluctance came from the simple fact that sitting still didn't suit my natural propensity for movement. Why sit still when I could run? Besides, how could I sit still when I had exams to grade, dishes to do, kids to raise, and laundry to fold? Time seemed a luxury that I couldn't really budget for.

If I did find the time and wanted to meditate, however, I could not always find the place. I'd visit a meditation center in the city from time to time, where I'd find that I was usually one of the only women of color present. I'd also discover that most of the Asian American Buddhist temples that I visited didn't include a lot of meditation; most of the practices were devotional in nature and meditation seemed an afterthought.

In retrospect, I seemed to have forgotten that meditation or deep looking into the nature of one's mind, heart, and body did not have to take an entire hour or two every morning, but I still admired the monastic life for its simplicity.

"As a monk, I only have to wear one outfit for all occasions. I never open the closet and sit there scratching my head—What do I wear for a wedding? What should I wear for a funeral? For a pilgrimage? I just wear the same thing each day," my friend who is a Thai monk explained. "Also, I never have to worry if I gain any weight because the robes are so loose no one will notice," he added smiling as he pointed to his own round belly. Ah, to be a man with a single robe and not a care about what his body looked like.

Aside from dressing in one robe each day for simplicity's sake, the seemingly endless cycles of walking, sitting, and walking that Japanese monks and nuns do for upwards of seventeen hours a day during the special winter season session neither appealed to me nor seemed possible. There's a reason monks and nuns have no kids to drive to and from after-school activities and no daily jobs outside the temples! Without worrying about where their next meal will come from or if they are having a bad hair day since they shaved their heads, monks and nuns have a lifestyle maximized for silent contemplation.

But not me. I may have dreamed once or twice about how nice it would be not to worry about what I look like, and how great it would be to have but a few requisites for daily life (robes, food, medicine, and lodging plus a single alms bowl and a few razors), that lifestyle was just not in my karma. Instead, my interest in a Buddhist life was first framed around my intellectual life, and it was only in the past few years that I decided to give the meditation practice a serious effort. Part of the reason for this transition is simply that I had to divest myself of the misperception that meditation has to last for hours on end and include only sitting or walking ever so slowly. I attribute this realization to the one time I sat on a panel discussion on Buddhism and feminism with the feminist author bell hooks and she reminded me in her syrupy sweet, soothing but powerful voice, "Now look, you only need two minutes to meditate. That's all that matters; who says you have to sit for hours on end? That's it—just two."

When the foremost African American feminist scholar, public intellectual, *and* Buddhist practitioner tells you that you only need two minutes, then indeed two minutes is enough of a starting point. Through baby steps that included a short meditation session in the morning and a few at night, to eventually longer sits, I have come to see that the practice of developing awareness can begin on one's cushion but then extend to the ordinary phases of the day. In other words, there is more to meditation than simply sitting on one's ass; the point is to expand the awareness that comes from observing the nature of the mind and the stories it tells about us that are not based on reality. "You shouldn't have eaten that. Those pants are too tight. Why didn't you drink a smoothie instead of eat that box of chocolate? You have no self-control." Recognizing that these stories are fictions and not facts can be transforming. When we do so, we suffer a little less and create a little less suffering for others.

"In what ways are we conditioned to think the way we do about ourselves? Why and how do we see ourselves in the ways that we do, and in what ways have we managed to substitute external eyes or the external gaze for our own?" asks Sharon Salzburg, one of the most famous visiting insight meditation teachers. She was in Seattle for one of her annual Buddhist talks and workshops on meditation, and since she is so personable and down to earth, I was ready to spend the day meditating and chewing on some Buddhist food for thought with her. As I sat on my cushion at the front of the room, I thought about the all-powerful gaze that culture and media place upon our bodies, and wondered why it is that we invest so much more veracity in the external gaze or labels placed on our bodies, without subjecting that skewed gaze to too much questioning. In other words, why do we simply absorb that which is said about us without ever really questioning why the words are spoken?

After all, the Buddha encouraged his disciples to consider the ways they spoke to one another and how to cultivate right speech—he even gave discourses about the five conditions that were supposed to be met *before* saying anything. Do I speak at the right time? Do I speak facts? Do I speak gently or harshly? Do I speak beneficial words? Do I speak with a kindly heart or am I malicious in the ways I speak? In other words, as the Buddha taught, think before you speak to others, but it also seemed to me that we should also question before we take what we hear and turn it into some kind of truism about ourselves. Couldn't it be the case that the things people say about us and the labels placed upon our bodies are things said that we don't actually have to connect to and then absorb into our senses of self? I sat observing these thoughts and the sensations of my body as my legs began to tingle from sitting cross-legged on the floor. I began to examine how I constantly assess myself and make sense of who, why, what, and how I am, in light of social constructions of identity, cultural constructions of identity, familial constructions of identity, and the individual ego's constructions of identity. Yet all these labels are simply labels, words, judgments, and ideas proliferating external to me; whoever said that I had to cling to them and make them my own?

As with many religions, the female body has often been a source of both desire and anxiety for monks because they take a vow of celibacy. Many ancient Indian Buddhist texts therefore do not have very favorable things to say about women's bodies. But they also don't have that much to say about learning how to appreciate our bodies in general, regardless of our sex and gender. There has been so much important and significant attention spent on developing awareness of the body and all the sensations in the body and whether or not we overlay feeling tones on top of them. However, much of the discussion of the body in Buddhist texts has either been about how monks should avoid women's bodies, or how bodies in general are often seen as impure, or the body has been seen in a neutral (almost scientific) way. There hasn't been a lot of discussion of embodiment and learning how to tune in to, inhabit, feel, and appreciate our bodies. If society doesn't see us, if religion doesn't see us, and culture doesn't see us as we are, then who and what will? And why is it that we seem to cling to the negative comments that detract from our positive sense of self rather than those that inspire confidence?

It has been twenty-five years since my mother died and it is only now, nearly half of my life later, that I have begun to rewrite the narrative that she passed onto me. The stories she told me about my ugliness, about not being attractive enough to watch television with her, and not being worthy of her gentleness and emotional care, all rendered me a silent, passive, and guarded young girl who became a young woman, and eventually a mother of two teenaged girls, who now knows deeply impact that words, criticisms, and labels can have on a child's self-esteem. I have learned to practice what the Buddha referred to as "right speech," which is to refrain from saying that which will knowingly cause harm and to cultivate speech that is honest but gentle. I knew that my mother must have internalized many of the social pressures and cultural ideals of being a Korean woman and she passed that troubling inheritance on me. I had a choice, though, because I could see through meditation that I had the capacity to cut the strangling thread of her—and eventually my own—storylines and begin to rewrite the narrative for myself and for my daughters.

They have enough struggles being young women in America today where their identities are continually constructed through social media that both exhibits and makes spectacles out of female bodies for public consumption. The daily onslaught of idealized and unrealistic images of female bodies come to them each morning on their Instagram accounts which send them daily notifications that they should look like some airbrushed celebrity. They are tirelessly told that they should look like these beautified images of the ideal face and body and are compelled like all of us to compare how their own images reflect these unrealistic standards. As their mother, I have both the experience and the responsibility to help them see what has taken me decades to absorb—the stories and images that others project about who we are and what we should be are not an accurate reflection of who and what we are. They are but external phenomena conjured by a society, a culture, and its inhabitants, to try to label us and determine our value based on our physical bodies. These standards of beauty are not necessarily or inherently bad, but they are a powerful gaze that can shake us at our core if we don't see that they are images, labels, and thoughts imposed on our bodies from the outside.

The practice of meditation has offered me an opportunity to unpeel layers of internalized self-hate, for when I sat in quiet contemplation, I could begin to see that I had negative feelings about myself that were not based in any actual reality. By sitting and feeling my body at rest and rooted to the earth, I began to settle into the experience of being present in the only moment that was physically real—now. I came to see that I was not the stories of my past, nor the memories that I have of growing up in New York at the mercy of my mother's mental instability. These are things that happened to me but they cannot define who I am here and now. Similarly, I began to let go of my relentless, future-forward planning for my perfect self—a self that was always five pounds thinner, more toned, more this, less that—as yet another example of false advertisement imposed externally, that I didn't have to absorb and cling to. Sitting still in the present moment, I could see that it was possible to live in this very moment, in this very body, and somehow let go of the stories of the past that told me I wasn't good enough and those of the future that tell me that I could be better than I am now. Those powerful stories are but narrative overlays onto this body of mine that exists only in this present moment. It did not have to be beholden to the past or the future. It could be anchored in the present and I could see myself through my own eyes and my own internal gaze rather than constantly react to the negative messages that my culture and my mother tried to send me.

Through the act of sitting, which was no simple feat because I was basically stuck handling the contents of my own mind, I realized that I was not whom she said I was and that I could override the power of her silence with my own powerful voice.

"As the Buddha taught, we are always shaped by others in a seamless play of mutuality; in other words, we do not and simply cannot exist alone or in isolation. Our lives depend on all other beings," continues the guest teacher. The meditation hall was filled to capacity with all sorts of older, white meditators and while I was feeling awkward since there were only a few people of color, I took my meditation cushion and sat in the front row so that I could listen to one of the most popular teachers of everyday practice. As I sat with my eyes closed, she remarked, "It makes very good sense for us to observe how it is that we come to see ourselves, so that we can see what the add-ons are and in what ways we might cling to what it is that we find not good enough or what could be better."

Once again, a Buddhist teacher and relative stranger managed to get at the heart of my habitual tendency of determining my self-worth by virtue of how I was feeling in and about my body at any given moment. Old habits cast in childhood can calcify and narrow our field of vision, and my own gaze seemed to ever-fixate on what I was told about myself as a little girl.

"The narrative overlay of judgment, about not being good enough, or even the sentiment that 'if only I had the time, then I would…' is simply an unskillful use of time because that time will never come."

Her teaching reminded me right away of the tendency women have to suspend our happiness and self-value to some mythical time in the future when we lose five pounds or fit into our skinny jeans. How many of us chase these chimera and magical unicorns when we ought to know better?

"These narrative overlays are but fantasies that draw us away from accepting ourselves as and where we are in this very moment of time," she continued as she surveyed the rapt audience with her twinkling eyes— she seemed so convincing precisely because she seemed like she, too, had appended her worth to an unknown future rather than on the present moment at least once or twice.

I settled into my body during this Friday night workshop, my legs folded loosely on my cushion. I was immediately reminded of what I had just taught to my students the week before. "What we think of as the thing that will somehow make us better negates the very thing that Buddhism teaches us, which is that we are fine as we are."

My students gave me confused looks because we had been studying the seemingly endless rules that monks and nuns have to follow in order to achieve the end goal of enlightenment in Buddhism, and here was Shinran Shonin, one of the most profound lay Buddhist teachers, teaching his fellow Japanese Buddhists that there is no need to struggle for perfection for perfection is, as I continued, "simply a mental construct getting in the way of appreciating the present moment." As I sat in meditation at the Insight Meditation Society recalling this lecture, I laughed at how easy it was to teach something and still not practice it.

Boy, the more things change, the more they stay the same. Did Japanese people in the 12th century suffer from the same struggles with their bodies as we do today? my mind mused as it sat cross-legged at the feet of this warm and funny meditation teacher.

This maturing body of mine is the only one there is. Why not inhabit it now and appreciate it now rather than trying to make it better? I asked myself as I sat. I began to make the connection that by allowing external forces like social media and women's magazines to dominate my thinking, I was being tempted in the same way as the Buddha who was visited by Mara's beautiful daughters (Mara is the Buddhist demon of delusion) who personified greed, hatred, and delusion. External labels and illusory ideals have certainly tempted me to go down that rabbit hole of somehow not being good enough. In the Buddha's life story, Mara's daughters use their beautiful and charming bodies to try to sway the Buddha from his path to enlightenment by testing his resolve. Perhaps like the Buddha I can learn to use the strength of my mind, my *virya*, to simply say, "No, Mara of marketing and popular culture. I will not be buying into your false advertising of what will make me happy." As I sat there with my own body starting to sway a little from exhaustion, I resolved, "I can learn to step away from culture's mirrors and see myself from an internal gaze (what the yogis called *drsti*)." I then made a mental note to teach my students that if the Buddha encouraged us to carefully look at ourselves and see who we really are, then I believe that we are capable of looking beyond the social gaze and seeing ourselves with our own eyes.

This body is all I have. Why not inhabit it now and ease up on the inner critic rather than trying to make it perfect and living for the future? I consider again as the evening wears on. I have often wondered why it is so hard to cultivate compassion for myself, especially since Buddhist tradition teaches that compassion is the crucial ingredient for ending suffering. Maybe it is because Asian cultures often tell us that self-love and self-care are selfish. There is a lot of pressure placed on us to be good daughters, sisters, mothers, aunties, and grandmothers; still, we know that in order to be truly available for others and to be able to hear their cries, we need to be willing to acknowledge our own needs. Perhaps learning to care for ourselves and nurture ourselves will allow us to dispense with the myth of self-sacrifice which often means that we elicit other people's respect for how much we are willing to harm ourselves for the sake of the other. I do not believe that this kind of self-harm is the selflessness that the Buddha had in mind because really it becomes a contest of sorts over who has given up the most.

Perhaps there is a deeper lesson in the Buddhist teaching that we do not have to detract from ourselves through excessive sacrifice to be somehow less than we are. If we are, in the language of Buddhism, "fine as we are," then why must we try to be less than we are? This means that perhaps we can say that our bodies are good as they are, we do not need to be less than we are by dieting, losing weight, over exercising. That desire to be less means that perhaps we have not thoroughly integrated the idea that we are good as we are, and lovable as we are.

When we claim that we will fix something if we have the time, we negate the gift of presence that we have. Now is the only time, the present is a gift, as Buddhists are often to say. Patriarchy, sexism, racism, all have combined historically to make it hard appreciate our bodies as they are. Hollywood, popular culture, and white supremacy have all leveled an impact on us, the likes of which we are often not even aware. We simply react and believe what external forces tell us. Instead of asking why we feel this way and looking for the root causes and conditions, we simply lament and say, "what is wrong with me?" Social distortions are the work of Mara. As a woman, why don't I love myself as deeply and as compassionately as I do others? This paradox is one that seems to pervade all corners of the world and one that meditation has been helping me to explore.

I return home that evening and gaze into the mirror as I practice some yoga postures and check my form and alignment. As I do, I remind myself that this body of mine is more a process than a "thing" that endures through time. I don't recall the Buddha ever teaching that this female body of mine is beautiful; what he taught was just the opposite—he suggested our bodies are repulsive collections of tissue, bones, blood and pus—something from which we should want to detach ourselves. I used to agree, but for different reasons. The Buddha taught that we should transcend our attachment to our bodies in order to experience liberation. Therefore, the body became an important vessel to nourish but not one to get overly hung up on. Looking on my own body in the mirror, observing the way it has softened here, hardened there, loosened in some parts, grayed in others as it evolves through time, I am reminded of the Buddhist nuns over 2500 years ago gazing at their own bodies as object lessons in impermanence.

The Buddha taught that attachment to the body can give rise to suffering because our own bodies and the bodies of the others we admire, desire, and love, will inevitably change. Men were taught to gaze upon the female corpses in cremation grounds if they were particularly lustful and encouraged to poke at the bodies with a stick to see what it is that endures and what it was that so attracted them in the first place. According to the Buddhist texts, there were some horrific and gruesome moments of deep realization, or what the Buddha referred to as that big "ah-ha" moment, when one understands the nature of impermanence and sees reality as it is.

Nuns were never exhorted to stare at male corpses to uproot their sexual desire; instead, they were taught to look upon their own bodies and in the passing of time etched into their bodies, they were to have direct and immediate insight into the nature of the reality as ever changing.

I have done the same thing but perhaps for a different purpose. My observations in the mirror are probably no different from most of those nuns and even most other women today as we learn to deconstruct our bodies into their component parts and then judge each part as too thin, too fat, too wobbly, too bony. The difference, though, is that I am no longer interested in observing myself as a composite of pieces presented for judgment by myself, and I am no longer as interested in the social gaze that is relentless in its criticisms. I am far more interested in observing my body from the inside out, so that I can develop awareness and mindfulness of how it feels in the present moment without all the external chatter.

The Buddha taught his disciples that there is ultimately no permanent self, and that we are propelled through time as an ever-changing composite, and no matter how hard we look, we won't be able to find an enduring self. As many a religious master has said, we are like rivers that constantly flow and therefore we can never step in the same river twice. Thus, we would do well not to get too attached to this fleeting body.

This lesson in impermanence has always made logical sense to me, but somehow it didn't really help me come to terms with how I felt about my body, nor did it teach me to consider how my body feels. In fact, the Buddha's teachings about observing the body can sometimes seem downright negative for someone who has struggled for years with wanting to occupy her body. In other words, I have never felt that transcending my body was a desirable goal. I have spent way too many years silenced and made invisible to ever want to let go of my desire to feel this body from the inside out. I have always been looking for a way *into* my body and appreciating it in the present moment.

I carry these thoughts with me to Karuna studio early the next morning as I unfurl my mat and prepare for class, which I have come to refer to affectionately as going to church. Carla starts to play some soft Indian devotional music and heads to the front of the class with her mala beads draped around her neck, her long gray hair flowing. She begins to speak without much fanfare.

"Yoga is about showing up and arriving on your mat. No need to look around at what anyone else is doing. There is no perfect posture, which is why we don't have mirrors in the studio. There is no such thing as perfection and when you give up that idea, then you can really find some freedom and appreciation for these beautiful bodies of yours."

I take in a full breath and try to imagine my diaphragm contract because I know that a big, full breath will help relax my body and bring my mind along for the ride. Buddhist meditation has developed my capacity for mindfulness and calming my mind, but there has been little talk about coming to appreciate and find beauty in this body of mine, and so I headed to the yoga studio. What I have found in many studios though is almost the opposite of what the Buddha taught. If the Buddha taught us to basically ignore our bodies, some forms of Western yoga have taught us that we should focus on developing beautiful, perfect bodies.

Part of the reason that I signed up for this yoga teacher certification at Karuna had to do with the realization that this practice of mindful movement offered me such respite from negative self-image and body dysmorphia that I thought I might have something to offer others who might benefit in the same way. Although I couldn't manipulate my body into the various pretzel-shaped poses or balance my whole body in a side crow posture like some of the twenty-something-year-olds next to me, I did know that yoga could be liberating for all people, no matter their age, size, and physical ability. I could feel its effects in my own life and thought that combining seated meditation and mindfulness through yoga was the next logical step in my vocation as a teacher. I wanted to begin to teach what I have benefitted so greatly from, and create spaces where women of color were no longer made invisible or even hyper-visible by virtue of their race and gender. I also wanted a practice that wasn't focused on transcending this body or criticizing it by holding up unreachable standards of yogic beauty. I wanted to live inside my body, to occupy my body, and begin to share the potential that I have found in the dual practice of meditation and yoga.

Yoga provides me the opportunity to appreciate this body and to learn how to feel this body in every move that it makes. I have come to find that for the first time in my life, I can envision my body as a safe space that I don't need to change or escape, and I can ease up a little on my life-long practice of self-discipline through excessive measures.

"Can you soften the gaze? There's no need to look so hard with your eyes when balancing. And maybe the face will soften some too. You might relax a little more into your pose that way," Lili says with a smile as she takes us into Eagle pose, the pretzel-like pose where my right leg is crossed over my left and my right arm is twisted under my left. I am in eagle pose but feel no way near as regal as an eagle. I am gripping my feet into my yoga mat hoping that through sheer force of my mind, I can grip and balance enough to not topple over.

"What's the worst thing that can happen? You wobble, you fall over. Maybe you laugh and try to get back in. It's not so bad," she adds with a gentle chuckle.

I am beginning to topple over some; my ankle is bearing a lot more weight than it can gracefully manage since I injured it a year and a half ago. People around me are swaying back and forth in all sorts of falling eagle forms and nothing bad happens—nobody judges. Not even me. So I take a few deep inhales despite the fact that I am twisted up like an asymmetrical pretzel and when I feel my ankle buckle, I do what I can to steady myself—I simply let go. I lower my right foot that has been balancing off the ground and do what once might have seemed unthinkable to me—I put that foot down so that it finds balance. My eyes have softened and I realize that my internal gaze and inner critic have softened as well. I fall a little, gently land, laugh at my desire to be perfect and realize that perfection is someone else's projection to live up to. I'd rather feel my way into my pose, and my body, not into someone else's pose and someone else's body.

I have learned in yoga that softening the gaze is really important and wonder how much benefit there can be in softening the gaze on others as well as in myself. Looking in the mirror might help me if I were to look at my spots I don't love and see them with a softer focus. But it's not with rose-tinted glasses that I wish to gaze; I want to see what is actually is there and accept where I am today. I am learning to occupy this body and to look at it from within, and what I have learned in yoga training is that the body is so much more than I thought it was.

"Yoga philosophy teaches us that we have more than this physical body, we have three—the physical, a subtle energy, and a bliss body—representing oneness with all phenomena. Through breath and posture, *prana* and *asana*, we built the foundations to access the bliss body or the experience of oneness," Carla explains as she walks around the crowded, mirrorless room.

Treat this body well because it is the way to liberation, I think as I try to keep up with all new terminology coming my way.

Focusing on the breath in yoga has been an exceptionally effective tool for me to let go of all the mental chatter and the inner critic. Rather than looking to see if the pose is in alignment, my teachers want me to feel it, but feeling into an experience is quite new to me—I have been conditioned since birth to shut down, go silent, or flee for emotional safety by battening down the hatches on my emotional life. Vulnerability and I are new-found friends, and sometimes I forget to heed its invitation. If I am indeed shaped by my past mental conditioning, then I will continue down the same path, which means I might as well stay put without movement.

But yoga teaches me to breathe into the sensation and to develop some curiosity, to begin to explore what happens if I tell my ego to let my body back off a pose or make an adjustment. If things aren't working right, it makes sense to shift, doesn't it? As on the mat, so in life. Feel, assess, and shift if it doesn't feel right. And no one else can do that for me.

Through all the miles I accumulated while discipline my body I developed gratitude for my strength, endurance and fortitude. And with yoga I learn to be with my experiences—the graceful, the wobbly, the inflexible, and the focused—and realize that I cannot savor the benefits of one without the other. I finally have some way to understand the meaning of Carla's words to us at the opening of our practice a few months ago. As she sat at the front of the yoga room, she explained, "I finally learned the importance of arriving in my body. I had worked on my mind, I worked on my spirituality, but something was missing. Once I started my yoga practice, I realized that that was the missing piece. I needed to be in my body. I hadn't really paid any attention to it and didn't really feel it."

As she said these words, I began to feel my toes on the ground and paid attention to how they felt. I thought about all the wonderful things that my body allows me to do, and after chanting a resounding *Om* in unison with the rest of the class, I whispered a gentle thank you to my body and surrendered into a child's pose.

Meditation as Self-Love

In Buddhism, there is a lovely term, *kalyanamitra*, which means a "good spiritual friend," who helps one along the pathway toward freedom, and Malia, my meditation teacher, had become that for me. She offered wise counsel when I finally decided to leave my marriage, and encouragement that I would make out okay as a single mother. And she always seemed to know the right words to say each time I'd meet with her to discuss a class of mine she'd guest lecture in, or when I'd see her at a meditation session in town. With her own life experience as a single mother who grew up in poverty and whose own family of origin included violence, I had found an informal role model who helped me see that I could break away from the daunting fear that our culture likes to generate—that women cannot make it on their own, that we cannot support ourselves, and that no man would want to be with a single mother. In her own humorous and generous way, she helped me dispel the myth that I frantically held onto before I ended my marriage, the one that goes like this: "I will never be able to make it on my own. I have no idea how to manage my finances. I have no idea how to live on my own and support my children." Through the compassionate counsel that defines a good spiritual friend, Malia helped me see that those fears were simply stories I clung to, and that I had the capacity to think and live otherwise.

A year and a half after I was officially divorced, I sat outside at the Raye Street Café, and Malia carefully eased her body into the cold metal chair to protect her back. "Sometimes the tension I hold in my body can be seen as a gift because it makes me stop to notice what's going on," she said as she explained that she was nursing some recent back pain. "It comes with the territory of being an older woman," she laughed and grimaced at the same time. She didn't casually flop her body onto the chair like I did, but rather gingerly allowed gravity to gently ease her into an upright position.

The Seattle sun was shining and nearly blinding us, so we pulled out our sunglasses and I settled into receive some tips for preparing for the five-day silent retreat for people of color that I have signed up for. In between bites of food, Malia pushed her dreadlocks out of her face and, like the retired prosecuting attorney that she used to be, she proceeded to list point by point what I should and shouldn't do on retreat. She was and remains, after all, one of the many Buddhist women whom I consider my teachers, and it is no surprise that she is an older woman of color. Somehow, I seem to seek out the Buddhist teachers with enough years in them to be my spiritual mothers. It also helped that she had done the retreat several times and was the perfect coach to help me develop my survival strategy.

"Listen, when doing the walking meditation, be sure not to take the easy way out. Don't take that time to sneak off and have tea, because that is just your mind telling you that you want to have tea. In that moment, going for the tea is a convenient excuse to distract you."

I jotted down some notes so that I could remember this ever important piece of advice; I wanted to be prepared and not waste my time on retreat. I was trying to get as much as a could out of this immersion.

"Eventually you will find yourself getting tea anyway and realize, darn! I did it again. Remember, it is the mind that has trained you to want to fill the time."

I repeated her words in my head so that they would become part of my mental muscle memory, because I didn't want to look like an obvious newbie on the retreat.

Then she said something I would have no trouble remembering, "Also, you want to practice long enough that you begin to trust the body's capacity for awareness more so than someone else's overlay on that experience."

Here is where all my academic training in Buddhism would be tested, when it met the wisdom of practice on retreat, for it became clear that the mind absorbs projections and delusions about the body, and that my job would be to notice that the mind was playing tricks on me when it said my body was no good. The memories of all the instances when I was told by my mother that my body was no good, the images I replayed in my head of being force-fed as a young girl, the anxieties I had around eating too much, and the times that boyfriends would hint that my body was less than perfect, all bubbled up to the surface as I began to feel, and not just know on an intellectual level, how much I had internalized the judgments of others. I had taken their stories about me as objective fact and in so doing, let my mind play tricks on me. I would need to sit and carefully investigate the nature of my mind and to pay attention to the things that caused me to feel uncomfortable.

"Remember too, all your yoga is great for you because yoga mindfulness can always help you find and move toward comfort. But mindful meditation is going to help you be aware of discomfort and investigate where it comes from. Understanding the origin of suffering and discomfort is the key to healing," she said as she stuck her headphones in her ears, carefully lifted her body off her chair, and bid me a good journey.

Two weeks later, I am in the meditation center surrounded by fellow people of color listening to Asha address our group with a dharma message perfectly (or as Buddhists like to say, skillfully) tailored to our needs. She walks her soft and slightly rounded body slowly back and forth in front of the Buddha statues at the front of the hall and makes barely any noise. Her smile is as relaxed and effortless as that of the statues behind her and I wonder how much meditation it will take for me to have the same kind of comfort in my body. Her body is beautiful—and I realize that what makes it so is the confidence and ease with which she carries it, and of course her brilliant white teeth that seem to shine with light.

"As people of color, we need to learn to be present in our bodies and practice taking up space too," she reminds us. "Isn't this why we are here? To learn to take up space where we often feel excluded? In public, in the office, and sometimes at home?"

I begin to wonder if I can learn to occupy my own body through meditation and mindful awareness, and as I do, Asha explains, "It is important to take up space with a gentle and softened heart that can withdraw from the onslaught of socially-constructed *dukkha* (suffering) and outer harm that tells us that we are somehow less than the norm or the ideal."

I wonder, too, if we can learn how to be accepting of all women's bodies, which we immediately measure ourselves up against. Yet even if we looked kindly and lovingly upon other women aging—their bodies growing old, their bodies transforming in middle age—and wouldn't dare criticize them, we still make negative comments on our own and reject our own worthiness of gentleness and care.

Once again, I am reminded of how lucky I am to have signed up for this retreat, for never in my life have I so felt that the words of a teacher could really offer me relief. *How radical is it to occupy our bodies and challenge the oppressive notion that we must somehow automatically be what those external labels of racism and sexism say we are? I can learn to occupy other spaces beyond the racialized, gendered ones. If I withdraw and pay radical attention, just maybe, I can develop the courage to sit without buying into mediated images of what I am supposed to look like. Wow, meditation really*

*can be a radical act of freedom and self-love and help me let go of clinging to
my mental distortions.*

I am relieved beyond measure because my hunch and faith that meditation can really help me come to terms with this body of mine have been
confirmed by some of the most amazingly hip women-of-color teachers
that I have ever met. They get the struggles, the stresses, and the paradox
of both invisibility and hypervisibility for women of color and offspring of
immigrants, caught between conflicting cultural norms and idealized images. Buddhists take refuge in the Buddha, the Dharma, and the Sangha
(community) when they declare themselves Buddhist, and it is here on
retreat that I begin to realize that this group is in fact a refuge and a safe
haven where I can begin to explore the causes and conditions of my unkind thoughts toward myself. It is here that I can learn how to gently
accept myself as I am and stop clinging to a future moment of perfection
which simply doesn't exist. It is, as the Buddha said, a mental construct
with no corollary in actual reality.

It is day three of the retreat and my stomach has been feeling bloated.
We are sharing bathrooms and so the lack of privacy has been a little rough
on my ability to relax and use the toilet whenever I feel like it. The result is
a stomach that needs relief. The day's dharma lesson is to be careful about
what one asks for and to find humor in things when the body goes somewhat awry. In an effort to reduce the discomfort in my stomach and the
feeling that my belly was pooching out in an unattractive manner, I went
over to the tea station in the dining hall and saw some natural laxative tea.

*Well, it looks organic and healthy. What bad could come of something
that the Buddhist kitchen puts out for everyday use?* I convinced myself,
as I made two very strong cups of this tea that I thought could be my
savior. There were no directions for how much one should take, which
to my desperate mind meant that it was a gentle kind of relaxant. So I
quaffed at least two cups after breakfast and another after lunch. I was a
little impatient for things to get moving but thought that I should just
distract myself with a pleasant hike in the sunny hills after lunch. Off I
went, huffing my way up the hill, excited to feel my heart rate increase for
maybe I could get some exercise in, too. However, as I quickly stepped
up the mountain, my gut began to rumble as if setting off a warning
beacon in my body. But as usual, I ignored the signals my body was
making and decided to override the alarm so that I could keep going up
the mountain—I was almost at the summit anyway. A few more steps
couldn't hurt, or so I thought.

A few more steps and I began to break out in a sweat as I panicked. *Oh no. I might not make it. Oh no. I am going to be the meditator who humiliates herself on retreat! I might not make the toilet in time.* I made a quick turn around and hastily but gently descended the mountain and prayed that no one would be in the public bathrooms. I found an empty stall and immediately realized that just because something seems naturally derived, it doesn't necessarily mean it is a good idea. I also learned, to my great dismay, that the clingy ego that wanted me to reduce the poochiness of my bloated belly was getting her comeuppance because the folks who volunteered to clean the bathroom as part of their service work during the retreat were waiting in silence to wash the toilets. After a few extended visits to the bathroom, I turned my gaze down like the good Buddhist I hoped I was and didn't make direct eye contact as I exited hastily. My cheeks were flushed with embarrassment as I hoped that like a good Zen practitioner, I left no trace of myself.

"To be seen as whole, full, enough, and fine as you are—this view of the self becomes the proximate cause for love and beloved community." Dee Dee's voice reverberates through the silent meditation hall and I imagine that there must be many others in the room who might feel the same way as me—full of hope that begins to melt the edges away around the self-doubt. I begin to tell myself and others silently, "*Live* in this body in this moment! Not tomorrow's body. Occupy *this* body. Occupy *this* space in wholeness."

My mind was racing and I was practically jumping out of my body in excitement. *Hey, we have all been marginalized, rendered invisible, seen through the frame of racism, sexism, heteronormativity, and therefore we have all been fragmented. Didn't the Buddha tell us that we should let go of the projections thrust upon us by the dominant culture that we react to, and stumble with discomfort as we sometimes make that projection our own?* I imagine that I have a bullhorn and am, of course, shouting silently to the choir. Meditation becomes a way to occupy my body and no longer feel invisible, unfit, and marginal, and I realize that it does take courage to take up space. On this retreat, it becomes crystal clear that meditation, a practice I used to consider abstract or even self-indulgent, is in fact the best way to wake up and begin to appreciate my body as it is—ever-changing, and fully perfect, because it is mine.

Retreat and Take Up Space

It is Sunday afternoon, the second to last day of the retreat, and I am on kitchen duty, chopping organic lettuce leaves dirty from being freshly unearthed from the garden out back. The heads of romaine are full of little bugs that we try to keep alive and put outside—gnats and other things with wings that I know I am supposed to set free. Busy worker bees are we—the four of us women who chose the post-lunch vegetable chopping job so that the commuity could have fresh food for dinner. Chop, chop, chop, chop. I was honing my "chopping vegetables silencing the mind skills," the knife gracefully slicing its way through our upcoming dinner greens. I was feeling rather proud of my rhythmic knife cutting. I was like Cook Ting, the famous Taoist butcher who could cut through a slab of meat and never touch bone because he was so aware and able to yield to any potential obstacles. He was one of the renowned Taoist teachers, Chuang Tzu's most well-known characters, because he always went with the flow of nature rather than against it.

As I fixated on becoming the Zen Buddhist with a Taoist-flair chef of all chefs, I looked down at my trail of slickly-sliced greens only to make contact with a giant pair of eyes staring up at me from the lettuce. This was no little gnat! The eyes took up most of the real estate on the perfectly round head of what I finally realized was a frog. Its quarter-sized head was frozen still and had me in its deadlocked guilty gaze. Was it dead? What is this thing? Why the hell is it here? *Oh, my god, I have killed a frog in my attempt to not kill a living thing!* My calm cool demeanor quickly faded.

There's been a murder in the vegetarian-loving-kindness-to-all-living-things kitchen, and I had committed it, or so I thought. I threw my knife down with a loud thud on the stainless-steel counter. The tabletop echoed with a shrill scream as it seemed to point its fingers at the guilty party. I backed away as quickly and silently as I could with my hands up in the air, but everyone in the kitchen looked over at me and the commotion I created. Being the good silent meditator that I was, I verbally said nothing, but I frantically gestured toward the murder scene of hacked

193

lettuce, my finger pointed madly at that terribly dead something that lay within its folds. My kitchen mates silently approached to peer over my shoulder thinking perhaps that this city meditator was afraid of a few bugs. But no, it was no bug! As I pointed wildly at my transgression, the real go-with-the-flow cook came soft-footed out of the kitchen, peered into my lettuce head, and swiftly picked up what I was sure were the remains of the frog that I had decapitated. I turned my eyes as she picked up the body in her calm, nurturing hands and carried its head and body to the outdoors.

I shrank away in shame and disgust with myself, and in a few moments she returned to put a gentle warm hand on my shoulder, looked directly into my eyes and said out loud, "Don't worry. The frog was alive; it was just frozen in fear."

I felt immediate pressure release from my heart. "I didn't kill it? Are you sure?" I asked, hoping that I had heard her correctly.

"Nope, it's fine. The frog is now resting in the garden."

Relief washed over me as the real Cook Ting walked purposefully back to her kitchen station. I could hear Tara let out a grand guffaw in the distance. She was witness to my imagined tragedy and broke the silence that I had tried so hard to keep. That laugh was an invitation that opened up the kitchen hall with more laughter and relief and I felt evermore grateful to be part of this community. They had my back.

Later that afternoon, fresh off the heels of that rather funny and embarrassing kitchen escape, I returned to the meditation hall, my home away from home, and sat atop my cushion. Asha came in and put on her microphone headset, and told us that the day's dharma lesson was on the importance of acknowledging and facing painful moments, embarrassing events, and bad memories. I wondered if she had heard about my silent outburst in the kitchen, and smiled.

"This stuff gets lodged into our mind-body processes," she began. "If we ignore painful memories, we end up constricting our lives into smaller and smaller spaces," she continued as she took a piece of paper. "Each memory, each painful experience we try to ignore and hide, compresses our identities." She folded down the corners of the paper each time she mentioned a memory or shameful moment we might suppress. Then she held up the once large piece of paper which was now a small, tightly-folded wad of paper for us all to consider.

"You see, eventually like the paper, we get so small and compressed because we hide so much of ourselves out of shame and embarrassment that we end up having very little space to breathe and to live out of our full identities."

I was amazed that a blank piece of paper could become one of the most significant teaching tools that I had ever encountered. "Look, as a queer woman of color, I have done the exact same thing. But instead of compressing the self, maybe we can acknowledge, feel, and shine the light of awareness on the parts of our identities that we think we should keep in darkness. Meditation is like a lighthouse that sheds light on things in the sea like the fish in the ocean."

Asha's words remind me that shining the light of mindfulness on experience allows for the recognition of pain and loss, but also for healing and wholeness to develop—especially for those of us whose suffering is often dismissed. Maybe being open and honest about my own past suffering could be an antidote to the unkindness I have shown my own body. Here in the meditation hall, I realize that the practice of mindfulness can lead to breath and body awareness that can help me create stability and equanimity in response to all of life's vicissitudes and challenges. As Asha's voice enveloped me in warmth and hopefulness, I thought back to my mother and how far away in time her words seemed to me now. She was long gone and, while her memory will not fade, the sting of her words slowly dissolves. It has also become so much easier now that it used to be to turn the volume down on my inner critic. "Meditation does not take the suffering away, but it does make it easier to endure," the smiling teacher continues.

That is true, I do think I have developed a little more resilience and confidence in meeting painful events face to face, I think as my mind wanders to losing my father a year and a half ago.

My father left New York Hospital for home hospice care the day I turned forty-six, just a few days after I left Manhattan for one of the several cross-country trips I took from Seattle to New York to stay with him as he finally succumbed to the cancer that developed in his liver over twenty years before. Those final weeks I felt like I was on a continually looping conveyer belt between flying to New York, raising my kids, teaching, work, dealing with the detritus of a marriage that had fallen apart, and trying to help manage my father's care and attend to his final wishes to spend his remaining days at home.

Unlike what I thought a cancer patient would be like, my father was quite vocal about not wanting to die. He was desperate to figure out a way to keep living and did not relax until my aunt called in his Korean priest, who presided over worship services in the Catholic church next to my dad's apartment. My dad had converted to Catholicism not too long before because my stepmom had done the same thing after being a Buddhist for a number of decades, which was not so unusual for Korean immigrants. Father Shin came to my father's bed in the Intensive Care Unit wearing a black shirt, crumpled black cotton pants, and a wool cap. He went straight to my father's bed, looked directly into his eyes, grabbed my father's tired hands into his and said, "You cannot make this decision to die or live right now my friend. It's not up to you. This one is up to God."

The priest's words seemed to give my dad some relief because he suddenly didn't have to be in charge of everything, including how to make things better for my stepmom who would soon be twice widowed. My dad always felt a tremendous amount of responsibility to take care of people and he didn't want to leave until he felt like we could take care of ourselves.

After teaching the first week of the new quarter, and just three days after my father arrived home and his gurney bed had been set up in the living room of his midtown apartment, I got a call from his homecare nurse.

"Your father is in a coma; it's time."

I knew the travel drill since I had been preparing for his death. I would go home, throw some clothes in the carry-on that had been waiting open in my living room, and grab the next flight out.

The nurse listened to my fears as I cried into the phone, "What if he dies before I get there?" But she assured me that he would stay with us until I got to his bedside.

"He told me to let you know that you shouldn't come to New York because you were too busy. But he'll hang on until you get here. I see this with people all the time, especially men like him."

I flew straight out of Seattle the very next morning and arrived there just two hours before my brother's plane touched down from Hong Kong. I dropped my bags by the front door and immediately collapsed onto the bed next to my father. He looked serene, although his breathing had become labored and jagged.

I glanced over at the nurse who reassured me, "He is comfortable. He isn't in any pain."

I sat and stroked his hand as I continued to whisper into his ear that I loved him, and stayed by his bedside until my brother arrived. The two of us sat flanking my father and I kept one hand on his chest while I stroked his hair. "Dad, we're here. You have been a wonderful father. We love you. It is okay to let go," we softly repeated. And ten minutes later, he did just that. He slipped away quietly when my brother went to the kitchen. I sat on the bed with both of my hands on his chest and I felt his body relax as I tracked his breathing with the rise and fall of each inhale and exhale into my palms. In a few moments, his breathing became lighter and lighter until it was barely perceptible and with his final, gentle exhale, he slipped away. I sat still as I let this moment sink into my body and kept my hands on his chest until the cool of his departure crept up his torso. I sat there amazed that I could hold him as he died. It was the most tender, painful gift that I had ever known. He couldn't choose to remain with us, he couldn't choose not to die, but he could choose when to let go, and I am to this day grateful that I could be present to him as his breath and consciousness left his body. His death still does weigh heavy on me and grief can catch me instantly, but most of the time, I let that sadness wash over and through me and emerge grateful that I had such a lion of a man as my father. He had great confidence in my ability to weather any storm and come out a little better for it, and I believe I have done so even in his death.

I have been fortunate enough to inherit my father's tenacity and endurance and am confident that he is smiling now as he watches me go through my day as a professor I always dreamed of becoming. Each time I give a presentation or a book talk, I see my father beam with pride and imagine him laughing as he reminds me that I got my public speaking skills from him. I imagine him once again ordering multiple copies of my most recent book and giving them to just about all of his friends as a sign of pride in my accomplishments. I imagine him delighting over my recent promotion to full professor and decision to stay in Seattle at the small liberal arts university that has been my academic home for 17 years. I can also feel my father's joy and happiness that I have settled into my life as a mother of two teens who is living independently and who finally has a little more time to herself. And I also can feel his joy and curiosity in my new-found love—an artist. I imagine my father trying to understand the creative energy that motivates the man to whom I am engaged and I laugh in return as I imagine him asking me, "What *exactly* does your fiancé do?" I assure my father that I will be fine and that I do not need a doctor or a lawyer to be happy. I have fallen in love with someone who loves, admires, and accepts me as I am, Zen flaws and all. And then I feel my father relax, for he knows that I am doing well, that I am happy, safe, and secure.

Occupy This Body

WHERE *does my physical body begin and end? What about my cultural body?* These questions swirled around my head for much of my time on retreat. These questions have also been crucial to understanding the gift that Buddhist practice brought to help loosen the grip that body dysmorphia, obsessive thinking about my body, and disordered eating, have had on me. I found the answers through silent meditation where I could understand the difference between internal feelings in my body and the external world where my body is defined by labels I did not make. Although it has been nearly a year since I sat in silent retreat, I continue to practice as a reminder to cultivate a kinder attitude toward my body and about food, for I know how easily an untrained mind can become distracted and give in to distorted thinking. I am not looking for perfection; I am looking for the mental and emotional steadiness and ease that can carry me through the vicissitudes of everyday life. Through the practice of Buddhism, I am working to appreciate this body as it is, a body that will change and evolve over time.

Through my studies, I have read that monks were often taught to detach themselves from their egos and from physical desire for others through a deconstruction of the female body. But such a practice has little to offer many women like me who struggle to come to terms with the labeling and assessment of our bodies as "less than." These Buddhist teachings offer me little succor for a body so ravaged by culture and family. As I inch closer to my fifth decade of life, I know my body will change; it will become softer, weaker, and creakier because it is impermanent. "Shift happens" as many a t-shirt and bumper sticker claim, and each time I sit in meditative silence or step to the top of my yoga mat with my hands in prayer position at my heart center, I set an intention to accept that shift with gentleness, grace, and perhaps a little humor thrown in for good measure. This intention serves as a reminder to refrain from absorbing the gaze of others as the ultimate arbiter of the truth of who, how, and what I am. This body of mine will never again be what it was, and who knows what it shall become. It is a body in process and the process is to be accepted as just simply that. It is but a fleeting moment in time that is not actually caught and entangled by the past; it is only my mind that that sometimes still thinks it so. As the concluding lines of the beloved Buddhist text, the *Diamond Sutra*, remind me:

> All composed things are like a dream,
> a phantom, a drop of dew, a flash of lightening.
> That is how to meditate on them,
> that is how to observe them.

Memories of my childhood abuses have inscribed themselves upon my body and the way it moves through space but, as the Buddha taught, that inscription does not have to be indelible. That indelible permanent nature of my body as not good enough is simply the mind's clinging to an image rather than a reality, the eyes seeing with someone else's vision and not my own. Thus, Buddhism has the power to radically re-vision how I see myself, by requiring me to look with my own eyes and to hold my vision of myself with gentleness and ease.

I continue to practice the compassionate body scan I learned on the people-of-color silent retreat, through which I feel where my body touches the ground, and observe where the breath originates and dissipates. I experience myself settling down by breathing from the depths of my belly rather than the surface shallow breaths that I used take when I was under stress. The anxious breath is the one that remains only in the chest and does not take over the fullness of my body. But when I engage in meditation I experience my true self, my resilient self, a self that does not blindly heed to the expectations of the external world with its overlay of cultural and social expectations. Through gentle observation of how my body feels from the inside out, I turn off the judging mind and embrace my body as it is rather than chase some spectral image projected through the lens of cultural norms and ideals that discipline and judge rather than accept and hold.

> May I be happy.
> May I be well.
> May I be safe.
> May I be peaceful and live with ease.

I recite these words of the Buddha silently to myself when that old familiar voice begins to poke at me again with its negative chatter, offering assessments about my body that I haven't asked for. In remembering these words of loving-kindness, I breathe in slowly and imagine my breath gently carrying this prayer throughout my body, from the crown of my head to the tips of my toes, where it can begin to soften the hard edges of self-criticism. I have grown wise enough to know that negative mental chatter is part and parcel of being human, but now I am prepared to meet that hardness with a softened heart that reminds me I am fine as I am. Through my breath, I enter into my body anew, a body I now know is ever-changing and fluid in its constitution. I expand my body with each inhalation, I exhale the thoughts that no longer serve me, and I settle in as I gradually take up more space and occupy this body from the inside out.

Although I have studied and taught Buddhism for over thirty years now, it took entering into the Buddhist meditation hall and sitting still for me to experientially understand that just as the body fluctuates and can be gently trained through mindful movement, so too the mind. Breathing in and breathing out on the meditation cushion and on the yoga mat have brought me to stillness and gratitude for this body that by its very nature will never again be the same from moment to moment. If I occupy this body in the here and now, it may in fact offer me the gift of presence, peace, and calm—no clinging to the past and what would have and should have been. No clinging to the future of what should be and what will be. It's just me on the cushion and on the mat, enjoying for the first time the body that is now.

Epilogue

It's a Tuesday afternoon in late winter and I am sitting in an urban meditation hall in Seattle's Capitol Hill neighborhood as the stereotypical Seattle rain streams down the windows. The meditation space is a tranquil dark oasis in the midst of heavily tattooed and pierced passers-by. The candles emit a dim glow as nine women of color sit in a circle on meditation cushions; their eyes are gently closed and their hands rest upon their bellies as they practice a meditation of gratitude toward the body. As they generate loving kindness and offer a compassionate touch to parts of their bodies that they have been conditioned to ignore, dislike, or even loathe, a few of them begin to cry. As they confide in me later, they have never brought such kind attention to parts of their bodies they had grown to distrust and despise; the act of compassionate touch is radical, soothing, and startling, they say. They begin to wonder when, how, and why they learned to dislike their own flesh and bones. Anger, frustration, sadness, and then hope emerge as they openly discuss how racism, sexism, and cultural and family norms have dictated how they should look on the outside, and have dictated what they should and shouldn't eat.

Over the past eight weeks they have been been students in my Mindful Eating Method course to explore how their innate and intuitive hungers have been overridden by social norms, cultural conditioning, and family of origin, and to learn to trust their own hungers and bodies again. We are at the end of the course, and the women are excited and a little nervous to continue the journey toward re-establishing a joyful and trusting relationship to food and their bodies, on their own without the safety net of a weekly meeting in the company of others. "Trust yourselves; you have the innate capacity to feed yourself in a loving and gentle manner. Pay attention to your internal hunger cues and feed your hunger, not anyone else's desires, well-meant or not, for you," I remind them. After writing letters to themselves about things they might wish to remind themselves of (that I will mail to them in three months), we close the program with a meditation, and end the day with a round of heartfelt hugs, and off they go.

For many women, myself included, learning how to tune out external authorities such as diet culture, mothers, partners, and friends who love to weigh in on what they should eat and how they should look, becomes a radical act of self-love and care that instills trust in one's own decision-making abilities. Over the past two months, we practiced to how to check in with our hunger, ask ourselves what we would like to eat, and how much we wanted. Most importantly, we practiced feeding ourselves what we wanted and treated ourselves as beloved guests at the table, learning to eat by bringing all senses to this act of joyfulness. As in all things, the proof is in the process; for many of us, deciding what and how much to eat becomes a lesson in self-respect and courage to make our own choices about what to put into our bodies and what messages and social pressures to tune out. In so doing, the table becomes the meditation cushion where we drop into the body and become fully present to what sensory experiences unfold on our plates.

I am the last person likely to have believed that I would be leading other women in meditation, gentle movement to return to the body, and mindful eating practices; it was not something I planned long ago, but here I am, leading workshops throughout the city, on campus, in yoga studios, and meditation centers. After decades of struggling over how to figure out my own hunger level, re-learning how to determine if I was satisfied at the table, learning how to occupy my body and feel it from the inside out rather than judging it from the outside in, I found my way to a Mindful Eating training program led by a Zen Buddhist priest in Oregon. I discovered her by chance at a bookstore during a particularly rough day where I just had to get out of my house. I drove to the local bookstore and perused the Buddhism section, as was my usual practice. I quickly scanned the regular titles I knew quite well and stopped upon a book on mindful eating written by a pediatrician-priest, Jan Chozen Bays. I opened the book and read the introduction that revealed the ways we are conditioned to eat in patterns that override our own internal cues to satisfy external forces.

In that moment, I knew that I had found a Buddhist practice that spoke to me and the suffering I had been carrying for decades. It was not my fault, I read; my suffering was conditioned, and as the Buddha taught, if I could see the origins of my suffering then I would also find liberation. I bought the book, devoured it in a day, cried my eyes out because finally there was a book about Buddhism that helped me understand my struggles over food and my body, and, like I do with most things that fascinate me, I took a deep dive and signed up for a teacher training so that I could learn and teach simultaneously. I knew that I was not the only one with food- and body-related suffering. I first wanted to heal myself and knew that my own unique trauma around food, body, motherhood, and culture would allow me to engage in the Buddhist practice of compassion or co-experience. Like all healing, it is never a single road toward progress, but like most things, there is a push-pull forward and backward; still the path unfolds. I like to think of it in Buddhist terms, that like a lotus blossom remains rooted in the mud for its survival, I too have taken the mud of trauma and transformed it into nourishing particles for myself and the other women with whom I practice and teach. No mud, no lotus.

About the Author

SHARON A. SUH is a Professor of Theology and Religious Studies at Seattle University. Suh earned her Ph.D. in Buddhist Studies from Harvard University and is the author of *Being Buddhist in a Christian World: Gender and Community* (University of Washington Press, 2004) and *Silver Screen Buddha: Buddhism in Asian and Western Film* (Bloomsbury Press, 2015).

In addition to her academic work, Suh completed her 200-hour yoga teacher certification training, Transcending Sexual Trauma through Yoga, Yoga for Trauma (Y4T training), and level I Certification in Mindful Eating – Conscious Living through the UCSD Center for Mindfulness. She serves on the board of directors of Yoga Behind Bars, advocating for transformative justice, and offering yoga for resilience and trauma recovery. A popular speaker on the topic of feminism and Buddhism, she has also developed and presented workshops on mindful movement, meditation, body image, body acceptance, and mindful eating practices. She resides in Seattle with her two teenaged daughters, three dogs, and husband.

Acknowledgments

WRITING A MEMOIR of my experiences as a second-generation Korean American daughter raised in Long Island, and learning to embrace my body through the practice of Buddhism, has been on my mind for a long time. In writing this memoir, I wanted to reach out to fellow women whose familial, cultural, and social bonds often make it seem impossible to reveal what life is really like on the inside, in order to save face. I share my own story with the hope that it might offer some measure of hope that we can begin to inhabit our bodies and see ourselves from the inside out rather than react to external judgments. It is my deepest hope that this memoir will resonate and provide some support for others who have endured in similar ways.

It takes a wide community to nurture a writer and I have been blessed with several *kalyanamitras* or "good spiritual friends" who have offered me the unwavering support that I needed to take the courageous step to write about my own experiences around food, eating, and body image. I'd like to thank a few of those special people in no particular order of importance of course. Thank you so much to my incredible friends and colleagues of the Asian Pacific American Religions Research Initiative (APARRI) that has been my academic refuge since it began in 1998. We have known each other for over twenty years and I have always thought of you as my true academic family. In particular I'd like to thank Khyati Joshi, Tammy Ho, Carolyn Chen, Jane Iwamura, Joe Cheah, Mimi Khuc, Rita Nakashima Brock, and David Yoo, for your thoughtful conversations about the memoir, humor, endless support, wisdom, and damn good conferences! Special thanks as well to our Wabash Mid-Career Summer Colloquium hosted by senior scholars Jeffrey Kuan, Benny Tat-Siong Liew, and Kwok Pui Lan, who encouraged us to stay true to what we really wanted to pursue and to be authentic in our desires to help others through our teaching and scholarship. A special thank you to Mark Unno for reading an early draft of this memoir and offering such wonderful support.

A huge heartfelt shout out of gratitude to Ellen Newhouse! Your book, *Nothing Ever Goes On Here: A Memoir*, was the exact thing I needed to inspire me. You are one of the most generous, intelligent, spirit-filled women I know, with the best laugh, who let me know that sharing one's life can also be about saving a life. Special shout out to the Fancy Ladies Writing Group and your willingness to welcome a newcomer and relative stranger like me—Emily, Stephanie, Olive, Paula, and Ellen, all heard me tentatively share from my memoir and offered the most incredible support and skillful critique to help me get it done. I owe a huge debt of gratitude to Janice Harper, Ph.D., for her ongoing support of my writing, incredible coaching, and truly discerning eye. I would not have been able to write this memoir were it not for you. I would also like to thank Jan Chozen Bays, MD, and Char Wilkins, LSW, for creating and offering an incredible program in Mindful Eating – Conscious Living through the UCSD Center for Mindfulness, that has been transformative. Char, thank you so much for your mentorship. It has changed me for the better and taught me to always KISS, or Keep It Simple Sweetie! To my first cohort of Mindful Eating – Conscious Living practitioners—you were an incredible group of fierce and compassionate women!

I would also like to thank Tynette Deveaux from *Buddhadharma: The Practitioner's Quarterly*, for her initial interest in a chapter from my memoir, and Andrea Miller for her support in publishing that short piece in *Lion's Roar: Buddhist Wisdom for Our Time*. Special thanks to Seattle University and the department of Theology and Religious Studies where I have worked since 2000. I have had the great fortune of holding the Pigott-McCone Endowed Chair in the Humanities for two years, which afforded me the time and resources to do the research in trauma studies, Trauma-Sensitive Yoga, Transcending Sexual Trauma through Yoga (Zabie Yamasaki—you are such an inspiration!), retreats at the Spirit Rock Insight Meditation Society's annual People of Color Retreats, and advanced training in yoga and mindfulness needed to write this book. And last, but not least, I would like to offer my sincerest gratitude to my editor and publisher, John Negru, of The Sumeru Press, for seeing the potential in this memoir, for being such a ready supporter of this work, and for your great patience in getting this memoir out the door!

I know that the list of people to thank is really endless and there are so many more people to express my gratitude toward; please know that you are in my heart and any negligence on my part to name you is simply the result of my own sometimes faulty memory.

Finally, this book is dedicated to my parents, my incredible daughters who have given me the gift of mothering, and my wonderful husband, Jimmy Johnson, whose unconditional support, openhearted optimism, and great sense of humor never cease to amaze me.

Printed in the USA
CPSIA information can be obtained
at www.ICGtesting.com
LVHW102356220823
755946LV00001B/32